BELONGING
AND BELONGINGS

"*Belonging and Belongings* provides an extraordinary portrayal of the experiences of children living in multiple households. It is especially laudable that the book by Laura Merla and Bérengère Nobels takes a multimethodological explorative approach capturing the very words, images and connections of families while they are getting transformed by shared custody arrangement. Family scholars and professionals will find it extremely insightful."
Laura Bernardi, Ordinary Professor of Demography, University of Lausanne

"I LOVE this book. It is rich in ground-breaking insights, and a must-read for anyone interested in the latest research on shared parenting. Children have a way of telling it like it is, and the authors have clearly heard them."
Bruce M. Smyth, Professor of Family Studies, Australian National University

"A thoroughly researched, sensitive account of children's lives in post-separation families, crucially taking children's points of view as the starting point. This is a ground-breaking sociological text."
Virginia Morrow, Visiting Professor, University College London

"Shared custody has increased rapidly, yet we know little about how it actually works. In this path-breaking study, Merla and Nobels center the lived experiences of the children involved, which, when combined with their thoughtful reflections, provide critical information for all those who care about the future of children living in diverse family forms."
Daniel Meyer, Professor Emeritus of Social Work, University of Wisconsin-Madison

"This is a fascinating book on a neglected subject, about how children who live in multilocal families make themselves 'at home'."
Ida W. Winther, Associate Professor of Educational Anthropology, Aarhus University

"Deeply insightful, this book captures the nuanced ways children adapt to life between two homes. It invites us to rethink stability and home through the lived experiences of children in shared physical custody arrangements and offers practical and emotional insights for families and practitioners."
Jani Turunen, Associate Professor of Social Work, Södertörn University

Sociology of Children and Families

Series Editors: **Esther Dermott** and
Debbie Watson, University of Bristol, UK

This series brings together the latest international research on children, childhood and families and pushes forward theory in the sociology of childhood and family life. Books in the series cover major global issues affecting children and families.

Also available in the series:

- *Reimagining Stepmother*, by Patrycja Sosnowska-Buxton
- *Turning Global Rights into Local Realities*, by Afua Twum-Danso Imoh
- *Understanding Muslim Family Life*, by Joanne Britton
- *Thinking Through Family*, by Janet Boddy with Fidelma Hanrahan and Bella Wheeler
- *Critical Perspectives on Research with Children*, edited by Sarah Richards and Sarah Coombs
- *Race, Class, Parenting and Children's Leisure*, by Utsa Mukherjee
- *Childcare Provision in Neoliberal Times*, by Aisling Gallagher
- *Black Mothers and Attachment Parenting*, by Patricia Hamilton
- *Sharing Care*, by Rachel Brooks and Paul Hodkinson
- *A Child's Day*, by Killian Mullan
- *Designing Parental Leave Policy*, by Berit Brandth and Elin Kvande
- *Social Research Matters*, by Julia Brannen
- *Nanny Families*, by Sara Eldén and Terese Anving

Find out more at:
bristoluniversitypress.co.uk/
sociology-of-children-and-families

BELONGING AND BELONGINGS

Children's Sense of Home in Shared Custody Arrangements

Laura Merla and Bérengère Nobels

Bristol University Press

First published in Great Britain in 2025 by

Bristol University Press
University of Bristol
1–9 Old Park Hill
Bristol
BS2 8BB
UK
t: +44 (0)117 374 6645
e: bup-info@bristol.ac.uk

Details of international sales and distribution partners are available at bristoluniversitypress.co.uk

British Library Cataloguing in Publication Data
A catalogue record for this book is available from the British Library

ISBN 978-1-5292-3658-3 paperback
ISBN 978-1-5292-3659-0 ePub
ISBN 978-1-5292-3660-6 ePdf

Cover design: blu inc
Front cover image: 123rf/sasun1990
Bristol University Press uses environmentally responsible print partners.
Printed and bound in Great Britain by CPI Group (UK) Ltd, Croydon, CR0 4YY

Contents

List of Figures and Tables   viii
Acknowledgements   ix

1   Shared Custody and Sense of Home: The Child's Point of View   1
2   Parental Islands   25
3   The Journey Between Islands: Transitioning from One Dwelling to the Other   58
4   Routines and Rituals of Return   91
5   Making Each Island 'One's Own Island': Defining and Negotiating One's Place   109
6   Maintaining One's Place during Absence   142
7   A 'Singular-Plural' Sense of Home   161

Concluding Reflections   186

References   193
Index   203

List of Figures and Tables

Figures

1.1	Socio–Spatial Network Game (Lewis, aged 16; photo taken from his vantage point)	17
1.2	Socio–Spatial Network Game (Eliot, aged 14; photo taken from his vantage point)	18
1.3	Emotion Map of mother's house (Marie, aged 12)	19
1.4	Emotion Map of father's house (Chloé, aged 12)	19
6.1	Socio–Spatial Network Game (Coralie, aged 12; photo taken from her vantage point)	156
6.2	Socio–Spatial Network Game (Théodore, aged 13; photo taken from his vantage point)	156
7.1	Socio–Spatial Network Game (Félicien, aged 12; photo taken from his vantage point)	167
7.2	Socio–Spatial Network Game (Chloé, aged 12; photo taken from her vantage point)	170

Tables

1.1	Characteristics of study participants	15
2.1	Typology of post-separation parental styles	28
2.2	Typology of 'parental islands'	31
4.1	Definitions of routines and rituals	92
4.2	Definitions of routines and rituals of return	95
7.1	Definition of a 'singular-plural' sense of home	163

Acknowledgements

Thank you to the families, parents and children who trusted us and shared their stories with us.

Thank you also to Annette Dubois for her insightful comments and excellent editorial work on this book.

This book is part of the MobileKids project, funded by the European Research Council and led by Laura Merla. This project has received funding from the European Research Council under the European Union's Horizon 2020 research and innovation programme under grant agreement no. 676868. This book reflects only the authors' view. The European Commission is not responsible for any use that may be made of the information it contains.

1

Shared Custody and Sense of Home: The Child's Point of View

Lewis

Lewis is 16 years old; his parents separated when he was three. For the first few months after the separation, he lived mainly with his mother, in the triplex where he and his parents had lived since his birth. Both parents retained ownership of this property after the separation. During this time, Lewis's father lived nearby and spent time with his son several times a week after school, but Lewis stayed with him only occasionally. It was eventually decided to set up an egalitarian shared custody arrangement (seven days with each parent, with a transition on Tuesdays after school), with a clear and structured organization that offered more stability to all family members.

For the past eight years, Lewis's mother has lived with her new partner and their daughter (Lewis's half-sister, Clémentine, aged ten) in a house on the outskirts of the city, more than 25 kilometres from the triplex where Lewis's father now lives. The triplex is in the city, close to Lewis's school, his friends and the urban amenities he finds essential to his daily life. These different living environments allow him to enjoy a variety of activities. While Lewis enjoys the liveliness of the city, the cultural events and the outings with friends when he is living with his father, he also appreciates the peace and quiet of the countryside for resting and having time with the family when he is living with his mother. He has his own bedroom in each of his parents' dwellings. Although he has not put much effort into decorating these rooms, he spends a lot of time there playing on his computer or composing music.

His mother's move out of the city has made the weekly transition from one residence to the other more time-consuming and complicated, representing something of a burden for Lewis. While he used to make these journeys on his own by tram or on foot, he must now determine each week whether his mother will drive him to her house or whether he will make the hour-long

1

journey alone by train. This is the only reason he and his mother call or text one another when Lewis is living with his father. When his mother picks him up at a meeting point off the motorway, the teenager enjoys the journey with her, sharing a snack in the car. The trip allows the two of them to take stock of the past week before meeting up with the other members of the 'new family'.[1] When he returns to his father's apartment after a week away, Lewis goes there by tram after school and spends a few hours alone there. In the evening, after his father has returned from work, they have dinner together.

At the start of the school year, Lewis asked his parents to adapt his alternation schedule to his new course schedule because of the distance between their dwellings and the travel time involved. This year his courses finish at 5:30 pm on Tuesdays, and he found travelling by train at that time to be extremely inconvenient. His request was granted, and the alternation was modified from seven days with each parent to a 'quasi-egalitarian' arrangement of eight days with his father and six with his mother. Lewis now stays with his father on Tuesday evenings, going to his mother's house on Wednesdays at lunchtime after his courses finish.

Lewis has a wardrobe at each of his parents' dwellings, and can manage his belongings as he sees fit. However, he does not take any clothes or other personal belongings with him on the day of a move – only his books and his computer, which he keeps in his school bag at all times to ensure he will not leave them behind when he moves.

Annelyse

Annelyse is ten years old; her parents split up when she was four. Since then, she and her sister Chloé (aged 12) have been moving between their parents' residences every Friday. On the day of a move, Annelyse goes to school with her bag containing the personal belongings she wants to bring with her, and the parent with whom she will be staying picks her up by car after school. When she arrives at her parent's residence, she arranges the contents of her bag in her wardrobe, and then leaves the open bag in the hall of her mother's apartment or under the desk in her bedroom at her father's house. Over the course of the week, Annelyse gradually returns the things she no longer needs (her sports equipment, a book, clothes she particularly likes) to the bag to ensure she will not forget them on the day she leaves.

For the first three years after the separation, Annelyse found it difficult to be away from one of her parents for a week at a time. She used the phone of the parent she was living with almost daily to contact the other parent, to check in with them or to be comforted. For her tenth birthday, her parents gave her an iPod Touch to help her communicate with them independently, but today she no longer feels the need to reach out to them as regularly. They are now the ones who make contact with her, once or twice a week – a rhythm that suits her well.

Annelyse has had to adapt to the differences in routines, rules and environments between one residence and the other. Whereas she eats and goes to bed at set times at her single mother's apartment, she leads a less structured life at her father and stepmother's house, eating at a different time each night and going to bed late. Moreover, at her mother's apartment she has her own spacious bedroom in which she feels comfortable, whereas at her father's house her room is so cramped and cluttered with toys that she sleeps on a mattress in her older sister's room, being afraid to sleep in her own room alone.

Cédric

Cédric is 15 years old. His parents separated eight years ago and immediately set up an egalitarian custody arrangement, with Cédric spending the same number of days with each parent. The teenager has never wanted to change this arrangement. On Fridays, the day he moves between residences, he returns after school to the dwelling where he has spent the week. He collects his school things and his various sports equipment, and then travels to the other parent's residence. Cédric's father usually drives him to and from his mother's house, so he will not have to carry three or four bags; his mother cannot do this because she works on Fridays. When his father is unable to drive him, Cédric walks to the other parent's residence. At his mother's house, he meets his stepfather and his three half-brothers, who live there permanently, while he lives alone with his father, who is single.

For seven years, Cédric's mother lived in a *commune* (municipality) adjacent to his father's, but further away from the town centre. As a result, during his time with her Cédric had no way to access any of the town's amenities other than a bus every hour, on which he depended for all his transportation needs. After the separation, his father moved into an apartment a stone's throw from Cédric's school, and a five-minute walk from the town centre and the train station. This proximity meant that Cédric could walk or cycle to school, his sports club or his Scout meetings on his own. A year ago, his mother and stepfather moved closer to the neighbourhood where Cédric lives with his father; their dwellings are now within a 20-minute walk of one another. The teenager has his own bedroom in each parent's residence. He has decorated each of these rooms soberly, surrounding himself with objects that reflect his tastes and interests (like photos of great athletes and from Scout camp), but uses each room differently because he does not have the same equipment at each residence (for example, a PlayStation at his father's flat and a computer at his mother's house).

Every day, Cédric sends a message to the parent he is away from to say hello, check in with them and wish them a good day. They also call each other at least once a week for a longer conversation. Although the subjects of conversation are sometimes trivial, it is important for him to have regular contact with both of his parents.

★★★

All three of these children alternate living with each of their separated[2] parents for approximately equal time periods, in what is commonly known as an *egalitarian shared physical custody arrangement*. However, their experiences of this arrangement differ, revealing different ways of structuring their family and personal lives. By allowing children in this situation to speak for themselves, we will explore a number of questions raised by these portraits. What does it signify for Lewis to carry only his 'computer kit' when he moves from one residence to another? How does he perceive the time spent travelling with his mother, and how do these moments of togetherness help to maintain their family ties? What does it mean to Annelyse and the other members of her 'new family' when she puts away her belongings upon arrival, and how does she define her place in a family and a residence where she lives only half of the time? How does Cédric adjust to moving between his mother's house, which he shares with a large 'new family', and the flat where he lives alone with his father?[3] How do these three children manage to feel 'at home' when they are constantly moving between two residences?

Shared physical custody: a growing phenomenon

In this book, we are interested in the lives of children in egalitarian forms of *shared physical custody* (SPC). SPC, also known as 'joint physical custody' or 'shared parenting', is a childcare arrangement following parental separation in which children live alternately, and for at least 30 per cent of their time, with each parent (Bernardi and Mortelmans, 2021). The children at the heart of this book live in 'egalitarian' or 'quasi-egalitarian' forms of SPC, a terminology used when children spend at least 45 per cent of their time with each parent.[4]

SPC is based on the principle that parenthood should be shared between separated parents, and that children are entitled to ongoing relationships with both their mothers and their fathers – both of whom are responsible for providing them with accommodation and practical care, as well as for their upbringing and maintenance (Hakovirta and Rantalaiho, 2011). It is both the result and the source of a societal trend towards greater equality between men and women in the care and upbringing of children post-separation.

This arrangement is becoming increasingly common in Western Europe, North America and Australia, although to varying degrees. Within the European Union, it is estimated that one in five children with divorced/separated parents lives in SPC (Hakovirta et al, 2023). Around 5 per cent of children with separated parents live in SPC in countries where there is no legal framework favouring this arrangement, such as Croatia, Romania and Italy; this figure ranges from around 12 per cent (in France and the UK) to around 20 per cent (in Denmark and the Netherlands) where SPC is considered as an option but not as a preferred model, and reaches 40 per cent or more where legislation strongly encourages this arrangement, for example in Belgium, Sweden or the US state of Wisconsin (Steinbach, 2019; Recksiedler and Bernardi, 2021; Meyer et al, 2022; Hakovirta et al, 2023).[5]

Interestingly, the vast majority of SPC arrangements in many countries are set up by mutual agreement between the parents, with judges intervening only to ratify these agreements (Cretin, 2015; Godbout et al, 2015; Solsona and Ajenjo, 2017; Fransson et al, 2018). This shows that SPC has become a recognized option for parents, regardless of the legal framework in place. However, its use is not evenly distributed across social classes. Recksiedler and Bernardi (2021) note that while SPC is generally considered as a priority by the better-off and more educated middle classes, it tends to spread over time to other social classes in countries that support this system. However, it is not feasible for all parents who might wish to implement it. SPC poses many challenges, not only as a new way of life but also because of the relational, logistical and material costs and constraints associated with its implementation. Existing research suggests that SPC is most common among parents who are highly educated, have dual incomes, own their own homes and live close to one another (Flaquer, 2021; Biland, 2023). Access to SPC may be particularly difficult when parental separation is highly conflictual, and for less-privileged segments of the population where parents may have neither the financial resources to pay for double accommodation for their children nor the opportunity to be properly heard in case of a dispute between ex-partners (see, for instance, Fierens, 2008; Bessière et al, 2013). In her study on the implementation of family law in divorce cases in France and Quebec, Biland (2023) observed that judges tend to be guided by a normative vision of co-parenting that reinforces existing inequalities of class, gender and race. Paternal involvement tends to be assessed according to the cultural standards of the (white) upper middle class, where investment in the development of educational and cultural capital plays a key role. Thus, fathers from working-class or migrant backgrounds have more difficulty in gaining recognition for their investment in their children's upbringing, and are less likely to be encouraged to set up SPC.

Over the last 20 years, SPC has been included in many legislative texts, either as one of several possible options (as in France and Spain) or as a solution to be examined as a priority (notably in Belgium and in Wisconsin), and in many countries, large sections of the population are in favour of this form of arrangement (Braver et al, 2011; Godbout et al, 2018; Flaquer, 2021). However, sole maternal custody remains the dominant post-separation childcare arrangement across Western countries.

Even where SPC is to be considered as a priority, a case-by-case approach prevails, with the best interests of the child as the guiding principle. SPC is therefore not considered appropriate in all circumstances. Nevertheless, in countries/provinces such as Belgium, France, Quebec and Sweden, this type of arrangement is gradually becoming a model of what some people call a 'successful divorce' (Godbout et al, 2015; Wagener et al, 2021): a new normative standard that may stigmatize other custody arrangements, particularly sole custody. Even in these countries, SPC remains a subject of debate. While its introduction was guided by a concern for establishing greater equality between fathers and mothers in case of separation (Flaquer, 2021), some feminist and anti-domestic violence movements have denounced what they see as a way of prolonging men's power over their ex-partners and of downplaying violent behaviour. Although legislation and case law often recognize that SPC should not be implemented in cases of domestic violence, research tends to show that violence may be taken into account insufficiently by the courts (Bruno, 2018; Fehlberg et al, 2023).

The idea that fathers and mothers should be equally able to bring up their children is also confronted by a more traditional view of gender roles, particularly where babies and very young children are concerned. Some courts and professionals are thus reluctant to set up SPC for children aged under three years, or even under five years (Godbout et al, 2015; Austin, 2018; Bernardi and Mortelmans, 2021; Merla et al, 2022). This debate relates more broadly to the question of whether SPC has a negative impact on children's well-being, which occupies a central place in research on divorce and child custody.

The numerous works in the social sciences, demography and psychology that deal with children's living arrangements after separation tend to concentrate on the impact of these living arrangements on children's well-being and on gender inequalities, mainly using quantitative methods based on the parents' perspective (Steinbach, 2019; Bernardi and Mortelmans, 2021; Zartler, 2021). Berman and Daneback (2020) list more than 111 references dealing specifically with SPC. These studies are mainly based on quantitative methods (questionnaire surveys or analysis of existing databases), and are strongly focused on the impact of parental separation on children's physical, psychological, social and emotional well-being, reflecting the prevalence of theoretical approaches and frameworks rooted in psychology. These issues are approached through three main prisms: the level of conflict between the parents and its impact on the child's well-being and resources; the effect of the socio-demographic characteristics of families using this type of arrangement (in particular, socio-economic level and presence of a step-parent), and the impact of communication on the parent–child relationship after separation and more broadly on the child's well-being. The authors note that only a small number of qualitative studies have looked at the well-being of children in SPC from these children's own perspective.

The conclusions of this body of literature are mixed, with some authors suggesting that the well-being of children in SPC is improved relative to that of children living in other post-separation arrangements and others pointing to specific difficulties, particularly where the level of conflict between parents is high. Taken together, therefore, they do not settle the sometimes-heated public debate on the advantages and disadvantages of SPC, but rather highlight the need to consider specific situations, whether national, local or within families themselves. Berman and Daneback (2020) also call for the strong psychological focus of previous research to be transcended by developing more sociologically based research that begins from the children's point of view and broadens the analysis beyond well-being to include issues such as interpersonal relationships, geographical and emotional mobility, and the cultural and normative constructs of the family. This is the approach that will be adopted in this book.

The relevance of studying shared physical custody in terms of children's sense of home

This book contributes to the study of SPC by focusing on the key question of the meaning of 'home'. The concept of 'home' has been studied in a wide range of disciplines, including sociology, anthropology, psychology, human geography, history, architecture and philosophy, which testifies to its richness but also to its fragmentation into multiple and sometimes contradictory definitions. Depending on one's perspective, 'home' can be considered, simultaneously or independently, as one or more place(s), space(s), feeling(s), practice(s) and/or way(s) of being in the world (Mallett, 2004). However, these disciplines all agree on the constructed, relational, multidimensional and processual nature of home:

> Home is 'not a given but a creation'. Home is generated through the interaction of shared cultural understandings and personal practices, relationships and embodied experiences – which are in turn enabled and constrained by biography, identity and socio-economic structures. Home is neither given nor static: it is something people build and alter through their actions, emotions, relationships, connections with objects and sensory experiences associated with a specific location. (Fehlberg et al, 2018: 5)

In this book we will focus on children's sense of being 'at home' in their family dwellings, paying particular attention to the practices they use for 'making themselves at home' (Winther, 2009: 57). We understand a 'sense of home' as a unique sense of identity, stability, security, peace and belonging to one or more places – and by extension, to the people, objects and ideas that inhabit that (or those) place(s) (Winther, 2009). We acknowledge that 'home' can be a place of danger and violence and a source of alienation (Price, 2002; Blunt and Dowling, 2006), although this situation did not arise in our study. We also recognize that a 'sense of home' can be attached to other places and to people who are not family members (Massey, 1994; Ahmed, 1999). However, we have chosen to focus on family dwellings to explore the ways in which children anchor themselves in these places and negotiate a sense of family belonging in the specific context of SPC. In other words, we are interested in the ways in which children 'do family' in and through the space of their two residences (Morgan, 2020) and, in turn, how the spatial characteristics of these residences help to define their place in the family. Our book thus contributes to the understanding that creating and maintaining a sense of home is an ongoing and complex process involving concrete practices in which the material and the relational play important roles.

The sense of home is a crucial aspect of the process of empowerment and identity building for adolescents, and living in SPC calls this process into question.[6] Some psychologists and legal experts consider living in a single stable home to be a necessary condition for children's development, believing that the absence of such 'stability' puts them at risk of 'identity fragmentation' (de Singly and Decup-Pannier, 2016: 276). In reality, living in and between two residences challenges the normative model of sedentarism characteristic of Western societies, in which the management of populations is largely based on identifying people according to a single place of residence (Merla, 2018). This paradigm is reflected in the standard institutional model of the family: according to this definition, the contours of the family are delimited by the walls of the dwelling, which houses members connected by physical co-presence (Morgan, 2011).

For social scientists, the family dwelling crystallizes the three dimensions of what Bonnin (1999: 23) calls a 'house-domus', namely:

1. the localized material capital of the dwelling;
2. the functionalized living space as a necessary instrument of domestic practices, which may be everyday, festive, repetitive or exceptional; and
3. the symbolic expressions of identity (collective and individual) that it supports.

The second and third dimensions emphasize how individuals 'do family' through daily interactions with – and within – the space of the dwelling, engaging in practices that define them as members of a family and nurture their sense of belonging (Morgan, 2011), thereby constructing and negotiating their individual and collective identities. This process is particularly important during adolescence, a period that sociologists define as a time of learning autonomy (Galland, 2010), when young people reflexively examine their family ties and distance themselves from the 'family-we' in order to construct their personal identities. The dwelling provides adolescents with a sense of ontological security and a place to socialize with family and peers, and is therefore a key resource in the construction of their identity and sense of belonging.

The bedroom occupies a prominent place in work examining the process through which adolescents develop a sense of belonging within the family dwelling and the role that this sense plays in construction of identity (Bacon, 2018). De Singly (2006) and Poittevin (2005) describe this space as a complex universe that supports processes of empowerment, belonging and construction of relationships with parents, siblings and friends (see also Bovill and Livingstone, 2001; Zaffran, 2014; Ramos, 2018). Adolescents tend to see the bedroom as their 'home', an intimate space apart from shared family life and constituting a personal territory (Ramos, 2018). It provides them with a refuge from the outside world, where they can be themselves and express their personality and lifestyle (Lincoln, 2014). The bedroom is thus a symbolic and meaningful space that allows them to define and express their identity (Zaffran, 2014), as manifested through the control exercised over the space (by closing or not closing the door; by furnishing, organizing and decorating it in a certain way), the time spent and activities pursued there, and the people who are allowed – or forbidden – to enter at certain times (Zaffran, 2014). Rather than a place of withdrawal that is completely closed to the other, Amphoux and Mondada (1989) see the home – symbolized here mainly by the bedroom – as a meeting place, 'a place of the identity of the "I" welcoming the other' (1989: 5), which allows young people to welcome those with whom they share social references. 'It thus allows them to assert their belonging and to recognize themselves in those who come there' (Zaffran, 2014: 2).

Adolescents develop a sense of home by appropriating not only a bedroom (shared or otherwise[7]) but also other spaces within or beyond the dwelling, by means of furnishing and decorating these spaces and by using, owning and surrounding themselves with certain objects rather than others (Poittevin, 2005; de Singly, 2006). In this way, they create a space of significant and meaningful symbols that permits them to maintain a certain form of continuity in their life course and that reflects their particular identity (Csikszentmihalyi and Rochberg-Halton, 1981; Gyger Gaspoz, 2014). Adolescents' sense of being 'at home' in the family dwelling is thus rooted in the space-times of both non-family practices (what they do in their bedrooms, in a favourite spot like a desk or sofa or on their phones or computers), when they are in 'their world', and activities shared with family members, whose importance stems from 'being together' and/or 'being present' with one another (de Singly and Ramos, 2010: 12).

What happens then when children have *two* residences? How do they develop a sense of home that can positively support the formation of their identity and their sense of family belonging? This question is all the more crucial as the resulting separations and blending of families blur family boundaries and undermine feelings of belonging (Zartler, 2011). Although to date only a limited number of studies have examined these questions in terms of the meaning of 'home', the existing body of work attests to the importance of feeling 'at home' in the processes of identity construction and belonging (de Singly and Decup-Pannier, 2016; Palludan and Winther, 2016; Campo et al, 2020). For example, Palludan and Winther (2016) argue that Danish children living in SPC are recognized in their family relationships by claiming the right to have their own room and their own belongings in each of their parents' dwellings, thus making these two dwellings 'their house'. The 'socio-material weight' (Palludan and Winther, 2016: 40) that this process gives them determines their status as hosts, guests or regular visitors in each dwelling.

For their part, de Singly and Decup-Pannier (2016) emphasize that young French people in SPC do not necessarily put their two dwellings on an equal footing: some of them 'prioritize one of their two bedrooms, recreating a "habitual" residence' (de Singly and Decup-Pannier, 2016: 276). This duality does not necessarily lead to a fragmented sense of belonging, as children adopt tactics to reinforce the feeling of having only one 'home', whether in a private bedroom or in a broader territory (de Singly and Decup-Pannier, 2016: 276). It is also important to note that children who do not have their own room in one or both of their parents' dwellings can create a sense of home for themselves by, for example, 'delimiting their "spot" by their bed and what is within reach of that bed (a personal element of "my spot")' (Ramos, 2018: 58).

Blending of families calls existing relationships into question, and also raises spatial issues (Fehlberg et al, 2018). In these new family configurations, the renegotiation of children's and adults' respective positions may be accompanied by competition over the allocation of bedrooms or the demarcation of shared and private spaces in the dwelling, as well as by other spatial and material strategies and practices signalling the acceptance or rejection of 'newcomers' (Marquet and Merla, 2015; 2018; Merla and Nobels, 2019). These family changes therefore challenge children's sense of 'home' and contribute to the reconfiguration of their familial identity.

By bringing adolescents' agency to the fore, these studies contribute to demonstrating that having more than one living space can potentially constitute a resource rather than a handicap for the construction of identity. As de Singly and Decup-Pannier note, 'sociologists (particularly Erving Goffman) claim that having several living spaces is necessary for the individual. From the multiplicity of spaces, the possibility of independence is born. ... Having several addresses is one of the ways in which an individual seeks to avoid being reduced to a single identity' (2016: 275). Serfaty-Garzon (2006) observes that individuals can identify with and become attached to multiple residences, which contribute to the positive definition of their identity. Even when they are geographically distant, these residences are bound together by the meanings that the resident attaches to each of them, thus constituting the resident's 'global' home (Serfaty-Garzon, 2006: 19). Having several places of residence where one feels 'at home' provides access to a heterogeneous repertoire that could thus enable the construction of a unique and original self at the intersection of these multiple identities (Merla, 2018).

As these studies have shown, exploring how children in SPC create and maintain a sense of home offers us a way to better understand how they construct and define a place for themselves within each of their residences, how they appropriate (or do not appropriate) this alternating way of life, and how they articulate their two residences and families into a whole, a 'global home' synthesizing their multiple spatial and familial affiliations. We will see in this book that living in and between different places of residence confronts children with obstacles and difficulties in their daily lives, such as the physical burden of transporting their personal belongings, the distress of missing a parent when they are apart, the distance they need to travel between dwellings, and the need to navigate between different or even conflicting family cultures. However, we will also see that through their socialization in this particular context, the children we encountered in our study have developed skills, strategies and ways of being and doing that are specific to this way of life and help them to cope with their periods of presence and absence. These practices integrate the different spaces of residence, which are seen as distinct, binding them together to form a coherent whole: an all-encompassing and unique sense of home. Far from taking the appropriation of this way of life for granted, our aim here is to understand its underlying mechanisms. We will also show how certain practices are facilitated or, on the contrary, made more difficult – or even impossible – by the material, cultural, social and temporal conditions that constitute the structure of opportunities and constraints with which children must contend on a daily basis.

In taking this approach, our work is part of an emerging body of research that considers SPC starting from the points of view and practices of the children themselves. Our goal is not so much to determine whether this form of arrangement is 'good' or 'bad' for children as to understand a way of life experienced on a daily basis by hundreds of thousands of children in Europe and beyond, which challenges not only the foundations of the family as it has been constructed over the last two centuries but the way in which the social sciences study the family (Merla et al, 2021b; Thomson and Turunen, 2021).

We will therefore analyse the ways in which children who move between two residences can construct a sense of home and of belonging to a family through an intersection of individual and family practices within, outside and around each of their dwellings, and we will examine the ways in which these practices contribute to 'doing family'. Our aim is to understand the mechanisms underpinning this appropriation, as well as those that make it difficult or even impossible. We will also look at how the 'family practices' (Morgan, 2011) that they deploy within and around each place of residence make it possible to create a distinct family life in each dwelling. Considering that children in SPC also move between educational practices that are 'contrasting (or not)' (Michaud Delahaye, 2009) and heterogeneous family cultures (Merla, 2018), we will observe how children develop different strategies and skills to adapt, appropriate, negotiate and position themselves in relation to different family environments. We will approach this way of life as a potential resource for children in a context where the family is undergoing multiple processes of spatio-temporal, relational and emotional reorganization. By doing so, we are distinguishing ourselves from the dominant Western ideology of childhood which considers a child's natural place to be the house – a unique and fixed place where the child finds stability and security within a united family – and which consequently views parental separation and child mobility as automatically problematic and alienating.

Belgium: a key case study

We have chosen to study children's sense of home in SPC based on research carried out in Belgium between 2016 and 2021. The choice of Belgium is no coincidence, as this country presents a particularly interesting context for the study of separation and SPC for a number of reasons.

First of all, parental separation has become a relatively common experience for children and adolescents in Belgium, to the point of losing its exceptional character (Marquet and Merla, 2015). Historically, the country's divorce rate has been very high compared to the European average, reaching a maximum of 3.3 in 2008 compared with a European average of 2.0. Since then, the divorce rate has gradually decreased, reaching 1.9 in 2021, but remains higher than the European average of 1.7 (Eurostat, 2023).

Belgium also stands out among Western countries for its early adoption of SPC as the preferred model following divorce or separation, which has had a significant impact on child custody arrangements. Under the Law of 18

July 2006 (henceforward, the 2006 Law)[8] SPC became the primary form of custody to be considered by the court in cases of parental separation where this arrangement is requested by at least one parent. Article 374(2) of the Civil Code states that:

> In the absence of agreement, in the case of joint legal custody, the court shall, at the request of at least one of the parents, consider as a matter of priority the possibility of determining the child's residence on an equal basis between the parents. However, if the court considers that equal accommodation is not the most appropriate arrangement, it may order non-equal accommodation.

Custody can be apportioned in a number of different ways under this system. Van Houcke (2017: 5) distinguishes between egalitarian SPC, where the child's time is divided equally between the two parents (50 per cent with each parent, with alternating periods of 3.5 days, seven days or 15 days, for instance), and quasi-egalitarian SPC, where the child resides for 65 per cent of the time with one parent and 35 per cent with the other parent (for example, with alternating periods of nine days and five days, respectively).

It is important to note that this legislation has reversed the burden of proof: a parent applying for SPC must no longer prove that it is beneficial, whereas a parent opposing such an application must now prove that it is contrary to the best interests of the child (Merla et al, 2022).

This law was enacted following recognition of the legal concept of 'joint exercise of parental authority' or 'joint legal custody', which was introduced in the Law of 13 April 1995 (henceforward, the 1995 Law).[9] These changes in legislation emerged from a social discourse that included arguments about parental equality, the feasibility of such custody arrangements (Marquet, 2008) and the best interests of the child (Casman et al, 2010). It is worth noting that the 2006 Law appears to have formalized a pre-existing social trend, as an increase in the practice of egalitarian SPC was observed even before legal support for this practice was in place (Côté and Gaborean, 2015; Van Houcke, 2017).

The consequences of this legal framework include a continuous increase in the prevalence of SPC (Van Houcke, 2017). By 2020, more than four in ten parents in Belgium had experienced divorce or separation, and one in three separated couples shared physical custody equally (Ligue des Familles, 2020). This means that, despite the predominance of the 'traditional' nuclear family, which represents some 57 per cent of family configurations, the number of parents with SPC after separation is now nearly equal to the number of parents with sole custody (Ligue des Familles, 2020). This shift, given that sole custody was previously the default option, underscores society's evolving preference for SPC. Belgium therefore provides a key case study for understanding how SPC works on a day-to-day basis, and offers important lessons for societies where this type of arrangement is on the rise.

Introducing the children at the heart of our research

This book is based on data collected from 17 Belgian families between October 2017 and August 2019. A total of 21 children were interviewed: ten girls and 11 boys, aged between ten and 16 years.[10] As stated elsewhere (Merla and Nobels, 2021), children in this age group were chosen for this study because they are experiencing important transitions, such as that from primary to secondary school, and they are gaining more autonomy, especially in terms of travelling, using information and communication technologies (ICTs) and managing their personal belongings. To be included in our study, children had to reside in the Walloon and/or Brussels regions, have lived for at least one year in SPC and have at least one re-partnered parent.[11]

As shown in Table 1.1, the majority of the children in our study (13 of 21) alternate residences weekly (7/7 days), four alternate every five days (5/5) and four have a quasi-egalitarian rhythm, with three alternating every six and eight days (6/8) and the fourth every nine and five days (9/5). SPC was established when the children were under three years old in seven cases, between three and six years old in three, and over six years old in 11. Ten parents are single, while 24 are in new relationships. Among the cases of family blending, seven children have one parent who is single and one who has a new partner, either with children (in four cases) or without children (in three cases). Where both parents are in new couple relationships, five children have a blended family with children on one side only, while seven others experience this situation of blending in both parental residences. The degree of conflict[12] between parents is low in three cases, medium in seven and medium-high in seven. In all cases, the decision to set up SPC was taken amicably. All parental couples had separated or divorced (if married) by mutual consent. Six parental couples had their agreements recorded by the family court and divorce decrees issued; four worked out a written agreement with the help of a notary (mainly if they shared property) or a mediator, without having it approved by the courts. The other seven settled for a verbal agreement.

Most of the families are middle class, with the exception of two fathers who describe themselves as upper middle class, but there are some differences in terms of the parents' educational qualifications (11 parents have a secondary school diploma, 21 have a university degree and two did not provide this information) and perceived standards of living ('modest' for four parents, 'intermediate' for 24 and 'high' for six). The parents of 12 children live less than 25 minutes by car from one another (that is, less than 15 kilometres

Table 1.1: Characteristics of study participants

Characteristics of children surveyed (n = 21)

Age	10–12 years: 10 13–14 years: 6 15–16 years: 5
Gender	Female: 10 Male: 11
Age at implementation of SPC	Under 3 years: 7 Between 3 and 6 years: 3 Over 6 years: 11
Alternation rhythm	7/7 days: 13 5/5 days: 4 6/8 days: 3 9/5 days: 1
Distance between parental residences	Less than 25 minutes by car: 12 More than 25 minutes by car: 9
Family composition*	Both parents single: 2 Single parent/parent with new partner: 3 Single parent/parent with new partner and child(ren): 4 Parent with new partner/parent with new partner and child(ren): 5 Both parents with new partners and child(ren): 7

Characteristics of parents of children surveyed (n = 34)

Family situation	Single: 10 Re-partnered: 24
Educational level	Secondary education: 11 Higher education/university degree: 21 Missing data: 2
Perceived standard of living**	Modest: 4 Intermediate: 24 High: 6

Degree of conflict between ex-partners (n = 17 parental couples)***

	Low: 3 Medium: 7 Medium-high: 7

Note: * Neither the father nor the mother of Joseph (aged 16) and his sister Amandine (12) is re-partnered; these children therefore do not meet this eligibility criterion for our study. However, we decided to retain them because they meet the other criteria (age, distance between homes and time of separation) and because analysis of their discourse reveals relevant profiles for our research. ★★ Here we follow the *Institut national de la statistique et des études économiques* assessment of 'perceived standard of living' based on the parents' and children's perceptions rather than a statistical measure (Clerc, 2014). We thus distinguish three levels (high, intermediate and modest) based on the descriptions given by the parents and the child of their 'living conditions', which are understood as representing a high, intermediate or low level of material well-being. The quality of housing and the purchasing power devoted to the child's possessions (clothes and toys/games) are the main factors considered. ★★★ The term 'parental couple' (Marquet, 2010: 55) refers to the idea that the child's father and mother continue to fulfil their parental roles after separation. Our use of this term when referring to both of them reflects the responsibility they both retain for the child.

apart); the parents of the other nine live between 20 and 50 kilometres apart. All live in urban or suburban areas.

Although none of these family configurations is characterized by significant economic insecurity or extreme levels of inter-parental conflict,[13] their profiles challenge the preconception that parents practising SPC have high educational and income levels and relatively low levels of conflict (Berman and Daneback, 2020).[14] As we have described, there is indeed a diversification of these profiles in countries where SPC is encouraged by legislation – although SPC remains difficult to implement for disadvantaged families. None of the parents we interviewed would consider setting up another type of arrangement, such as exclusive custody in one parent's dwelling.

Using participatory methods to hear children's voices

Few sociological studies have specifically examined children's experience of mobility and multilocality, or their sense of home. It was therefore necessary to develop a methodological approach tailored to these issues and to this specific target group. Our choice was guided by our wish to offer the participants tools adapted to their age, their level of maturity and their diverse ways of expressing themselves. We therefore opted for participatory, creative and flexible methods (MacDonald and Greggans, 2008; Weller, 2012; Schier et al, 2015), which were used in several sessions with the children. We also chose to interview at least one of the parents before the first session with the child; data were therefore collected in two stages.[15]

We started with a semi-structured interview with at least one parent in order to understand the child's family context and culture. We then conducted two or three semi-structured interviews with each child individually, each structured around a participatory method. The Socio–Spatial Network Game (SSNG; Schier, 2017) consists of a game board on which children lay out and construct the different places that are important to them, the people associated with these places, and how they move between these places. This technique enables us to look at the children's family and residential network and how they circulate within this network. In the Emotion Map (Gabb and Singh, 2015), children are asked to draw each dwelling in the form of a plan as seen from above. They identify the rooms/spaces in the dwelling that they consider to belong to them with coloured stickers, and draw emoticons to reflect how they feel there. They then proceed in the same way for the other residents, identifying the rooms/spaces that belong to each family member with a coloured sticker (one colour for each person) and drawing an emoticon to describe how they feel in the rooms/spaces that 'belong' to the others. This technique enables us to look at the processes of territorialization and the tensions and negotiations that accompany them as well as the family relationships within each dwelling. Finally, the

Figure 1.1: Socio-Spatial Network Game (Lewis, aged 16; photo taken from his vantage point)

Go-Along Method (Kusenbach, 2003) consists of accompanying children on a typical journey between their two residences. This technique provides rich information on how children leave one residence, travel to and arrive at the other, and the emotions associated with this journey.

To give the reader a better idea of the first two tools, we will present some of the children's creations. The first (Figure 1.1), an example of the SSNG, was made by Lewis (aged 16), whose parents live about 30 kilometres apart. In the interview, Lewis says that the distance between their dwellings complicates his daily life, although he is beginning to get used to it. His comments are reflected in his construction where, after placing a red block symbolizing his father's triplex on the board, he explains: 'My mum's house [the green block], I'd put it over there [the opposite corner of the room], but I'm going to put it here [the opposite corner of the board].' He also points out the many means of transport that he uses to get from one residence to the other (train, tram/underground, car). At his mother's house, he places pawns to represent his mother (orange), his stepfather (blue) and his half-sister Clémentine (ten; a small white pawn hidden by the two large ones), as well as his cat and his mother's car. At his father's apartment, he places a pawn symbolizing his father (green) and one representing himself (black), with the black pawn on a small wooden disk to indicate how important this place is to him.

The parents of Eliot (14) both live on the same street. He puts his mother's apartment and his father's house (pink cards) next to each other on the same green card to symbolize the fact that he feels at home in both his mother's and his father's dwellings (Figure 1.2).

In the SSNG, we approach our research questions through the children's own constructions and the explanations they give when they place an element

Figure 1.2: Socio-Spatial Network Game (Eliot, aged 14; photo taken from his vantage point)

on the board. These constructions are not set in stone: the children often use them to illustrate and clarify their comments during the interview. Some participants illustrate the journeys they make regularly by moving the small car, bus, pedestrian, bicycle or tram represented on the board.

The second methodological tool we used in the interviews is the Emotion Map. On the map of her mother's house (Figure 1.3), Marie (12) represents the areas that she considers to belong to each member of the family, symbolizing her mother with a green sticker, her stepfather with a red sticker, her half-brother Oscar (six) with a blue sticker and herself with a white sticker. When we ask her to associate the emotions she feels with the type of interactions that take place in each area, she draws a lightning bolt on the living room sofa, explaining that she often fights with her half-brother to occupy that space. The adolescent wants to sit there comfortably and watch television, while the boy marks 'his territory' by scattering all his toys.

Chloé (12) draws an Emotion Map of her father's house, showing the rooms that belong to each member of the family and how she (symbolized by a green sticker) and her sister Annelyse (ten; represented by a white sticker with the initial 'A') feel in the different rooms (Figure 1.4). She also lists the objects in her bedroom that are particularly important to her (her telephone, her bed and her yoga mat).

Our research takes a qualitative and comprehensive approach, investigating how a small number of children, interviewed in depth, appropriate their

Figure 1.3: Emotion Map of mother's house (Marie, aged 12)

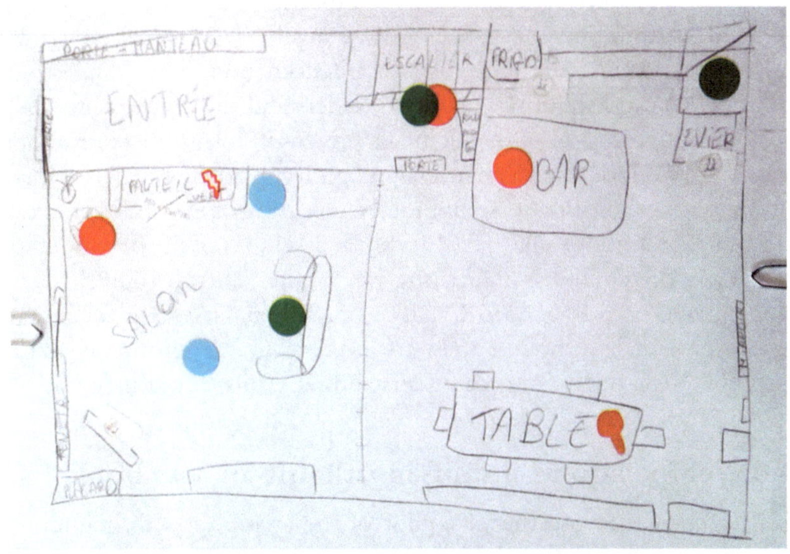

Figure 1.4: Emotion Map of father's house (Chloé, aged 12)

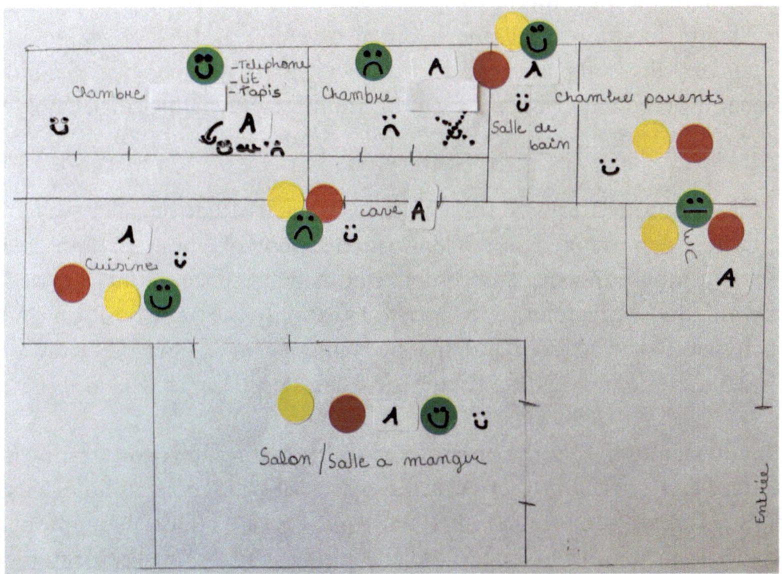

alternating way of life and construct a home based on the meaning they give to their practices. The aim of this approach is to interpret 'social reality as it emerges from the experience of those involved' (Marquet, 1991: 205). Thus, understanding the meaning of a phenomenon is not a question of explaining its causes, but of seeking to understand the context in which it appears, considering all of the elements present in relation to one another. We are therefore adopting a phenomenological approach, which is primarily descriptive and consists of 'scrupulously reporting the manifestations and modes of expression' (Paillé and Mucchielli, 2021: 42) of the phenomenon – in this case, the children's alternating way of life. This method sheds light on complex processes that are difficult to capture in large-scale quantitative surveys, and that, although they are specific to the group of children approached, can open doors to understanding similar life situations.

The archipelago as a unifying theme in this book

We have chosen to use the metaphor of the archipelago throughout this work to characterize the children's two dwellings. This image allows us to understand these places of residence as interconnected 'islands' in the children's experience, between which they navigate and at which they anchor themselves on a daily basis. This metaphor was originally developed in the field of multilocality studies by Duchêne-Lacroix (2014).

By living in more than one habitual dwelling and by engaging in an 'active daily life' (*vita activa*) in and between their residences, the children we encountered experience a form of 'multilocal dwelling' that Duchêne-Lacroix (2013) defines as:

> [T]he appropriation of the multi-residential situation as a way of life, not experienced as transitional, transient or abnormal but as a way of inhabiting space, a discontinuous lived space, 'contaminated' by rhizomic practices, appropriated through the transposition and activation of resources and the permanence of a portable array of instruments for daily life. (Duchêne-Lacroix, 2013: 159)

This concept highlights the processes of appropriation, territorial familiarity, practices and continuity between the spaces of residential multilocality to examine the ways in which individuals – in this case children – appropriate the social and family practices and the physical spaces of their multilocal lives. Physical space is considered here not only as an objective reality, but as a 'lived space' (Di Méo, 2012) in which the lived, perceived, felt and value-laden dimensions of reality are also taken into account. This 'lived space' is understood as an intimate network of places and territories, both real and imagined by each individual (Di Méo, 2012). By practising, representing, thinking about, redefining or avoiding these spaces, individually or collectively, people give them a particular meaning.

The notion of multilocal dwelling invites researchers to examine the ways in which practices of physical mobility are linked to practices of local anchoring (Duchêne-Lacroix, 2014). The 'archipelization of living spaces' (Duchêne-Lacroix, 2014: 52) thus describes the articulation between stable, immobile places of anchorage (routines, expectations, strong ties) and mobile, immaterial spaces within which people, objects and ideas travel, ensuring continuity between living spaces. The in-between is thus central to the experience of multilocality, as it creates continuity between places. Indeed, multilocal living implies regular, circular mobility between at least two habitual places of residence, with a certain degree of habit; this circular mobility allows the individual to connect these places of interest through regular use of a physical passageway. This 'transitional space' (Duchêne-Lacroix, 2014: 38) is appropriated by individuals who develop routines and rituals as they travel, initiating certain activities that are then continued in the fixed places where they arrive (such as reading a book or starting a discussion). What happens 'in between' connects the dwellings and gives meaning to the lived spaces of multilocality.

This in-between space is thus a 'constitutive part' of multilocal living in SPC (Schier et al, 2015). During their travels, children establish family and social relationships in various ways (for example, when travelling with their siblings or meeting friends along the way): 'via the movements of bodies, things, ideas with varying intensities, including stillness; through mediating technical devices ... by the assemblage of heterogeneous materials used for the living arrangements and by the multiple encounters of people here, there and on the move' (Schier et al, 2015: 441). The perspective of multilocality therefore considers both stability and mobility to be integral to the experience of multilocal living arrangements.

Moreover, relationships between family members are no longer confined to physical, embodied spaces – they extend beyond the walls of the dwelling through virtual means of co-presence. As Wellman notes, digital media 'have afforded household members the ability to go about on their separate ways while staying more connected' (Wellman, 2018: xix). The development and democratization of ICTs have thus had a profound impact on the ways in which family members stay in touch, providing new forms of virtual co-presence that create opportunities to maintain family and social relationships across space and time (Merla et al, 2021a).

We propose to consider the two family residences of children living in SPC as two 'islands' that form an archipelago symbolizing the children's multilocal dwelling. This metaphor invites us to focus on what happens within each 'island' as well as the practices deployed between the two. In other words, we will explore various practices taking place 'here', 'there' and in between the 'islands', which are interrelated as in an archipelago. This metaphor does not imply, however, that the archipelago is made up of islands that are similar, homogeneous and equally invested as 'home'. We will see that each island can have its own characteristics and properties, that specific and distinct practices and subcultures can develop there, and that tensions and contradictions can arise between them. However, this does not prevent them from forming a whole, a global home, in the children's experience.

Before embarking on our journey with the children who have told us their stories, we will first set out some contextual elements relating to the family environments in which they are growing up, in terms of norms, values and educational practices. We will introduce a typology of parental 'islands' based on styles of parental functioning and the types of boundary, more or less impermeable, that parents draw between their own dwellings and those of their ex-partners (Chapter 2).

In subsequent chapters, we will invite the reader to follow the children on a journey that begins with the transition from one residence to another, involving the management of belongings to be taken or left behind and the journey between the two dwellings (Chapter 3). The journey continues with the arrival at the destination residence, where 'routines and rituals of return' are carried out (Chapter 4), and with the time spent there, as the children define, negotiate and appropriate a place within the family and a particular sense of home (Chapter 5). The journey will end with a new departure, raising the question of maintaining the children's symbolic presence in a dwelling during their absence (Chapter 6). We will then return to the question of the children's sense of 'home' in SPC, and will propose a model incorporating the dimensions and modes of experience according to which children define a sense of 'home' that is both singular and plural (Chapter 7). Finally, in our Concluding Reflections, we will begin by summarizing our main contributions to the study of children's sense of home. We will then move beyond our specific study to relate our findings to the question of children's socialization and habitus formation in a multilocal context, discuss the contributions of our research to the broader study of children in SPC beyond the Belgian case (and its limitations), highlight some key lessons for practitioners, and present possible ways to broaden our analysis to a wider range of family situations, spaces and significant others.

Notes

[1]   We will use the term 'first family' to designate the members of the initial nuclear family (that is, the parental couple to whom the child we encountered was born, as well as the brothers and sisters also born of this union). We will use the term 'new family' to designate the biological parent and the children born of the same union where the parent is now single, or in case of family blending, the biological parent, the children born of the first union, and the new partner and their children, if any, as well as any

children born of the second union. We refer to the mother's side as the 'new maternal family' and the father's side as the 'new paternal family'. It should be noted that none of the families we met had adopted a child, which is why we refer to biological ties in our definitions. There were also no same-sex couples among our participating families.

[2] In this book the term 'separated' is used in a generic sense to include both separated and divorced couples.

[3] We are asking these questions as part of the MobileKids project, funded by the European Research Council and led by Laura Merla. The aim of this project is to understand how parental separation and the mobility and multilocality that result from the establishment of shared physical custody affect children between the ages of ten and 16. In particular, the aim is to understand how these children cope (or do not cope) with this way of life, to uncover the diversity of the children's experiences and to identify their needs based on their own accounts. This involves identifying how and under what circumstances these children appropriate this lifestyle and develop new ways of acting and being in the world, or a 'habitus' (Bourdieu, 1979; 1997), specific to multilocality, mobility and the experience of intermittent co-presence and absence.

[4] In this book, 'SPC' is used as a generic term for both egalitarian and quasi-egalitarian shared physical custody arrangements.

[5] It should be noted that there is a dearth of statistics that quantify and compare the importance of SPC at national and international levels. For instance, data on the prevalence of SPC in Western Europe come from a range of sources and are based on different statistical indicators, making it difficult to make valid comparisons (Flaquer, 2021). The recent study by Hakovrita et al (2023), based on a new module on the living arrangements of children from the European Union Statistics on Income and Living Conditions survey, is an important exception.

[6] The meaning and the challenges of home for children in SPC have been reviewed by Merla et al (2021a), whose main arguments are presented and further developed here.

[7] It is important to note that the importance of having one's own bedroom is a recent cultural and historical construct, and therefore varies across space and time, including in Western countries (see, for example, Bovill and Livingstone, 2001; Palludan and Winther, 2016).

[8] *Loi du 18 juillet 2006 tendant à privilégier l'hébergement égalitaire de l'enfant dont les parents sont séparés et réglementant l'exécution forcée en matière d'hébergement d'enfant* (Law of 18 July 2006 to promote equal accommodation for children whose parents are separated and to regulate the enforcement of orders for the accommodation of children).

[9] *Loi du 13 avril 1995 relative à l'exercice conjoint de l'autorité parentale* (Law of 13 April 1995 on the joint exercise of parental authority).

[10] In this book, we will use the terms 'child', 'adolescent', 'teenager' and 'young person' interchangeably to refer to individuals in this age group.

[11] The challenge of recruitment was to vary the profiles of the families, particularly in terms of where they lived (urban, suburban, rural), the distance between the parents' dwellings, their socio-economic levels and the gender of the children. Our aim was not to create a representative corpus of interviews; this non-representativeness is inherent in qualitative research, where 'the aim is to understand situations, [and] not to estimate values in a survey population' (Berthier, 2010: 176).

[12] The degree of conflict is assessed according to the criteria defined by the psychologist Ahrons (1979) and the sociologists Brunet et al (2008) to characterize the nature of the relationship between parents after separation. These works each propose a typology with three broad categories of parents practising SPC, distinguishing among friendly and close, cordial and polite, and conflictual and distant relationships between parents. These qualifiers define co-parenting styles based on the ways in which parents do or do not invest

together in the child's upbringing, based on questions including whether or not the parents still communicate with one another, whether they spend time together and whether they value and seek out these contacts and shared moments. Here we use the responses to these three questions to define four levels of conflict: the level of conflict is considered low when parents maintain a friendly relationship, communicate, jointly spend time with the child and enjoy these moments. It is considered moderate when they maintain a cordial and polite relationship, communicate and jointly spend time with the child, but do not seek these exchanges or moments together. A medium-high level is defined by parents who have a conflictual and distant relationship and avoid communicating or seeing each other as much as possible, except when they need to make important decisions affecting their child (such as choosing a course of study). We did not encounter any situations where the level of conflict is high, as all of the ex-partners are able to talk and see one another without the intervention of a third party (such as a mediator or lawyer) when they feel this exchange is necessary for their child's well-being.

[13]   This may be partially due to selection bias, in view of the ethical requirements of the project: each of the two former partners had to agree to the child's participation in our research.

[14]   Other research also challenges the idea that only parents with low levels of conflict implement SPC (see in particular Sodermans et al, 2013; Merla and Dedonder, 2019).

[15]   All of the interviews were conducted by Bérengère Nobels, in close collaboration with Laura Merla.

2

Parental Islands

In this chapter, we will explore the kinds of boundaries that the parents in our study draw between their own dwellings and those of their ex-partners, based on their own parental styles. Through these boundaries, each gives their 'island' a particular shape, which forms an important framework that the children must deal with on a daily basis.

The typology of 'parental islands' that we have developed from our data was constructed in two stages. We first identified each parent's 'parental style', which characterizes the style of interaction between parent and child with reference to a set of inter-individual norms, values and practices deployed within the 'new family' centred around a dwelling (an 'island'). We then analysed the forms of inter-dwelling boundaries drawn by each parent, corresponding to specific 'styles', which shape five islands of varying contours.

A typology of parental styles post-separation

Analysis of the children's discourse, contextualized and reinforced by that of the parents, revealed five distinct 'parental styles', defined on the basis of values, routines, practices and limits or freedoms granted by each parent. This typology extends the classification of 'family' functioning and 'conjugal interactions' in nuclear families defined by Widmer et al (2002), building on the work of Kellerhals et al (1982; Kellerhals and Montandon, 1991). We will briefly present the typology developed by this team of Swiss sociologists before adapting and transposing it to parent–child relations in post-separation families.

Family functioning and conjugal interaction in nuclear families

In their study of family and conjugal interactions in nuclear families, Widmer and his team (2002: 16) identify four major axes used to define family functioning in the sociological literature: *autonomy/fusion, openness/closure, expressiveness/instrumentalism* and *regulation*.

The 'autonomy/fusion' axis refers to how individual resources are pooled and how they are controlled by the family group: families whose members tend to favour the sharing of similar attitudes and points of view and who advocate values of consensus and similarity fall on the 'fusion' side of the axis. In contrast, those who value the maintenance of individual differences and pursuits and who interact based on these differences emphasize the autonomy of family members. The 'openness/closure' axis concerns whether exchanges with the outside world are valued or limited: a family group that encourages external exchanges to nourish internal dialogue demonstrates 'openness', while one that turns inward to maintain internal patterns shows 'closure' to the environment. To a 'closed' family group, the outside world may be seen as a threat – a potential source of new ways of thinking and doing things. The 'expressiveness/ instrumentality' axis reflects the family group's primary goals, opposing expressiveness and prioritization of internal, relational goals like empathy and support to instrumentality and prioritization of external goals such as social integration and mobility. The fourth axis, that of 'regulation', refers to the way decisional power and household tasks are divided between partners. Regulation is considered 'normative' when day-to-day life is guided by general rules that are often established on the basis of status (wife/husband, woman/man), resulting in a strong gender differentiation. In contrast, 'communicative' regulation favours dialogue, negotiation and analysis of situations on a case-by-case basis without defining rights or duties associated with status.

Widmer and colleagues (2002; 2006) draw on these axes to define five types of conjugal interaction within contemporary couples: the *parallel*, *bastion*, *cocoon*, *association* and *companionship* types.

'Parallel' couples emphasize a strong gendered division of domestic and relational roles, strong fusion and strong closure. They see the external environment as a threat to their internal equilibrium. Behaviour is guided by a concern for order, distinct individual spheres of activity and introversion.

'Bastion' couples place a high value on internal relationships, limiting exchanges with the outside world as much as possible for fear of upsetting their conjugal model. These couples tend to be home-loving and fusional. Rules are established mainly on the basis of status, reflecting a strong gendered division of domestic and relational roles. The 'we-family' takes precedence over the 'I', and consensus and tradition are valued over self-expression.

'Cocoon' couples show a high degree of fusion and moderate closure. Unlike 'bastion' couples, their internal models are not based on a strong division of gender roles. These couples value communicative rather than statutory regulation, and seek to establish intimate, comfortable surroundings.

'Association' couples value autonomy and individual differences and pursuits. Exchanges with the outside world – often individual – are valued as ways to reinforce internal solidarity and communication. Rules are flexible, as they are not based on gender roles but are the subject of constant negotiation between the partners, who are considered to be on an equal footing. Behaviour is guided by the quest for self-expression and by negotiation of individual rights.

Finally, 'companionship' couples value a moderate degree of openness and communicative regulation. In contrast to 'association' couples, they value fusion and similarity in the sense that the couple's ways of doing and thinking take precedence over individual differences and pursuits. Behaviour is guided by values of solidarity, external integration and community.

Post-separation 'parental styles'

We drew inspiration from these axes and this typology in our research, transposing and adapting them to describe 'parental styles' in post-separation families. Our aim was to grasp the specific parental style of each ex-partner based on the testimonies we collected. This enabled us to identify five post-separation parental styles, namely *bastion, cocoon, companionship, association* and *anomic parallel*, which are presented in Table 2.1. It should be noted that where a parent is single, that parent's style influences and shapes the functioning of the 'new family'.[1] In our study, where there was re-partnering, the parent's and step-parent's styles gradually converged towards a style specific to the 'new family'.

These five styles are based on the same axes of family functioning identified by Widmer et al (2006), namely openness/closure, autonomy/ fusion, regulation and expressiveness/instrumentality. Thus, for each style, we specify the type of interaction maintained between parent and child within the 'new family', defined by the parent's degree of openness to the external environment, the degree of fusion desired among members of the 'new family', the preferred type of regulation and the core values.[2] These styles are developed at length in the following pages; we present them here in broad outline.

'Bastion' parents seek a strong sense of fusion among the inhabitants of their 'island'. They prefer to establish few external relationships – particularly avoiding their ex-partners – as they want their 'island' to be an important point of anchorage for their 'new family'. Rules are established based on each inhabitant's status according to age and gender, and each inhabitant is expected to invest in the domestic sphere and to spend time with the family. Strongly ingrained family routines and habits are typical, such as sharing a meal at a specific time every evening in order to be together.

'Cocoon' parents also seek a strong sense of fusion, and do not value the establishment of external relationships. However, rules are established based on communicative regulation that leaves room for negotiation and

Table 2.1: Typology of post-separation parental styles

<table>
<tr><td></td><td></td><td>Bastion</td><td>Cocoon</td><td>Companionship</td><td>Association</td><td>Anomic parallel</td></tr>
<tr><td rowspan="2">Openness/ closure</td><td>Norms</td><td>Strong closure</td><td>Moderate closure</td><td>Moderate openness</td><td>Strong openness</td><td>Strong closure</td></tr>
<tr><td>Practices</td><td colspan="2">Information (such as advice) from within the family;
Little interest in external relations</td><td colspan="2">Information from outside the family;
External relations considered essential to internal dynamics</td><td>Information from within the family;
Little interest in external relations</td></tr>
<tr><td rowspan="2">Autonomy/ fusion</td><td>Norms</td><td colspan="3">Strong fusion in the 'new family';
We > I</td><td colspan="2">Weak fusion;
Autonomy of members of the 'new family';
I > We</td></tr>
<tr><td>Practices</td><td colspan="3">Priority given to family time;
Consensus;
Home-loving</td><td colspan="2">Priority given to time for oneself;
Individual differences and pursuits</td></tr>
<tr><td rowspan="2">Regulation</td><td>Norms</td><td>Statutory</td><td colspan="3" align="center">Communicative</td><td>Anomic</td></tr>
<tr><td>Practices</td><td>General rules based on status;
Strong family routines, culture and habits;
Investment in the domestic sphere for the family</td><td>Rules negotiated between equal members;
Case-by-case approach;
Strong family routines;
Investment in the domestic sphere for oneself</td><td colspan="2">Rules negotiated between equal members;
Case-by-case approach;
No family routines;
Investment in the domestic sphere for oneself</td><td>Absence of rules;
No family routines;
Disinvestment from the family sphere</td></tr>
<tr><td rowspan="1">Expressiveness/ instrumentalism</td><td>Core values</td><td>Loyalty to the family and respect for family rituals</td><td>Affection, comfort and intimacy</td><td>Family solidarity, external integration and community</td><td>Exchanges, self-expression and negotiation of individual rights</td><td>Distinct individual spheres of activity, introversion</td></tr>
<tr><td></td><td>Parents (n = 34)</td><td>4</td><td>7</td><td>7</td><td>12</td><td>4</td></tr>
</table>

case-by-case analysis of situations. Family members invest in the domestic sphere for their own reasons, and find affection and comfort within the family group.

'Companionship' parents value external integration and involvement in the community. They want their 'new family' to be open to the outside world, believing that external relationships are necessary to nourish the family unit's internal dynamics. 'Companionship' parents seek to establish a strong sense of belonging among the inhabitants of their 'islands', and prioritize time spent together. Rules are negotiated between members, who are considered to be on an equal footing. Parents do not seek to establish family routines, and are more spontaneous than those in the preceding categories.

'Association' parents emphasize the autonomy of family members, and prioritize time for themselves. Relationships established outside the family group are considered essential to the internal dynamics of their 'new families'. Norms are negotiated between members considered as equals, and self-expression and respect for individual rights are valued.

Finally, 'anomic parallel' parents are characterized by a high degree of closure to the external environment and a low degree of fusion between members of the 'new family'. Introversion and distinct individual spheres of activity are valued, and priority is given to time for themselves and to individual expression. It should be noted that the definition given here is similar to that proposed by Widmer et al (2006) when they define the 'parallel' type of conjugal interaction, but with one major difference. The 'parallel' type in the original typology is defined by status-based regulation, which implies a strong gendered division of domestic and relational roles. This is not the case for 'anomic parallel' parents, who value the absence of rules. This anomic form of regulation – or absence of norms – is reflected in the parent's disinvestment in the internal relationships of the 'new family' and the absence of family routines. We have therefore added this third form of regulation to the axes of family functioning identified by Widmer and colleagues (2002).

Parental islands defined by differing boundaries

Once we had established this typology, we re-examined the boundaries that each parent defined between their own 'island' and that of their ex-partner. Analysis of the children's accounts of their life experiences reveals that parents represent and delimit the boundaries of their own 'temporal territories' (Zerubavel, 1981, quoted by Hachet, 2014: 31) with varying degrees of permeability.[3] While Zerubavel uses the term 'temporal territoriality' to differentiate between moments of accessibility and of inaccessibility, Hachet (2014), who is concerned with the parental experience of part-time custody of a child post-separation, applies this concept to the context of shared physical custody (SPC) by defining the parents' 'temporal territories' as determined by the child's presence or absence in their dwelling. Following in Hachet's footsteps, and in line with our archipelago metaphor, we will use the territorial metaphor here to conceptualize the time children spend with each parent in a spatialized manner. This enables us to examine the ways in which children symbolically cross spatio-temporal boundaries and to measure the degrees of (im)permeability of these 'temporal territories'. In summary, by putting SPC into practice, parents accept certain passages between their 'islands', perceived as 'temporal territories', and those of their ex-partners. In so doing, these parents draw the boundaries of their 'islands', which, as we shall see, are specific to each post-separation parental style.

The intersection of the 'parental styles' we have described and the kinds of boundaries drawn by each parent defines the five types of 'parental islands' that we will describe in the remainder of this chapter. We begin by presenting the key elements of this typology.

Table 2.2 presents the main characteristics of the five types of 'parental island', defined by specific forms of inter-household boundaries: *wall*, *membrane*, *reef* and *flow*. Put briefly, the 'wall' is an impermeable boundary that does not allow any exchange between the two households. The 'membrane', while relatively impermeable, does allow some inter-household exchanges. The 'reef' is relatively permeable, regulating exchanges mainly through the strong fusion among inhabitants of the 'island', while in the 'flow' the two 'islands' are conceived of as being part of the same 'space–time continuum', allowing everything (children and belongings) to circulate freely between them. These forms of inter-household boundaries are specific to the different parental styles described in the previous section, and will be detailed in the following pages where we will describe and illustrate each type of 'island'.

Our analysis also considers the ways in which parents supervise their children's mobility and (digital) communication practices, which are also specific to each parental style. We give particular attention to mobility and to communication because they extend beyond the walls of the dwelling, both physically and virtually, and are therefore central to the study of inter-household boundaries (Merla et al, 2021a).

According to the degree of openness/closure of the 'new family', parents may perceive mobility as a threat or as a natural form of freedom. According to their position on the fusion/autonomy axis, they may restrict and monitor their child's movements, or may authorize movements without supervising them. Finally, according to whether their preferred form of regulation is statutory, communicational or anomic, parents may establish rules for movement based on the child's age and gender, negotiate the rules with the child or not establish any rules, leaving the child completely free.[4] The same trends can be seen in the use of information and communication technologies (ICTs). 'Bastion' parents worry about their children's use of

Table 2.2: Typology of 'parental islands'

		Fortress island	Cocoon island	Reef island	Open island	Wild island
Inter-household boundary		**Wall**	**Membrane**	**Reef**	**Flow**	
Definition	*Parental style*	Bastion	Cocoon	Companionship	Association	Anomic parallel
	Degree of permeability	Impermeable	Relatively impermeable, but passage is possible	Permeable, but with limits due to strong fusion	Permeable, without limits ('space–time continuum')	
	Spatio-temporal definition of family space	Family space defines time spent with parent			Time spent with parent defines family space	
Practices	*Child's mobility*	Mobility seen as a threat: Independent movement is limited and supervised. Travel seen as family time		Independent movement is authorized but supervised	'Natural' mobility	
					A form of freedom	A form of 'forced' freedom
					Independent movement is authorized and unsupervised	
		Rules defined by age and gender	Negotiated rules			No rules
	Child's use of information and communication technologies (ICTs)	Limited access and supervised use		No access limits or supervision of usage		
		No negotiation	Negotiation possible	Self-management if family time is respected	Self-management	
Spatio-temporal limits	*Travel limits*	Physical co-presence not sought on days of scheduled absence	Limited physical presence on days of scheduled absence. Negotiation possible	Physical co-presence on days of scheduled absence possible but must be negotiated	Physical co-presence possible on days of scheduled absence	
	Transfer limits	Transfer of objects not authorized	Transfer limited but negotiation possible	Authorized but negotiated transfers	Freedom to manage personal belongings. Transfers authorized without permission	
		Everything belongs to the 'island', so must go back to its original place			Everything belongs to the child, not to the 'island'	
	Limits to virtual contact	Little or no contact between 'islands'	Regular inter-'island' contact	Potential inter-'island' contact		
Parents (n = 34)		4	7	7	12	4

these technologies; consequently, they limit access to specific times of day and/or durations of time and monitor usage of games, social networks, messaging, and so on. 'Cocoon' parents operate in the same way, but allow their children to negotiate these rules. Parents with a 'companionship' style give their children the freedom to use ICTs as they wish, as long as this is not to the detriment of time spent with their 'new family'. Those with 'association' and 'anomic parallel' styles set no limits on access to ICTs and do not monitor their children's use: in the first case this is a recognition of autonomy, while in the second it results from an absence of rules.

These rules are not specific to the physical or symbolic crossing of boundaries to travel (or communicate) between 'parental islands'. It is therefore necessary to focus on those limits placed specifically on inter-'island' exchanges.

In this context, the degree of (im)permeability of the boundaries delimiting each 'parental island' is defined in terms of three types of spatio-temporal limits. *Limits on movement* refer to the potential for children to move between their parents' dwellings and for them to meet a parent on days when they are residing with the other parent. *Virtual contact limits* refer to whether or not contact is maintained through virtual means of communication (such as telephone or video calls, text messages, emails or messages on social networks) when children are at the other parent's dwelling. *Transfer limits* refer to whether or not children are allowed to take personal belongings with them to the other parent's dwelling.

It is important to remember that each parent has their own type of 'island' and parental style, which can be different from those of the other parent. A child can therefore live on, and between, two different types of 'island'.

The 'fortress' island

The *'fortress' island* is characteristic of 'bastion' parents. These parents, like the mothers of Marie (aged 12) and Romane (ten) and the fathers of Théodore (13) and Coralie (12), delimit their 'temporal territory' with walls that must not be crossed. They value fusion among members of the 'new family' and their retreat onto a 'fortress' island; they therefore circumscribe their living space and set predictable times to be with the child, structuring and ordering their homes by establishing rigid spatio-temporal boundaries. The child's two places of residence in SPC are considered mutually exclusive: these parents draw an impermeable boundary between the two islands, which they allow the child to cross only on the day of the planned change of residence. Parents in this category also value loyalty to the 'new family' and respect for family rituals, and establish inflexible family routines and habits: the time spent together in the home of the 'new family' is structured by precise schedules and defined rhythms. Marie emphasizes the importance of mealtimes at her mother's residence: 'Often we turn off the TV, because they like the four of us to be together and everything, and so, well, we eat and talk.'

'Bastion' parents perceive mobility as dangerous, being closed to the outside world and valuing their home base, and therefore restrict and monitor their children's travel times and destinations. The children generally depend on family transport, as they are often – if not always – accompanied by the parent with whom they are residing. These restrictions are based on the age and gender of the child. For example, Marie and Théodore have travelled to school on their own since they started secondary school. However, because of Marie's age and the fact that she is a girl, Marie's mother always drives her to her extracurricular activities at weekends or when she goes to a friend's house, to make sure she goes to the right place. Théodore's father takes care of most of his transportation, or calls on other family members (Théodore's grandparents or stepmother) or even the parents of one of his son's friends. This limits Théodore's independence:

> It depends … hockey is more often either my grandparents or a friend from hockey who takes me, or my dad. Mum, less often. Mum often picks me up. … For Scouts, every Saturday, it's Mum and Dad because, well, it's the weekend, so they don't do anything. … And for bass, well, often it's Fanny [his stepmother] who gets off work a bit earlier than usual and takes me. (Théodore, aged 13)

Romane explains that her mother is worried about her going to school alone or with her little brother Arthur (five). She explains that her father,[5] who lives a few houses away from their school, allows her to walk there, despite her mother's wishes to the contrary: 'Going to school by myself, she [her mother] didn't agree … and I did it anyway. … Going to school alone with my brother, well, she liked that even less … but we did it. Romane's mother has relented somewhat since Romane confided that she needed to get away from her little brother and do things on her own. She now allows Romane to go alone to her volleyball practice across the street, or to the bakery around the corner:

> In fact, volleyball is just across the road from my house, so I go there on my own, on foot. … I've asked … sometimes I go and get some buns or go to the shop. … What I like is … being on my own, because I'm kind of with my brother all the time. (Romane, aged ten)

Trips to the other parent's dwelling are seen as shared moments when family members come together. These trips are almost always accompanied and monitored: the children cannot go to the other parent's dwelling whenever and however they want. Parents with 'fortress' islands give priority to spending time among members of their 'new family', structured by family routines and habits: the child's unexpected arrival outside of scheduled times would disrupt this pattern. The children do not say explicitly that they cannot go to their parent's residence when they are not living there; rather, they talk about how these travel restrictions give stability to the time they spend with that parent in their dwelling. Romane, for example, is happy with her new alternating schedule (5/9 days) because it means that she does not have to 'change houses all the time' and that she can settle in with each parent without thinking that the next day she will have to go back to the one she just left.[6]

For his part, Théodore sees his father only on exceptional occasions outside the planned days: 'sometimes she [his mother] drops things off at the house [his father's], or sometimes Dad drops things off at the house [his mother's] so I see them, but it rarely happens. It's just occasionally'.

Parents in this category also limit their children's access to ICTs and monitor their use. For example, the children must ask permission to use their own phones or tablets. They are allowed to use these devices at certain times, but only outside of shared 'family time' (for example, while the parent is cooking); the type of use permitted is also specified (messages, calls, certain social networks, certain games), and is limited in time. Coralie explains that her father asks her to stop using her tablet when she reaches the time limit. These children must also leave their phones in a specific place at night, and are not allowed to take them into their bedrooms.

Other than Marie's mother, who allows her daughter to communicate with her exceptionally when she has problems with her friends and needs to be comforted, the 'fortress' parents avoid virtual contact[7] with their children when the children are not residing with them. As Coralie and Romane explain, their 'fortress' parents want to strengthen the relationships within their dwelling for a defined period of time, and do not seek out contact:

> Yes, by text. Sometimes we call each other [to make arrangements] or. … But since it's only two days and sometimes five days for the weekend [her alternating schedule is 2/2/5 days], it's not much. … It's not much and I'm used to it. (Coralie, aged 12)

> In fact, I don't really … like [to call them]. … But sometimes they'll call to wish me happy birthday or [to tell me] if things went well or if there's been a health problem. Not too much contact, though. (Romane, aged ten)

These parents also set up an impermeable transfer boundary, considering that the child's personal effects belong to the child, but only within the framework of their own 'island'. They therefore control the management of the child's belongings by limiting transfers from one dwelling to another, or by requiring the child to systematically return belongings to the parental residence to which they belong. These parents ensure that their child's material needs are met within their 'island' in order to avoid exchanges between dwellings. Coralie explains that her father encourages her to leave things with the parent who gave them to her: 'Often if it belongs to someone, the person who gave it to me, for example if Dad gave me something, it often stays with Dad, it doesn't go to Mum. Dad doesn't like it very much if I take too many things home to Mum, so …' (Coralie, aged 12). This is also the case for Théodore, whose father allows him to take some of the things that he has given him to his mother's house, but only on the condition that he brings them back the following week. Théodore explains that this is why on the day he moves (Friday), he makes sure he is wearing the same outfit he had on the day he arrived at his mother's:

> Clothes! I have a stash at Mum's and a stash at Dad's, and if I run out at Mum's or if I need a sweatshirt or two, I go and get them at Dad's and bring them here. … But generally they all stay at home, but sometimes I put on a T-shirt on a Friday so it goes to Mum's, and I try to put it on again the next Friday so it will go back to Dad's. (Théodore, aged 13)

Similarly, Marie must take the clothes she was wearing the day she arrived at her father's apartment back to her mother's house. Since she has started going from one dwelling to the other on her own, her mother has become slightly more flexible, so that she does not have to carry her bags to school:

> Before, I had. … It doesn't really matter now, but. … Before, I had clothes from my mum's at my dad's; I'd take them back to my mum's. But now I don't take everything back, because I had. … The other time I also had my gym bag, so I had three bags. … On public transport, it was a bit much. (Marie, aged 12)

The 'cocoon' island

'Cocoon' parents also build an island reflecting their parental style. The *'cocoon' island* is delimited by a relatively impermeable membrane that allows the 'new family' to withdraw into a closed space for a limited time. In our study, the parents with 'cocoon' islands are the mothers of Coralie (aged 12), Chloé (12) and her sister Annelyse (ten), and Émilie (ten), the fathers of Tristan (15) and Cédric (15) and both parents of Giorgio (16) and his brother Manuelo (13).

The 'cocoon' island's membrane protects the island while allowing certain passages. In contrast to parents with 'fortress' islands, who establish general rules based on status, those with 'cocoon' islands value negotiation among members of the 'new family' and allow potential openings of their 'temporal territory'. These parents are relatively closed to the outside world, promoting retreat within the 'new family' dwelling. They tend to be homebodies who value family routines, like Chloé and Annelyse's mother, who establishes family rhythms with strict timetables to be respected. Chloé explains:

> My dad's more, um … disorganized, he's more … you know? While my mum is all 'You have to go to bed early, you have to blah, blah, blah', and so, well, it's also different. And then my mum, as she only has the two of us [Chloé and Annelyse], she asks 'Oh yeah, how did your day go, blah, blah, blah?' So my dad, he asks that too. They also talk to each other [with her stepmother] … things we don't understand, so … [laughs]. (Chloé, aged 12)

This quote also illustrates how Chloé and Annelyse's mother, by being devoted and available to her daughters – to whom she dedicates all her time and attention when they are living with her – ensures affection, comfort and intimacy, the core values of the 'cocoon' parent. Émilie also describes her mother's attentiveness to her and the intimacy they share in her mother's small house: '[In the living room, at her mother's], I watch TV, draw, do my homework. … Lots of stuff like that … with Mum. It's a small house, so I'm more here [in the living room with her mother] than upstairs [in the bedroom]' (Émilie, aged ten). This strong sense of closure and fusion makes the children's mobility dangerous in the eyes of their parents, who restrict and monitor their independent movement. However, on the 'cocoon' island, children are able to negotiate these rules, which allows them to move around more or less freely. Cédric explains that his father drops him off when he has to go somewhere unfamiliar, but that he usually goes to school on his own (a five-minute walk from his father's house) or to his extracurricular activities (a ten-minute bike ride). Cédric says that he got his first mobile phone to keep his parents informed of his whereabouts, but that this practice was gradually abandoned as he grew older.

> I used to walk home on my own … from my dad's house and also from my mom's house, so I had to send them a message when I got to school and all. Now I haven't had to do that for at least two years, I think … but before, yes, I always had to do that. (Cédric, aged 15)

Manuelo is beginning to take the bus to school. His parents, he explains, still take him to his various activities, even though these are close to his father's house. When they cannot make it, they allow him to use public transport exceptionally. He finds that being accompanied by his parents suits him for now, and does not feel the need to negotiate for more freedom.

These children are restricted in their movements, but have some room to negotiate for more flexibility. They are not supposed to go to the 'cocoon' island outside of the planned schedule, but they can sometimes arrange to see the 'cocoon' parent outside of their residence. For example, Émilie's mother will occasionally travel to her ex-partner's village on Thursday (when her daughter is living with him) to attend one of Émilie's judo sessions and share a moment with her at the same time. Manuelo and Giorgio's father takes advantage of the proximity of his house to his sons' activities, sometimes greeting Manuelo as he leaves his Scout meeting or cheering on Giorgio at his rugby match at weekends, when they are living with their mother.

Parents in this category limit their children's access to ICTs and monitor their use; some set clear rules. Cédric said: 'With my dad, it's a bit more regulated. I can't go online after 9:30 pm, I have to leave [his phone] in the living room and all that.' Chloé is allowed an hour and 30 minutes of screen time per day. After this time, the applications freeze and she must negotiate with her mother to get some extra time. Coralie also explained that her mother limits her screen time to 20 minutes a day:

> I can't stay on it too long, otherwise Mum says 'Stop, that's 20 minutes!' It's 20 minutes of screen time a day, maximum. … And often I can divide … screen time into computer, TV or, well, we don't have a TV here, I only have one at Dad's. It's on the computer, Mum's … streaming, a film, that's OK too … because the computer is really big, it's like a TV. (Coralie, aged 12)

Manuelo and Giorgio's mother also regulates the use of telephones and video games. Her sons must switch off their mobile phones after 8 pm, and are not allowed to take them into their bedrooms. Manuelo explains: 'PlayStation is on Wednesdays, Fridays, Saturdays and Sundays at my mum's house.' At both parents' houses (both 'cocoon' islands), their use of ICTs is restricted mainly when it would interfere with time spent with their 'new family':

> At my dad's house, no [there are no rules], except when we're watching a film [together], he doesn't want that. … But at 8 o'clock [at his mother's house] … it depends, because sometimes when someone's having a wash or when it's 8 o'clock, we don't turn the phone off … we're on [the phone] because they're having a wash, so the family's not [all] there, so … it depends. But if we're watching a film. here [at his mother's] too, we don't use the phone. (Manuelo, aged 13)

Tristan's father does not impose time limits or schedules for using the phone or playing video games. He stresses the importance of time spent with the 'new family', and therefore recommends to Tristan that he not 'stay on it [the phone or computer] all day, or be on it all the time, or stay shut up in [his] room all the time. It's just that'.

The permeability of the 'cocoon' island's membrane concerns primarily the use of virtual contact to maintain relationships. 'Cocoon' parents communicate with their children several times a week when they are away from 'home', extending the fusion of members of the 'new family' across physical boundaries. When Tristan was still living in SPC,[8] he explained that his parents might call him to postpone a weekend or to organize his travel to their dwellings, but most of the time it was just to say hello.

Émilie also receives calls from her mother several times a week:

Yes, a lot … she calls me like every other day, but she's the one who calls me. For example, my dad, he works until 5:30 pm, so he doesn't have much time to call me, so I'm usually the one who calls him when I'm with my mum, and it's usually my mum who calls me when I'm with my dad. (Émilie, aged ten)

Unlike Tristan and Émilie, Cédric and Chloé actively maintain contact with their parents when they are not living with them, regardless of who takes the initiative:

Interviewer:	And when you're with your dad during the week, for example, do you still have contact with your mum on the days when …?
Cédric:	Yes, yes, of course … during the week, [they call one another] two, three times … and messages every day. … It's just to say hello.
Interviewer:	What about your father?
Cédric:	It's exactly the same thing … the same.

Yes, I call her [her mother] a lot. … Well, a lot – two or three times a week. There, she called me once, and she called me again, and I call my dad too. … Or I send messages, but before. … Before I really wanted an iPod so I could communicate; I always found it hard to leave them. Now, well, I don't really care. … Maybe my mum calls me more often [than her father, who has an 'open' island] but … it's maybe one more call. (Chloé, aged 12)

Manuelo maintains contact with his parents outside the days when they are together, but in different ways. He prefers to see his father face-to-face at weekends, after his Scout meetings, whereas he communicates with his mother by telephone on a daily basis:

Manuelo: I call her maybe twice a day, because whenever I have some little thing, seeing that she's a nurse or whatever, [when there's] a little thing I tell her straight away.

Interviewer: OK, so you contact her, but she doesn't necessarily call you?

Manuelo: My mum? Yes, yes, it's both of us. We can't go a day without calling each other. ... My dad, it's rare; we call each other maybe on Wednesdays. ... But not at weekends, because sometimes well, at Scouts ... maybe 500 metres away, I live right there with my dad, so sometimes he comes by, and sometimes I see him at Scouts, but otherwise, no.

In terms of transfer restrictions, 'cocoon' parents limit the movement of the child's personal belongings from one dwelling to another, but leave room for negotiation. Children are allowed to take personal belongings with them on the day of a move, though they are advised to bring them back to the 'island' where they belong. Émilie says that she often has 'problems with clothes ... like, for example, my knickers stayed at Dad's, and Mum, she complains'.

This was also the case for Tristan, who clearly distinguished between his wardrobes:

Tristan: I have [*sic*] my clothes here, my clothes at my mother's ... It was the separate thing. It was that each of them bought clothes separately; they were really different things.

Interviewer: OK, so let's say you came from your mum's to your dad's with clothes from your mum's. How did you handle that?

Tristan: I'd put them back on when I left. ... So we'd wash them and everything, and then I'd put them back on again.

Chloé also has separate wardrobes at each parent's residence, but she negotiates with her parents so she can take her favourite outfits, which she gets mainly from her father (or rather, her paternal grandmother), wherever she goes.

The 'reef' island

The *'reef' island* is typical of the 'companionship' parenting style. As with the previous two categories, priority is given to the 'new family' in that time spent at home with the family group is valued. Because of this degree of fusion, these parents spatially delimit their island in order to establish a predictable time with their child, surrounding it with a 'reef' that protects it from unwanted interference. Despite this spatio-temporal boundary, the children have considerable room for manoeuvre. They are seen as partners, on an equal footing with other members of the 'new family', and are invited to express their wishes, which are taken into account insofar as possible. Parents in this category include the fathers of Marie (aged 12), Émilie (ten) and Mélissa (ten) and the mothers of Mathilde (13), Joseph (16) and his sister Amandine (12), Théodore (13) and Cédric (15).

'Companionship' parents, open to the outside world, encourage their children to invest in the area close to home and to make it their own. Mélissa's father appreciates the fact that she participates in activities near his house as well as in her mother's town. Mélissa explains: 'That way I can have some activities in B and some in BT, because my father lives in BT, you see? … I sing and I take part in youth organizations.'

This is also the case for Marie, whose father lives in an eco-friendly co-operative. When she is staying with him, she spends most of her time with her neighbours, either in the building complex or in the surrounding area: 'Sometimes I go around alone with one of my neighbours from my dad's place; we go to buy sweets or just roam around the neighbourhood. There's a park near our house' (Marie, aged 12). The moments she shares with her father's 'new family' are nurtured by her external relationships and the time spent with the other residents:

> We do a lot of things together [with her stepmother], because my dad's apartment is in a co-operative, and so there's a lot to do there, there are a lot of things. … Sometimes there's work to do, because the place isn't finished yet, because we've been here less than a year … looking after the common room, tinkering with whatever, and sometimes we take the bins out together. (Marie, aged 12)

Marie explains that her father is teaching her to find her way around and to make short trips on her own, for example, to go to her dance class: 'I take the metro and the tram, and since I know the way, last time he asked me to be his guide and I didn't make a mistake … so he's thinking about letting me go alone' (Marie, aged 12). Similarly, Émilie explains that her father encourages her to go on her own to her judo class, which is just a stone's throw from his house, although he respects her fears for her safety:

> My dad takes me there, he drops me off and then I go. … And, well, he told me that because it's five minutes from our house, I could walk

there, but I don't really like walking there. … And besides, it's late, it's 5 pm. … So you see? (Émilie, aged ten)

However, parents with 'reef' islands still keep an eye on their children's movements, monitoring where they go and when. Mathilde explains that her mother contacts the parents of friends with whom she wants to go downtown after school, to make sure that the outing is 'OK with the moms, and the parents'. Marie's father asks her to text him when she goes to an activity on her own to confirm that she has arrived. Amandine must also keep her mother informed about her movements and any changes to the programme: 'My mum sometimes wants me to tell her when I'm leaving school, or when I come home, or when I'm going out with friends. … That way she knows where I'm going' (Amandine, aged 12).

Children can visit the 'reef' island outside of scheduled times, but these visits must be planned and negotiated beforehand. These parents demonstrate spontaneity, without seeking to impose routines, and are broadly open to transfers from one island to the other. Nevertheless, they prefer to keep to the pre-established alternation schedule, despite granting frequent exceptions. Théodore explains that his mother allows his sister Suzanne (20) to stay with her during exam periods, or on certain weekends when she does not necessarily want to go to their father's house. He finds that this flexibility does not pose a problem for their mother, as long as it is organized in advance:

So there's me and there's Suzy, who also goes from one house to another … but I go every Friday, and she decides whose house she's going to. So sometimes she goes to Mum's at the weekend because it's quieter for studying, and sometimes she goes to Dad's because, well, she wants to go to Dad's. (Théodore, aged 13)

Similarly, Joseph says that his mother does not mind if he or one of his younger sisters asks to stay with her for a few more days to have some special time with her:

After all, it doesn't really bother my mother if one of my two sisters stays at home, as long as it's not both of them, because if they're together they're a bit noisy and it sometimes gets on your nerves, but otherwise she [Amandine] can stay. So it's not a problem. (Joseph, aged 16)

However, extending a stay beyond the number of days originally planned should not be done unexpectedly or repeatedly. For the past month, Joseph has been going to his father's house by train directly after school on the day he moves. When he is too tired to take the train by himself, he waits until 7:30 pm, when his sister Amandine's acrobatics class finishes, and then travels with his father as he has done in the past: 'Either I stay at school for a while, so I revise my lessons … and then I leave, or I chat with friends outside school and then my father comes so I can go back with him.' To be more comfortable, he would prefer to wait at his mother's house, which is in the same town as the acrobatics class, but he does not feel welcome there 'because on Friday evenings I'm [supposed to be] at my father's, I have to wait until 7:30. I don't necessarily feel like it. … And so, logically, [since] I'm not [supposed to be] at my mother's anymore, I should be somewhere else'. Extending the stay at his mother's house must remain the exception, even though there may be many such exceptions.

Children on 'reef' islands enjoy a high degree of autonomy in their use of ICTs: they have no access restrictions, and are not monitored. They have room to manoeuvre, as long as these technologies do not interfere with the time they spend with their 'new family'. Théodore enjoys a great deal of freedom, but interrupts his video games as soon as his mother comes home from work so he can spend time with her. He explains that the day he returns to his mother's house,

> The first thing I do is my homework if I have any to do, or I study. … But usually she's not there [yet], so I'll either watch Netflix, or play on the PlayStation upstairs, or play a bit of hockey outside. … And then she comes home, and so. … She makes dinner, I set the table; I help her, and we have a quiet meal. … We usually watch a film together, or she tells me about her day and I tell her about mine. (Théodore, aged 13)

Other parents equip their children with tools that will be useful to them later in life, like Marie's father, who wants his daughter to make 'intelligent' use of her tablet and has therefore enrolled her in a computer course on Wednesday afternoons.

The autonomy that children are granted with respect to ICTs can be reconsidered if they are unable to limit their use on their own and their grades suffer. For example, Amandine and Joseph's mother takes away their mobile phones or turns off the Wi-Fi at bedtime to ensure that they do not keep playing online into the night.

These parents do not set limits on virtual contact, but do not all have the same relationship with ICTs. Some use these technologies to keep in touch with their children when they are away from their residence. Amandine explains: 'For example, when I'm with my dad or whatever, she sends me a little message to say, "How are things?" or something.' Her brother Joseph explains that he 'makes an effort' to stay in touch with his mother when he and his sisters are away from her. He tries to text her from time to time to chat, because he knows that 'she's a bit more sensitive about that'.

This is also the case for Mathilde, who keeps in regular contact with her parents, but mainly with her mother, 'because dads ask for a bit less information, but he still does it':

> We text each other [she and her father] and it's always one week, one week, so it's the same with my mum, that I don't see her, but we keep in touch. … To tell them how things are going with me, to say that things are going well with school … sometimes there are things I have difficulty with, so she [her mother] wants to know how that test went and all, you know. (Mathilde, aged 13)

Amandine and Joseph's and Mathilde's mothers value maintaining the fusion among members of the 'new family' beyond the 'temporal territory' marked by their children's physical presence. Other parents with 'reef' islands set temporal limits by not keeping in contact with the children outside their scheduled days, except when needed for organizational reasons. Nevertheless, they allow the children to contact them if they feel the need, as Émilie explains:

> I'm usually the one who calls him [her father] when I'm at my mum's, and its usually my mum who calls me when I'm at my dad's. … Sometimes it's to ask him for something, his permission for, I don't know, something … or it's to say hello because I miss him or whatever. (Émilie, aged ten)

Children also face few transfer restrictions. Indeed, parents with 'reef' islands allow regular transfers of objects between dwellings, after negotiation. An exception is Théodore's mother, who leaves her son completely free to manage his belongings. However, as Mathilde points out, these belongings must always be returned to the dwelling from which they came.

Mélissa systematically returns the clothes she receives from her paternal grandparents to her father's house, because, as she says, 'they have to go back there':

> He [her father] prefers that they stay with him because, when my grandparents give me clothes, I think they prefer me to wear them when, you know [she is staying with her father]. And so he tells me I have to take them home, even if they're dirty; I put them in a bag and we'll wash them at his place. (Mélissa, aged ten)

Furthermore, Émilie refers to the things she uses in each parent's house as if they belonged more to the 'island' than to her when she says: 'Often there are trousers that are at my mum's and that belong to my dad, or things like that.'

The 'open' island

The *'open' island* is characteristic of 'association' parents. In our study, these were the fathers of Mathilde (aged 13), Joseph (16) and his sister Amandine (12), Chloé (12) and her sister Annelyse (ten) and Romane (ten); the mothers of Lewis (16), Eliot (14), Remi (13) and Mélissa (ten); and the two parents of Jean (13) and his sister Anouk (ten) and Félicien (12). These parents advocate openness to the outside world and autonomy for the members of the 'new family', seeing their dwelling as part of a single large expanse whose spatial and temporal boundaries are difficult to define. Children are thus free to travel and to situate themselves wherever and whenever they wish within the 'space–time continuum' connecting the 'open' island with the other parental island. Rather than discrete 'temporal territories' to which children feel they belong, space is seen as being made up of networks to which they decide to connect temporarily, only to interrupt these connections and reactivate them later as they wish, as Lewis explains:

> One time I told my father that I'd stay an extra day with my mother, or something like that, but. … In fact I don't even ask, because both my parents tell me … especially my mother, that I really shouldn't worry, that they want me to be OK and so they're happy to see me, but in and of itself. I choose when I go to one's home and when I go to the other's; the alternation is just so we don't have to worry about it. (Lewis, aged 16)

In this way, the adolescent moves fluidly and continuously from one parental 'temporal territory' to the other. In contrast to the forms of parental island described previously, in which the family space – specifically, that of the dwelling – defined the time spent with each parent, here it is the time shared with each parent that defines the 'family space'.

Parents who function in this way also emphasize the autonomy and individuality of the members of the 'new family'. Because the degree of fusion of the 'we-group' is low, the child's bonds with the 'first family'[9] are valued. In fact, the uniqueness of the relationship between parent and child leads these parents to favour their relationship with the child during their time together, sometimes to the detriment of those with the other members of the 'new family'. This is the case for Félicien's mother, who hides her son's favourite snacks from his stepsiblings to ensure that Félicien will have them available when he stays with her. It is also true for Lewis's mother, who prefers to make the long journeys to the train station or to her ex-partner's town alone with her son (without the help of her new partner) so she can enjoy these moments of complicity. Moreover, she makes efforts to ensure that Lewis will feel at home with her, including relieving him of many domestic chores while expecting her daughter Clémentine (Lewis's ten-year-old half-sister, who lives with her full-time) to do her part. These attitudes are sometimes misunderstood by the permanent residents, and may lead to conflict.

According to Mincke and Montulet (2019), people's mobility across 'space-time continuums' (or 'flow forms') is defined as natural and as an individual freedom that contributes to their personal fulfilment. Parents with 'open' islands encourage their children's autonomy by following these same principles. They encourage children to travel independently, without relying on family resources, and give them the freedom to manage their own schedules and destinations. This is the case for Lewis, who is grateful to his parents for the freedom of movement they have allowed him since he was very young: 'I feel very free in that respect [that of the organization of alternation], because I think my parents know it's important for me to feel free, and they trust me, so … if at some point I'm supposed to be at their place and I'm not, they won't worry' (Lewis, aged 16).[10]

Eliot's and Remi's mothers and both of Jean's parents also encourage their children to travel on their own, thereby giving them a certain degree of independence, as Remi explains: 'When I'm going to do things with friends, I go there on foot or on rollerblades or by scooter, but often on rollerblades. Or I take the bus. However I can, you know? … I try to disturb my parents as little as possible' (Remi, aged 13). This high degree of autonomy means that children are free to move between islands as they wish. Children like Eliot feel free to go to their parent's 'open' island 'just to go say hello', or to look for things they have forgotten:

> Yes, a lot of times when I go to get my things, I'll see them [his mother and father], or sometimes I go to say hello, out of habit. … During the week I go to say hello, just to drop by like that. … Sometimes it's for particular reasons, but there are times when it's just to say hello. (Eliot, aged 14)

Jean says that he has become accustomed to this rhythm of life in alternation, and that he forgets his personal belongings 'less and less'. Until recently, he would systematically return to his other parent's residence when he forgot a notebook or phone charger on the day of the move. Today, he still sometimes goes to his father's flat while residing with his mother, 'to rest' and enjoy the 'beautiful view' from the third floor, to be able to catch the bus with a friend who lives nearby, or to find something to do:

> Because, actually, I like to take my time … to take my time going home, because that way I don't get too bored when I'm at my mother's. … At my mother's, in fact, there's still not so much to do … other than

reading, or drawing. Then there's also just watching TV, but I finally get kind of fed up. (Jean, aged 13)

These visits are not a problem for Jean's parents, as long as they are informed. In fact, when he goes to his father's flat on Mondays, 'they don't notice anything anyway' because both parents are away and 'they don't know that I'm here [at his father's]' so 'it doesn't change anything for them'. On other days of the week, Jean limits his comings and goings to avoid having to keep his parents informed of his whereabouts:

There are times when I feel like going to my father's, but I say to myself, 'No, no, I don't need anything … there's no reason'. And on Tuesdays, as my mother's at home, I need to tell her I'm going to my father's. … I always need to tell her. … On the other hand, when I go to her flat, I don't tell her. (Jean, aged 13)

Parents with 'open' islands, like Lewis's mother, trust their children to use ICTs responsibly, particularly screens. Lewis explains that he is free to use them as he wishes:

My parents are pretty confident about my relationship with screens in general, my phone or my computer. They know that I'm not addicted to my phone at all, that I don't spend my life on social networks, I don't really have any games on my phone or. … You see, it's pretty much 'practical' for me. … On the other hand, I do use my computer a lot, but my mother knows I'm not addicted to it because … as soon as it's time to do something else, it's not a problem for me to stop. … Or there are weeks when I don't really use it, unless I have to look at something for an assignment, for example. (Lewis, aged 16)

Some parents make sure their children are aware of the harmful effects of excessive ICT use. Mathilde's father allows his daughter to manage her phone, her tablet and her access to the various social networks, but he also teaches her about, for example, the importance of avoiding blue light from a screen for at least 30 minutes before bedtime, to avoid disturbing her sleep. These limits are often established through negotiation, especially for children aged 12–14. Chloé says her father sets a limit on her screen time each day: 'If I use my phone for more than an hour and a half, all my applications freeze, and I have to either enter a code or send a request.' She doesn't use all of her allotted time during the week, which allows her to negotiate for a bit more time on the weekend:

Sometimes I get bored on the train, so I go on my phone and then I don't have any more time. Or sometimes, just in class, I look at the time and then … that uses my screen time. And then I show my dad, 'But look, I haven't been on Instagram much', so he says 'OK, OK'. (Chloé, aged 12)

The 'open' island's negotiated space-time reduces the need for limits on virtual contact, allowing children to stay in touch with the parent with whom they are not residing. This spatio-temporal fluidity also means that some children, like Eliot, feel free to visit this parent's dwelling simply to say hello.

Some parents with 'open' islands maintain relationships over distance by communicating with their children repeatedly during the period of separation, encouraging virtual forms of co-presence (Baldassar, 2008).[11] Anouk explains:

Sometimes I call on Dad's phone, two or three times [a week]. … Sometimes it's Mum [who calls] … to ask Dad something and so I take the opportunity to call her. Or I call her [to tell her] if I'm doing well, if I got good grades at school. … And sometimes I ask her whether the rabbit is OK. (Anouk, aged ten)

Other parents check in on their children occasionally, but keep an otherwise low profile while they are apart. Chloé's and Mathilde's fathers will call in case of particular events like exams or doctor's appointments, but do not necessarily keep in touch otherwise.

Unlike his sister Anouk, Jean does not take advantage of the openness of their parents' 'temporal territories'. Instead, he settles in almost exclusively with each 'new family' for a few days at a time:

Actually, I won't communicate much with [his mother] … when I'm here [with his father], I really don't communicate a lot with her. When it's something I can say to my father, I say it to my father, when he comes home, but I never say it. … I don't talk much with my mother, actually. … But, well … no, no, with him [his father] either, I don't talk much [when he is with his mother]. (Jean, aged 13)

Romane and Mélissa do not communicate at all with their 'open' island parents (Romane's father and Mélissa's mother) while they are apart. Lewis does not 'really' contact his mother, except to make plans:

Because a week goes by so quickly for me, and for them, I imagine, we don't necessarily keep in touch, except in special cases, if there's an event or something like that. Otherwise, if it's something like … when I need to know that my mother won't be there on such-and-such a day when I come home, or something like that. (Lewis, aged 16)

Félicien, for his part, communicates with the absent parent only when their separation is prolonged, such as during a holiday:

> If we have something important to tell each other, yes, but otherwise no. Except during holidays … you know, if it's two weeks here and two weeks there, then yes, but otherwise no. … When I'm on holiday with my dad, it's usually Mum who will call; when I'm on holiday with Mum, it's more likely that I'll call [Dad]. Mum might call me three or four times during the holiday and I might call her once or twice. (Félicien, aged 12)

Concerning transfer limits, children are free to take the belongings of their choice to the other dwelling, as parents with 'open' islands consider these objects to belong to the child rather than to the 'island'. Remi takes a suitcase containing his everyday belongings each time he moves; Eliot goes back and forth between his residences to get the things he needs during the week; Chloé surrounds herself with 'everything [she] need[s]'; and Amandine sometimes takes clothes with her, even though she has a wardrobe in each of her parents' houses, simply because she 'likes to have a few more'.

The 'wild' island

Finally, the *'wild' island*, characteristic of the 'anomic parallel' parent, also has fluid boundaries. Like parents with 'open' islands, those with 'wild' islands demonstrate a low degree of fusion and give greater priority to time for themselves and to individual pursuits than to spending time with their 'new family'. However, whereas parents with 'open' islands invest in the domestic sphere for their own reasons, those with 'wild' islands[12] withdraw from this sphere into their own worlds. Their hobbies (for the father of Remi [13] and the mother of Tristan [15]) or their work (for the fathers of Lewis [16] and Eliot [14]) monopolize the time that they could devote to their children, who may feel abandoned. In fact, these family groups rarely spend time together in the living room, and may not even share meals:

> [In the living room] there's my stepmother when she comes home from work, but then she goes off to her computer. … There's my father who comes home from work, but he never really goes into the living room; he goes straight to the kitchen or to his computer, or to work on his models, and then my brothers come in, but, well, you know [they don't stay there long]. (Remi, aged 13)

> But during the week, what we do is we eat separately, so my mother is in the kitchen and my brother [Adam, 19] and I are in the living

room, or just me in the living room and my brother in his room. … We eat where we want. … When we were much smaller, it was like, we ate in the kitchen, but then after a while, little by little, we all split up and did pretty much what we wanted. (Tristan, aged 15)

There are a lot of times when my brother [his half-brother Kenzo, four] isn't there, [and] my dad comes back later in the evening, so … I don't cook much, although I kind of know how, but I don't eat so very well either. … It's often one big meal and then we eat leftovers for a few days and then, you know. (Lewis, aged 16)

It is clear from the interviews with their children and ex-partners that for parents in this category, it is the time spent with the child that defines the 'family space'. Lewis illustrates how children are thus free to situate themselves wherever and whenever they wish within this 'space–time continuum':

Actually, if I want to go to one of their places one day, I can, totally. My mother is totally fine with it, and my father wants to see me, but, well … I don't know how that works; it's like he doesn't think he's the one who decides, so. … Yes, I feel very free in that respect. (Lewis, aged 16)

However, children do not always feel welcome when they return to their parent's 'wild' island:

In fact, when I'm at my father's, the day before I'm going to go to my mother's, I call her … and my father, I never tell him because, well, I get home and he's there or he's not there. He knows more or less when I come home, so. (Lewis, aged 16)

As for those with 'open' islands, it may be concluded that parents with 'wild' islands perceive the children's mobility between islands as natural. However, in this case the children's considerable freedom of movement results more from the parent's reluctance to take responsibility for their travels than from valorization of autonomy as contributing to the children's personal development. Parents with 'wild' islands encourage their children to travel alone, without relying on family resources, and leave them free to manage their schedules and destinations without imposing rules. Thus Lewis, for instance, describes himself as 'pretty independent'. He is 'pretty familiar with public transport', having used it since he was in primary school to get to school while living with his father, to visit friends or just to ride around town without a specific destination.

Parents in this category relinquish their responsibility and commitment to their children, devoting themselves entirely to their own personal and/

or professional activities. They are too busy or absent to take care of the children, who learn to look after themselves and benefit from a high degree of 'forced' autonomy. This is the case for Remi, who used to take the bus to school from his father's house because his father did not want to drop him off. As the bus and school schedules are not well synchronized, Remi's mother now takes him back and forth – whether he is living with her or not – so he will not have to make the journey too early in the morning:

> Actually, it was more on my father's side, where I was already starting to take the bus a long time before [the beginning of the school day], because Mum didn't know to come and take us [Remi and his brothers] to school or whatever, so we'd take the bus to Dad's, we'd take the bus home and all that. (Remi, aged 13)

The absence of rules means that these children enjoy considerable autonomy and freedom of movement between their parents' dwellings. Indeed, there are no restrictions on their movements, in the sense that their comings and goings from one place to the other are not monitored by the parent. This is the case for Eliot, who moves freely between his two residences. When he goes to his father's house during the week, when he is residing with his mother, he stays there for only a short time because his father is too busy at work and is 'never' there:

> I go there [to his father's house] maybe two or three times a week, but it's not just to say hello, it's also to get … clothes or things I forgot the last time I was there, or whatever. … I stay ten, 20 minutes at the most. But often there's not really anyone there, so I stay even less time because there's no one to chat with or anything. (Eliot, aged 14)

Concerning the use of ICTs, 'there are no rules' with his father, says Lewis. 'There [were]n't too many restrictions' with his mother, says Tristan; 'she [was] much cooler about it' than his father, who has a 'cocoon' island. These parents let their children manage themselves, allowing them unlimited access and unmonitored use of ICTs, because they are too busy with their own personal or professional lives to be more involved. Remi and Lewis spend a lot of time in their bedrooms at the console or computer, except when their (younger) paternal half-siblings are present and they need or want to look after them:

> On the other hand, I use the computer a lot, but [with] my father, there are still no rules. But sometimes he thinks I'm on it a lot, and that … he'd like me to spontaneously spend time with him [the father] when my [four-year-old half]brother's there, because, you know, he'd

like me to spend more time with my [half]brother as well. So no, there are no rules. ... Nothing's set. (Lewis, aged 16)

I'm in the living room much more when, for example, she's there [his half-sister Elsa, aged 23 months]. When she leaves, I go upstairs. ... When she goes to sleep or has a bath, I go upstairs to my room ... [to play on the console]. (Remi, aged 13)

For his part, Tristan regrets not spending more time with his mother, who gave him complete freedom to use his screens and did not push him to do anything else:

We hardly ever do anything [with his mother] and that's also kind of why. ... Well, I don't go there much anymore because I'm starting to get tired of not really doing anything. We never go out. Well, seeing that we've got some — that she's got some financial problems, it's kind of normal, but we never even go for a walk or a bike ride or whatever. ... We never do that, we hardly ever go out, and, you see. ... Staying at home and playing on my PC or watching TV. (Tristan, aged 15)

We have already described the limits on virtual contact and transfer characterizing the boundaries defined by these children's other parents ('open' islands for Lewis's, Remi's and Eliot's mothers and a 'cocoon' island for Tristan's father). In terms of limits on virtual contact, whereas Tristan's mother has maintained contact with her son while he is living with his father, the other three boys' fathers do not necessarily maintain contact with them. However, they do allow them to make contact when necessary. Concerning transfer limits, as for 'open' islands, children's personal belongings are considered to belong to the children more than to the 'island'; the children are therefore free to take whatever they want to the other residence without the parent having any say in the matter. Only Tristan's mother, who is facing financial difficulties, asked her son not to leave the clothes she had bought for him at his father's, so she would not have to buy new ones when they ran out. As for his other belongings (console, computer, and so on), he was free to take whatever he wanted without approval from his mother, because his forgetting them at his father's house would not directly affect her.

Parental islands within a structure of opportunities and constraints

The particular form of inter-household boundary ('island') established by each parent is influenced by a number of factors, including *material*, *spatial*, *familial* and *temporal dimensions*.

The material dimension

The 'material dimension' refers to the perceived standard of living of each ex-partner and the material resources available to the child. Although the parents in our study had a relatively homogeneous profile in this sense, different strata could be distinguished, ranging from modest to comfortable standards of living. These perceived levels affect the kinds of boundaries that parents draw to demarcate their 'temporal territory'.

Parents with a modest standard of living tend to create 'fortress' and 'cocoon' islands. Because of their limited financial resources (and/or their desire to live modestly according to their values), these parents – who were mainly mothers in our study – draw strict transfer boundaries in particular, being unable to easily replace children's belongings if they are left at the other parent's residence. This was the case for Marie's, Romane's, and Chloé and Annelyse's mothers, who preferred that their daughters keep the things they had given them at home; Émilie's mother, who was angry when her daughter did not bring back the knickers she was wearing when she left; and Coralie's mother, who divides her daughter's belongings between wardrobes in each parental residence, asking her to keep them in balance by not taking anything from one house to the other.

'Reef' and 'open' islands are most prevalent among parents who perceive their standard of living as intermediate to high, considering that they have sufficient economic and material resources. These parents draw fewer boundaries between their islands and those of their ex-partners, and leave their children free to manage their personal belongings. If they lack something, the question of whether to replace it or buy more may be one of principle rather than economics, in contrast to parents with a more modest standard of living. It should be noted, however, that some parents who see their standard of living as modest will also create 'reef' and 'open' islands, as they value openness to the outside world, which distinguishes them from those with 'fortress' and 'cocoon' islands.

Finally, there is no clear relationship between 'wild' islands and perceived standard of living, as the profiles of these parents are very diverse. Parents with 'wild' islands are distinguished mainly by the priority they give to their own individual time, be it leisure or professional time.

The spatial dimension

The 'spatial dimension' refers here to the physical distance between residences. Ex-partners who live close to one another tend to create 'open' or 'wild' islands, allowing children to move freely between dwellings that are only a short walk apart. However, proximity does not entirely determine their practices. Cédric's parents, who live a 20-minute walk from one another, have 'reef' and 'cocoon' islands, while Romane's mother, who lives a five-minute walk from her ex-partner's flat, has a 'fortress' island. While some parents create an 'open' island because of the proximity of the parental dwellings, others choose this type of island because their dwellings are far apart. Travelling this distance on a regular basis requires particular family arrangements, and parents are often responsible for making the long journeys between residences. Parents with 'open' islands encourage their children to become independent and to take responsibility for these journeys in part to relieve themselves of this logistical burden, while others, like Coralie's father with his 'fortress' island, may see these car journeys as shared 'family time'.

The familial dimension

The 'familial dimension' relates to family composition, the degree of conflict between parents and the core values at the centre of family organization.

Family composition has an impact on the resources available to the 'new family'. Single parents, and particularly single mothers, often face financial difficulties, exacerbated by a lower income due to their often part-time jobs; consequently, they may have limited material resources. This is why the mothers of Romane (who has a 'fortress' island), Chloé, Annelyse and Émilie (who have 'cocoon' islands) and Mathilde (who has a 'reef' island) set limits on transfers of belongings between residences, although these may sometimes be negotiable.[13] These limits allow them to keep the few items they are able to give to their daughters in their own dwellings, and to avoid having to replace clothes or toys the girls may forget at the other parent's residence.

The degree of conflict between parents also influences the boundaries drawn between households. As Hachet (2021) points out, when the level of conflict is high, it is difficult for parents to maintain contact with their children when those children live with an ex-partner who does not answer the phone, or never calls. The level of conflict between Marie's parents is medium–high. The girl's mother (who has a 'fortress' island) maintains contact with her father (who has a 'reef' island) only by email; they avoid seeing one another, or even talking on the phone. When Marie did not yet have her own phone, this situation prevented her from communicating with the parent she was not residing with. With the exception of Lewis's parents, who maintain a friendly relationship (low conflict), the parents with 'wild' islands (Eliot's and Remi's fathers and Tristan's mother) barely communicate with their ex-partners, with whom they maintain medium–high levels of conflict. Now that these adolescents have their own mobile phones, they are free to communicate with their other parents as they wish.

The core values around which parents construct their family organization are also important in defining their 'temporal territories'. Coralie's father, who has a 'fortress' island, attaches great importance to general culture and education. When his daughter is staying with him, he spends a lot of time with her, and it is important to him to spend weekday evenings alone together at home.[14] They have a ritual that they never miss: they watch and then discuss the TV news together, and do further research on current affairs. In this way, he creates an impermeable boundary enabling him to spend time with his daughter. Théodore's father, who also has a 'fortress' island, has erected an impermeable wall between dwellings because he does not share all of his ex-partner's values or educational rules. He sets transfer limits to prevent his son from bringing home things of which he does not approve, such as a PlayStation. Concerned about the impact that new technologies can have on children, he sets clear rules about their use, and does not seek contact with Théodore when he is at his mother's house in order to limit his son's use of these technologies.

Émilie's and Marie's fathers each have a 'reef' island. The values of community involvement and external integration are central to their family organization. Indeed, they have both chosen to live in co-operatives, where they hope their daughters will be able to participate in various activities with their 'new families'. Parents with 'open' islands advocate values such as self-expression and negotiation, which they express by leaving children free to make their own choices. Consequently, they see their dwellings as being part of a 'space–time continuum' within which the children can move freely. Parents with 'open' islands are also characterized by a certain approach to life, taking it day by day and living each moment to the fullest. From this perspective, there is no point in setting limits in terms of time and space. Moreover, their children are invited to take part in discussions and to express themselves freely on all subjects, creating a warm and friendly atmosphere in a space where they can come and go freely.

The temporal dimension

The 'temporal dimension' relates to the age of the children, and also to the parents' desires to have time with the child and time for themselves.

The age of the child affects boundary formation primarily for mothers, who are likely to set impermeable boundaries when they have an eldest daughter aged 12 or under.[15] This is the case for the mothers of Marie (aged 12) and Romane (ten), who have 'fortress' islands, and for those of Émilie (ten), Chloé (12) and her sister Annelyse (ten), and Coralie (12), who have 'cocoon' islands. The mothers of Mélissa (ten) and Anouk (ten) have 'open' islands; we believe that this difference can be explained by the girls' positions as youngest siblings. Benefiting from their experience with the older siblings, their mothers seem to be more comfortable with the external environment and therefore more inclined to encourage their independence. Conversely, the 'fortress' and 'cocoon' mothers mentioned earlier tend to withdraw into the 'new family', setting impermeable boundaries to ensure that the family space is disturbed as little as possible. Fathers appear to be relatively unaffected by the child's age, and show less fear of the outside world with respect to their daughters. Similarly, when children are in secondary school,[16] their parents tend to create 'reef' or 'open' islands, seeing their children as partners and thus giving them more autonomy.

The desire to have time for the child and time for oneself, without the child, also influences the form of parental islands.[17] This observation echoes the work of Hachet (2021) on the parental experience of SPC in France. While Hachet describes a number of ways of conceiving of 'time without the children', the majority of parents see this time as 'time for oneself'. Some parents see this time as strictly delimited from time with the child – as time when they are not parents but simply people (which Hachet observed mainly among fathers). Others, while enjoying this time for themselves, maintain links with the child in a spirit of continuity (mainly mothers). Both of these types of behaviour were noted among our participants, but without a marked gender difference. Thus, some parents, such as Théodore's father ('fortress' island) or Manuelo and Giorgio's mother ('cocoon' island), set limits on movement to prevent the children from coming to their dwellings outside of scheduled days. They appreciate the egalitarian arrangement because it allows them to spend a week with their children and then have time to themselves, or private time with a new partner who has come to live with them. The mothers of Jean and Anouk ('open' island), Mathilde ('reef' island) and Amandine and Joseph ('reef' island) also value having a week without the children so they can have some time to themselves or with friends. While Jean and Anouk's mother is open to her son and daughter coming and going as they please, the others are not opposed to seeing their children outside the scheduled days, but prefer to be informed beforehand and for the decision to be discussed and taken together. For her part, Romane's mother ('fortress' island) appreciates having the few days without the children to compensate for her reduced working hours when she is looking after them. Other parents, such as Marie's mother and Coralie's father, who both have 'fortress' islands, set spatio-temporal limits in order to ensure a predictable time with their children while they are present. While Marie's mother does this to respect her ex-partner's desire for an egalitarian arrangement in which he has as much time with their daughter as she does, Coralie's father sets limits to ensure that his ex-partner does not interfere with his time with his daughter, even with a short phone call.

★★★

Understanding the environment of each 'new family', characterized by specific parental styles and degrees of (im)permeability between households, lays a foundation from which we will explore how children, defined as competent agents and placed at the centre of the family, circulate within complex family frameworks that offer both opportunities and constraints.

In the next chapter we will look at how these children themselves understand their mobile lives in and between two dwellings, highlighting the practices they use on a daily basis and the meaning of these practices.

Notes

[1] As a reminder, the 'new family' refers to two situations. When a parent is single, the new family is composed of this biological parent and the children born of the first union. In situations of family blending, the new family includes the biological parent, the children born of the first union, the new partner and their children, if any, and any children born of the second union.

[2] We have chosen to use the names of the family functioning styles proposed by Widmer and his colleagues to name the first four 'parental functioning' styles, because their definitions coincide very closely. Only the 'anomic parallel' style differs from the 'parallel' style defined by Widmer et al (2006).

[3] As our work focuses on the life experiences of children, we are considering here the boundaries imposed on the children, which may differ considerably from those imposed on the ex-partner. For example, some parents refuse to allow their ex-partners access to their dwelling, while allowing their children to visit them on days outside the custody schedule.

[4] These considerations echo Kaufmann and Widmer (2005), who note that family functioning, together with parents' economic, social and cultural resources, influences children's acquisition of 'mobility capital', defined as 'the way in which entities access and appropriate the capacity for socio-spatial mobility according to their circumstances' (Kaufmann et al, 2004: 750). This process becomes particularly complex in separated families with heterogeneous family environments (Widmer and Favez, 2012), where each household has different resources and ways of functioning (see also Merla, 2018).

[5] Romane's father has an 'open' island.

[6] Romane's previous schedule was 2/2/5 days, meaning that she moved on Mondays, Wednesdays and every other Friday.

[7] These virtual practices will be discussed further in Chapter 6, which deals specifically with children's maintenance of relationships at a distance. They are only touched on briefly here to give an idea of what children are and are not allowed to do.

[8] A month before we met for the first time, Tristan asked to reside exclusively at his father's house.

[9] As a reminder, in this book the term 'first family' refers to the members of the original nuclear family, that is, the parental couple to whom the child we encountered was born, as well as the brothers and sisters also born of this union.

[10] His father has a 'wild island', described in the next section, which also gives him a great deal of autonomy.

[11] The various forms of co-presence that are developed and maintained during periods of separation are further explored in Chapter 6.

[12] Parents are identified as having a 'wild' island based on strong concordance between the ex-partner's and the child's descriptions of the situation in this parent's dwelling: of the four parents having this form of territoriality, three were fathers who did not wish to be interviewed (only Tristan's mother agreed to be interviewed).

[13] Mathilde's mother has a new partner, but they do not live together.

¹⁴ Coralie's father has a new partner, but they see each other only at weekends so that he can enjoy a few days alone with his daughter.

¹⁵ Ten of the 21 children interviewed were aged 12 or under, and only one of these (Félicien) was a boy. We refer only to girls here because the parents of Félicien (12) both have 'open' islands. Although it is difficult to interpret this difference in parental behaviour on the basis of the child's gender, we hypothesize that the boy's parents have fewer fears for him in relation to the outside world and are therefore more open and less fusional than the mothers of the girls mentioned earlier. However, this hypothesis cannot be tested in the context of this study, as there are no data on other boys with the same profile.

¹⁶ In Belgium, secondary education begins with the first year of secondary school at around the age of 12, and ends with the sixth year of secondary school at the age of 17–18.

¹⁷ Merla et al (2020) note that according to family judges, one of the reasons why mothers request egalitarian SPC is to be able to have time for themselves. Bernardi and Mortelmans (2021) note that this type of arrangement reduces the pressure of needing to juggle paid work, family and leisure, in particular by allowing mothers to have time for themselves.

3

The Journey Between Islands: Transitioning from One Dwelling to the Other

In the previous chapter, we saw how parents create boundaries for their children that vary in terms of permeability and openness. The children we encountered in our study must navigate within these parental limits on a daily basis. However, they are not passive recipients of these limits, as they negotiate and develop their own ways of doing things. Indeed, children create their own 'islands' through diverse practices and investments that involve material possessions, emotions and family relationships. We will explore these practices and investments in the following chapters.

The belongings that children choose to take with them – or to leave behind – when they move between residences and the meaning they give to these practices can provide valuable insights into their ways of doing things and how they adapt to a multilocal way of life. As Duchêne-Lacroix (2013) observes, it is possible to appropriate residential multilocality not as a transitional or temporary stage but as a way of life, a 'multilocal dwelling', a way of inhabiting space 'through the transposition and activation of resources and the permanence of a portable array of instruments for daily life' (Duchêne-Lacroix, 2013: 159). These 'instruments' include the objects that children assign to a particular living space and those that accompany them as they move between spaces.

In this chapter, we will explore how children living in shared physical custody (SPC) create continuity in their daily lives. In the first three sections,[1] we will focus on how the management of personal belongings contributes to this process. We propose that children, whom we consider to be capable social actors in the sense of Danic et al (2006), make use of everyday objects to construct their relationship to their dual living space, to structure it and to give it meaning, thereby linking the two spaces into a coherent whole. The transition between dwellings, which is a regular part of these multilocal children's day-to-day lives, involves specific practices. These include planning which objects to take along to the other dwelling (for example, by putting them in a particular spot to avoid forgetting them); preparing the bag containing their personal belongings; travelling, alone or with family; unpacking their belongings, immediately or gradually; and finally, deciding whether or not to install personal items in each parent's dwelling. Our aim is to shed light on how the materiality surrounding these children enables them to structure their world into a 'lived space' and to establish links and continuities in their experience of mobility.

In the fourth section, we will explore the transitional spaces that children move through as they travel between residences. We consider space relational, as it 'takes on meaning not only in relation to other spaces, but also through the social relations and social relationships that take place there' (Lenel, 2018: 11). We are thus following in the footsteps of Remy, who defines space as 'a resource that enables individual and collective actors to assert themselves, to communicate with one another', but also to distance themselves from the socially imposed order (Remy, 2015: 43). Children's regular movement between living spaces and family environments allows them to maintain connections between their multiple living spaces and their 'new families'. This circular movement also means that they must adapt to a new family environment each time they leave one dwelling and return to the other. The children we encountered in our study express the need to suspend this connection during a transitional period in order to better adjust to the new residence. In the words of Winther (2015: 226), this 'floating space' represents a 'break, a time interval, a potentiality for something else, it marks an end and a new beginning'.

Materiality in the daily lives of multilocal children

It is essential to consider materiality when studying individuals, as Remy emphasizes (2015). Indeed, space plays a central role in social life because 'thinking about space is equivalent to thinking about the social in its materiality' (Remy, 2015: 155). The field of Material Studies pays particular attention to the dynamic interplay between subjects and objects (Miller, 2010), and to the role of household possessions in 'the construction and performance of the relationships, identities, histories and cultures of diverse groups of people' (Walker, 2020: 4).

Sacriste (2018a) stresses the importance of comprehending individuals' subjective experience when they interact with objects, and how they make use of them to overcome the challenges of their daily lives – such as alternating between two residences. She proposes considering objects as supports for our existence, which can help us cope with challenges but can also complicate our daily lives. In fact, objects play many roles – notably that of anchors, offering familiarity and stability in the social world and orientation in time and space. This is particularly useful in a mobile life, as objects 'delimit places, spaces and time. They do not disappear or vanish into thin air. Rather, they remain there, providing comfort and reassurance through their mere presence. They sediment our lives' (Sacriste, 2018b: 316). Everyday objects also carry memories and function as markers of our existence. They can provide aesthetic expression of our uniqueness, with clothes typically embodying the style of their wearer, their mood, or the circumstances of the moment. Lastly, they can be vehicles for liberation, permitting individuals to get away from their everyday life, amuse themselves, recharge their batteries or emancipate themselves.

The few studies that have focused on materiality in the lives of children in post-separation families reflect this multiplicity of functions. Most research in this field has focused on how the arrangement and use of domestic objects contribute to children's sense of home, and thereby to establishing their place in the family. A study by Palludan and Winther (2016) found that Danish children feel recognized as family members and appropriate their two residences as 'their homes' by asserting their right to have their own room and personal belongings in each parent's dwelling. Their status as hosts, guests or visitors in each dwelling is then determined by the 'socio-material weight' thus acquired (Palludan and Winther, 2016: 40). Our research has also shown that the personal items that children keep in each of their dwellings can create a sense of belonging and of attachment to their living space. These items create a spatial imprint of their presence, allowing them to reaffirm that they are returning 'home' each time they return and thus reflecting their place within the family configuration (Merla and Nobels, 2019). The objects in each dwelling play an important role in shaping family dynamics and creating feelings of inclusion/exclusion with respect to their new environment (Palludan and Winther, 2016; Fehlberg et al, 2018). By highlighting the ways in which materiality contributes to creating relationships and continuities, this research challenges the notion that alternation necessarily results in the splintering of identity and the loss of bearings.

The question of continuity is also addressed in terms of the logistics of moving between residences, shifting the focus from the appropriation of a 'home' to 'transitional space-time' and the in-between. Few studies provide in-depth logistical details, often relying on parents' accounts (Brunet et al, 2008); a study by de Singly and Decup-Pannier (2016), carried out in the late 1990s when SPC was still uncommon, is an exception. This study examines how French children in SPC manage the duality of their living space, and how they occupy their bedrooms differently in each parent's dwelling. For these authors, the question of how personal belongings move between residences is crucial in the lives of mobile children, whom they categorize into three groups based on their behaviour: those who carry a large bag containing their 'single mobile room'; those who make brief visits to the other parent's dwelling to collect items they have left there, as if they were at home in a 'large territory'; and those who are content with only a small bag, considering one of their bedrooms as a primary reference. The ways in which children move objects contribute to creating a 'lived space' (Rolshoven, 2008), where 'here' and 'there' simultaneously overlap and complement one another. In this chapter, we will revisit and extend de Singly and Decup-Pannier's work some 20 years later, focusing on the circulation of objects between residences rather than the appropriation of the bedroom.

The multilocal way of life of children in SPC involves two types of objects, which we will call '*parked*' objects and objects '*in transit*' (Merla and Nobels, 2021).[2] 'Parked' objects help to give meaning and substance to fixed locations, thus supporting anchoring processes, while objects 'in transit' travel within mobile spaces – where individuals and ideas also circulate – ensuring continuity between fixed locations. These relatively stable objects offer points of reference to mobile individuals, who can recognize them wherever they live. They can ease the burden of mobility, or help individuals to (re)integrate (Petersen et al, 2010). It is essential to consider not only the location of these objects, but also the relationships between 'here', 'there' and the 'in-between' (Schier et al, 2015): this transitional path, also known as a 'floating space' (Winther, 2015), helps to stabilize a life divided between dwellings, and gives meaning to the relationship between these places of residence. These objects, which help children to live, travel and transition between residences, stabilize practices both within each residence and in movement, making it easier to maintain routines. We will therefore consider multilocality as 'an act of connecting rather than an act of distancing' (Rolshoven, 2008: 17).

Adopting a multilocal perspective in which the 'in-between' is a constituent part of the new family arrangement, our research focuses on the reciprocal relationships between people and objects in everyday life. In particular, we are concerned with the crucial role of everyday objects in creating a 'lived space' that makes sense to children in SPC. These objects help children to order and structure their surroundings, enabling them to feel grounded and secure. Moving from one living environment to another can be a challenge for children, as it disrupts their daily routines and family life. It requires them to adapt, but does not necessarily destabilize them or disturb their points of reference. Alternation between dwellings involves both discontinuity – in terms of places, family cultures and people – and continuity 'in this regular and constant movement of sharing between two homes' (Michaud Delahaye, 2009: 154). While it undeniably generates some concerns, these are not necessarily experienced as a source of intense stress, as emphasized by Turunen (2017). Based on a quantitative study of Swedish parents and children in SPC, this author found that maintaining a relationship with each parent reduced a child's likelihood of experiencing high levels of stress. Moreover, alternation can be an opportunity for children to acquire multiple skills and identities (Michaud Delahaye, 2009; Merla, 2018). The difficulties of alternation can therefore be seen as not 'paralyzing' but 'challenging' (Sacriste, 2019: 50).

We hypothesize that objects – 'in transit' and 'parked' – are crucial elements of children's mobile lives, providing them with important points of reference. These 'humble things', to paraphrase Miller (2010), help them to ground themselves in their lives (Sacriste, 2018b) by orienting them and by delimiting the spaces and times spent with each 'new family' in a specific residence. Our purpose is to understand not only how children relate to objects in terms of utility, identity or sociability, or as a means of performing actions, but also how these objects assist them in adapting to their surroundings and coping with the challenges of their regular movement. It is important to note that children view everyday objects as both facilitating and (physically) weighing down their circular way of life.

Ordering a world in movement

As the children in our study prepare to move from one residence to the other, they begin to pack and sort their belongings, carefully deciding which items to take with them and which they can 'put on standby' (Marcoux, 2001) for a few days. Upon arrival at the other residence, they orient themselves within a familiar environment made up of the objects they 'parked' there before their last departure. The meaning that children give to these practices reveals two ways of managing multilocality. The first consists of ordering and distinguishing[3] their two dwellings and anchoring themselves in each one, with an emphasis on 'parking' objects in each place and limiting their circulation. The second consists of creating permanence and continuity of movement through objects 'in transit' that move with the child. These everyday objects include mainly clothes, but also school and sports equipment, toys and games, and objects with a strong emotional charge for them.

Ordering, distinguishing and anchoring by 'parking' objects in each dwelling

The children we will discuss in this section attach particular importance to 'parked' objects, which they associate distinctly with each residence. These objects remain fixed, always in the same place, and serve to delineate the spaces and times spent with each 'new family' (Sacriste, 2018a). They enable children to maintain a certain stability in their multilocal way of life, ensuring that they will find a familiar world each time they return to each dwelling. These distinguishing practices enable them to establish an order and a frame of reference that make sense to them (Marquet, 1991). In this way, limiting the circulation of personal belongings can help to enhance their sense of belonging in each parent's residence.

Children order their worlds according to a variety of rationales: some seek to differentiate between their residences, others to balance them and still others to reproduce similar elements while assigning each to a specific dwelling.

Ordering through practices of differentiation

Tristan (aged 15) used to move between his parents' houses every Friday after school, before moving in full-time with his father. Due to the distance between houses, the parent he would be staying with would drive him to the other parent's house to pick up the things he had left there. Although he could take advantage of this trip to carry more personal belongings, Tristan chose to take nothing but his school materials and the laptop he needed for his lessons. He clearly distinguished the belongings he kept at each house – including his clothes, which he separated into two wardrobes, each consisting of items bought by the parent in whose house it was kept. He said, 'I have [*sic*] my clothes here, my clothes at my mother's … it was the separate thing, [and] it was really different stuff.'

Tristan's mother always asked him to return the clothes she had given him, as she could not afford to buy him new clothes if he ran out, nor could she make an extra trip to his father's house. On the day of a move, in order to respect his mother's request and to maintain the distinction between his wardrobes, Tristan would change into the same clothes he had been wearing when he arrived.

The objects that surround a child in each parent's dwelling 'make' the child (Miller, 2010), in the sense that they determine a field of possibilities specific to each family space. They orient children socially, and delimit the time and space shared with each parent. This 'background' (Sacriste, 2018a: 317) enables them to anchor their family life within each space. The practice of anchoring oneself by distinguishing clearly between two dwellings reflects the 'tactics of differentiating' proposed by Petersen et al (2010: 271) in their research on methods used by mobile individuals to feel at home in multiple locations. In their study, they met a young girl living in SPC who wanted to maintain the distinction between her two residences to ensure that she could take a 'break' from the family members living in each dwelling. Through this practice of differentiation, she was able to fully disconnect from each dwelling every 15 days: this allowed her to take full advantage of the different elements available to her in each parent's dwelling, and to develop a distinct sense of belonging to each place.

One of our study participants, Romane (ten), whose parents live two streets apart, carries only her school bag with her when she moves between their dwellings. Most of her belongings are 'parked' at her mother's 'fortress' island. Her mother encourages her not to take any personal belongings to her father's flat (an 'open' island). Romane does not try to negotiate different transfer limits because her father's flat has little storage space, and she must share that space with her little brother Arthur (five), who has many clothes and 'takes up all the space'.

Romane wishes she had a single place to store all her clothes, but this is impossible:

> I would really like to have clothes in one place, because there are things I have at Mum's, and there are things I have at Dad's, and so when I have a jumper I want to wear with something from Mum's, well, I can't … and then there are most of the clothes from Dad's that I don't wear. (Romane, aged ten)

Romane has no intention of carrying a bag of clothes with her every time she moves, even though she does not really like the clothes available at her father's flat. However, she does manage to wear her favourite outfit whenever she moves.

Romane's mother's house appears to be the primary place of reference from which everything leaves – if necessary – and to which everything returns.[4] This reflects the fact that Romane spends more time at her mother's house than at her father's (9/5 days). The clear distinction that she establishes between her two dwellings is also reflected in other objects that she 'parks' at each residence, mainly because she is afraid of forgetting them in one residence and then wanting them in the other. These objects are markers that she has defined for herself and which she controls, which allow her to keep her belongings in an established order by place of residence – like the toys she has received at one or the other parent's residences, her favourite cuddly toy (which she prefers to keep at her mother's house to avoid misplacing) and her tablet.

Distinguishing in a spirit of fairness

Upon their separation, the parents of Coralie (aged 12), who have a 'fortress' and a 'cocoon' island, decided to split their daughter's wardrobe in half. At each change of season, Coralie and her mother rotate her clothes, dividing them equally between the two residences so she will always have appropriate clothing. Inspired by her mother's practice, Coralie has decided to divide her personal belongings between her two dwellings in a spirit of fairness. Some items, like her tablet, are left at one house, while others, like her Nintendo, are left at the other. She ensures that her personal items, including her clothes, are 'fairly separated'. Once their place has been determined, these belongings are considered 'parked' objects, and she no longer wishes to transport them back and forth as this may disturb the balance she has established.

In the same spirit of fairness, some children choose to carry only what they need for their day-to-day lives, temporarily leaving the rest of their personal belongings 'parked' at the other parent's residence. For example, Félicien (12) travels by train to his mother's house every Wednesday at midday. Although he is free to manage his personal belongings as he sees fit on his parents' 'open' islands, Félicien brings only his school bag with him on these trips. By ensuring that each object remains 'in its place' in each dwelling, he avoids introducing an imbalance between his two residences. Managing his belongings is Félicien's greatest preoccupation. He has learnt to avoid transfers so he will not feel encumbered, including that of something as simple as a sandwich box. During our third meeting, while we took the train together from the station near his school to the town where his mother lives, Félicien took a packed lunch out of his bag. He mentioned that he had exceptionally taken the previous day's leftovers in a reusable container instead of a disposable one, explaining, 'Often I take something I can throw away, so I don't have to take it back'. Félicien thus avoids having to think about taking items back to the 'right' parent and having to carry them back and forth on the train.

Théodore (13) has accumulated a 'reserve' of clothes at each of his parents' houses, which he wishes to keep intact. At the beginning of the separation, his father ensured that he would leave and return to his 'fortress' island with the same things he had brought with him.[5] Consequently, Théodore has continued this habit, although his parents have given him the freedom to manage his things independently since he started secondary school. To maintain the balance of ownership, he still makes sure to return any items he has taken with him to the 'right' parent, wearing the same clothes he arrived in when he leaves for school on the day of a move. Nevertheless, Théodore's approach to his two wardrobes differs from Tristan's: while Tristan considers his wardrobes to be mutually exclusive, Théodore strives for balance and fairness. Since he can move his belongings between parental 'islands' as needed, he is able to maintain balanced quantities of possessions on each. If he runs out of something at one parent's house, he can easily access the other wardrobe to restore balance between them.

Some children view 'parked' objects as 'supports for liberation' (Sacriste, 2018a: 321), while objects 'in transit' can seem heavy – both mentally and physically – and difficult to manage. As Théodore can attest, some children find it relatively easy to change residences and family environments at regular intervals. Each return 'home' provides an opportunity to break with the daily routine – or to take a 'break' (Petersen et al, 2010: 267) – by rediscovering a different world, made up of different 'parked' objects, at the other parent's dwelling. Théodore explains:

Théodore:	I change all the time. In other words, I'm not used to a particular room all the time, a particular house … I change. Sometimes I go here, sometimes I go there, so I have my two rooms.
Interviewer:	And what makes you want to go back to the other room?
Théodore:	At Mum's, it's mainly the PlayStation, and at Dad's, there are more books, or maybe it's that I'm fed up with the PlayStation, especially because at Dad's, I have more stories, more things to read, more things to do outside.

Dividing personal belongings between dwellings in a fair and balanced way is not always easy, however. Lewis (16), whose parents have 'wild' and 'open' islands, manages his belongings independently, but sometimes struggles with complex calculations:

> Sometimes there's too much of one thing at one [parent]'s place and not enough at the other's, so sometimes I try to count, just before going to the other's place, I write it down on a Post-it and then I write it down again at the other's place and try to balance it, but that doesn't really work. (Lewis, aged 16)

He 'parks' most of his belongings, with the exception of his 'computer kit' (his computer, power cable and headphones) and his lessons, which he 'almost never leaves parked in a house, [and which remain] in [his] bag all the time'. Lewis stopped taking music lessons just over a year ago, and now leaves his two clarinets 'parked' at his father's flat. Before, he would always take one clarinet to school with him on the day of a move, and then on to his mother's house. Both instruments now stay at his father's flat, because there are musicians in his mother's 'new family' who have clarinets he can borrow on the days he stays with them.

Ordering by creating similarity between dwellings

Émilie (aged ten) tries to create similarity between her two dwellings by negotiating with her father to have the same toys at his house as she has 'parked' at her mother's, or to wear the same style of clothing she considers to define her. However, her father, who favours second-hand objects, would like her to choose clothes that her half-sister Agathe (19) has outgrown, as her stepsister Capucine (12) does. This would mean that Émilie would have clothes in two completely different styles: one at her mother's house, where she can choose her own more tomboyish style, and another at her father's house, where the clothes available are more 'girly'. She explains:

> What annoys me about my dad is that before, there was Agathe, my older [half-] sister, and so she had clothes. But Capucine, she takes all [Agathe's] clothes, well, there are big boxes [of them] and when we get to that age, we try them on and see if we like them, but I have certain cuts, I have particular tastes, so my dad says, 'Oh, but you don't like anything!' … and so I say to myself, 'Well, sorry if I've got bad taste!'. (Émilie, aged ten)

Émilie finally convinced her father to buy her clothes identical to those she had at her mother's house. This replication of items recalls the work of Petersen et al (2010), who describe a strategy of 'doubling' (2010: 271) among mobile individuals that consists of owning duplicate items and distributing them among different places of residence, which allows them to feel at home in multiple locations.

Manuelo (13) favours 'parked' objects, which allows him to anchor himself in each dwelling and to limit the number of things he needs to carry with him each weekend. For this reason, he tries to have the same kinds of objects available in each parent's residence. Manuelo admits that he does not like other people (in this case members of his 'new family') to touch his personal belongings; he is very careful with the things he receives or buys with his pocket money. He therefore keeps his most valued personal belongings at his father's house, where he has his own room, while at his mother's house he agrees to share similar items like PlayStation controllers, a headset and a tablet with his brother Giorgio (16) and stepbrother Sandro (15) in their shared bedroom.

These objects can be considered as 'routine objects' (Sacriste, 2019: 57), defined as those that follow individuals everywhere, structuring their activities and thereby their lives. Manuelo finds identical objects in each of his parents' dwellings, although the objects themselves do not move. These objects are a stabilizing factor in the boy's life, providing him with a sense of familiarity and allowing him to pursue the same activities wherever he is living.

Taking 'nothing' along

It is interesting to note that these children's perception of the 'weight' of objects is socially constructed. When we asked them what they brought with them on the day they moved house, some of them, like Mélissa (aged ten), replied, 'Nothing. Well, my clothes that I have on, but otherwise nothing.' Apart from the clothes she is wearing, the only item she brings with her is her school bag. She uses the wardrobe and personal belongings 'parked' in each residence, although her parents allow her to move things from one dwelling to the other.[6]

Other children responded in the same way. However, it became evident during the interviews that in addition to the objects essential for their daily lives (such as school bags), children also travelled with a separate 'little bag' containing items that their parents wanted them to return: clothes bought by one or the other parent, sports equipment, food containers, and so on. The term 'nothing' in this context should be understood as 'nothing that belongs to the dwelling they are leaving' or 'nothing essential' that they would not have on the other side. These objects have become so familiar that they are taken for granted, and go unnoticed. This is what Miller (2010) calls the 'humility of things': these items that children may not talk about – or even notice – nevertheless affect their experiences of mobility. The objects may either help or hinder their movement, but the children accept their presence without giving them much attention.

Émilie (ten) and Marie (12), for example, say that they take 'nothing' with them. However, they each carry an additional bag containing items requested by the parent they are going to stay with. Upon arrival, both girls forget about the extra bag, which is left in the corner of a bedroom for Émilie and on the back of a dining room chair for Marie. Émilie opens the bag only on the day of her departure, to empty it and fill it with items to bring back to her other parent.

Every Monday after school, Marie travels by public transport between her mother's 'fortress' and her father's 'reef' islands. She finds that carrying an extra small bag 'is a lot' and 'it's annoying', although her parents try to limit its weight. While in the past Marie was always expected to take things back to the 'right' parent, her parents have recently allowed her to mix things more between their two dwellings. As a result, she no longer feels as much physical and mental strain from managing these objects:

> It doesn't really matter now, but. ... Before, I had clothes from my mum's at my dad's; I'd take them back to my mum's. But now I don't take everything back. ... The other time, I also had my gym bag, so I had three bags. ... On public transport, it was a bit much. (Marie, aged 12)

For de Singly and Decup-Pannier (2016), children's practice of carrying only a small bag containing very few belongings indicates that one of their living environments is more important to them than the other. However, in our study, we found a very different meaning for this practice. With the exception of Romane (ten), who prefers her mother's house, the children who favour 'parked' objects are not always content with having only limited possessions available at one parent's dwelling, and do not necessarily prioritize one residence over the other. Instead, their material practices contribute to finding a balance between two unique living spaces that they consider equally important. Having more than one dwelling also gives children 'access to a heterogeneous repertoire' (Merla et al, 2021a: 159) embodied in objects specific to each dwelling, which enables them to construct a unique and original home, as we will see later in this book.

Creating permanence and continuity in movement with objects 'in transit'

The children we will discuss in this section, unlike those who travel with only a small bag – or no belongings at all, travel with 'all their stuff', as if they were carrying a 'single mobile room' (de Singly and Decup-Pannier, 2016: 284). This 'all' takes on different meanings for each child, encompassing a wide range of practices that differ in terms of the quantities and types of objects taken along as well as how often these objects 'in transit' are moved.[7] When people say they are taking 'all their stuff', they usually mean everything that is important for their self-definition. Among these important objects, we will distinguish between '*shadow*' objects and objects '*on stand-by*' (Merla and Nobels, 2021). These two types of objects play different but complementary roles.

'*Shadow*' objects as supports for anchoring

In the Socio-Spatial Network Game (SSNG), a die is often used to represent important objects that accompany children in all their transitions. These are called 'shadow' objects because they are like a shadow that follows them everywhere, providing comfort and stability as they are familiar and always present. These 'supports for anchoring' (Sacriste, 2018a: 316) are usually unpacked upon arrival to become part of the child's new surroundings. Some children bring only a few objects with them between dwellings, while others bring almost everything they own.

Chloé and Amandine (both aged 12), Remi (13), Eliot (14) and Giorgio (16) bring all of their daily essentials – or considerably more – along when they move. They bring more clothes than are needed for the length of their stay, so they will have choice; they also bring complete toiletry bags, although they already have all they need at each parent's residence. Others use 'parked' objects to anchor themselves in each living space, but cannot resist taking along a few personal belongings that 'stick to them' – that they consider almost as parts of themselves. For example, Manuelo (13) has his tracksuit from his favourite football team, Joseph (16) has his headset and computer mouse, Tristan (15) has his PC and console, and Lewis (16) has his 'computer kit'. Joseph also takes his clothes to his father's house every week after his mother washes them, and then systematically takes them back to his mother's house; his father, being occupied with his work and with his renovation projects, does not 'have time to do the washing really regularly'. Surrounding himself with these 'routine objects' (Sacriste, 2019: 57) helps him to maintain a stable routine and adapt to weekly contingencies.

'Shadow' objects as supports for identity and singularity

'Shadow' objects reflect the personality of their owners and help them to develop and assert their identity. These objects – clothes in particular – enable children to express their unique style according to their circumstances or places of residence. Amandine (aged 12) explains that she does not always take the same clothes between her mother's 'reef' island and her father's 'open' island from one week to the next: 'Every week, I change my style a bit, so it depends. ... I have some at my mother's and [some at] my father's, but I like to have a few more.' Amandine keeps more of her clothes at her mother's house due to the quasi-egalitarian alternation of her stays (eight days with her mother and six with her father). She is careful to sort her clothes and to move them from one residence to another: this strategy enables her to 'have kind of the same [clothes] on both sides', and to express her personality through her 'unique' belongings wherever she lives.

Chloé (12) now packs her bag independently, and brings along all of her favourite clothes so she can always choose an outfit: 'All the clothes that I like the most. And I don't really take one for each day, I take a few. I really take too much, but that way I'll be able to choose what I want to put on.' Objects 'make us' as we think we are (Miller, 2010: 12). Clothing is not only a representation of one's personality, but plays an important role in defining it. The clothes that Amandine and Chloé carefully select provide 'aesthetic support' and individuality (Sacriste, 2018a: 314).

'Shadow' objects as means of reassurance

Annelyse (aged ten) surrounds herself with objects that she chooses more randomly, 'mix[ing] up a little of everything' based on her current mood and desires: '[I]f I want to have different clothes at my mum's, well, I take some clothes there [at her father's] that I'd like to have at my mum's, and the same for my dad's. ... I choose a bit at random.' Despite this haphazard way of managing her belongings, she is careful never to forget her cuddly rabbit Croquette, '*the* cuddly toy'. She is very attached to it, although she has other cuddly toys at her father's 'open' and her mother's 'cocoon' islands. This 'object of reassurance' (Sacriste, 2019: 59) soothes Annelyse and helps her cope with the hardship of being separated from one of her parents (mainly her mother) for a week at a time.

'Shadow' objects as means of liberation

'Shadow' objects, when they 'stick to' their owners, can also appear as means of liberation (Sacriste, 2018a: 321), allowing them to distance themselves from their surroundings regardless of where they live. On the day of a move, Joseph (aged 16) takes a few clothes with him, but more importantly, his headset, mouse and mouse pad. He is a big fan of online video games, and feels that 'it would be really stupid to forget [his] headset and mouse', as he would be unable to relax by playing with his friends. The frustration he feels when he forgets these things has made him realize how attached to them he has become. These objects, particularly his headset, allow him to retreat 'into his bubble'. In the past, he used the headset to isolate himself from his parents' shouting and arguments. More recently, he uses it to block out the noise when his younger sisters bicker, which he finds hard to tolerate:

> Sometimes she [Amandine, 12] annoys her sister [Lou, six], and I'm a relatively quiet person ... well, I really don't like noise. ... When I'm at home and I'm in the bedroom and I hear noise somewhere else, it really upsets me. So, I isolate myself with music, or I watch something [on the phone] to pass the time and forget about the noise outside. (Joseph, aged 16)

This 'object of escape' (Sacriste, 2019: 61) helps Joseph to cope with the pressures of his daily life and to recharge his batteries. Joseph's father expects his eldest son to assist with household chores. After a day at school, Joseph finds it challenging to engage in these activities, but as he explains, 'When I have music in my ears, I can do just about anything. I'm in my bubble, so I don't necessarily see the time going by or get bored with tidying up.'

Objects 'on stand-by' as supports for anchoring

Other children like Jean (aged 13), who is free to take whatever he wants to his parents' 'open' islands, take almost no belongings with them except for certain objects 'on stand-by' that they keep in their bags, ready to be used one day, as 'in-between reference points'. Children rarely take these objects out, to avoid forgetting them when they move:

> For example, I often carry pads of paper for school because. ... At my mum's I'm always afraid there won't be any, and here [at his father's] too. So ... there's always a pad of paper. Anyway, there's always one in

my school bag, but I carry one around all the time my bag, and I never take it out. It always stays in the bag. (Jean, aged 13)

These objects provide children with a sense of comfort and security, as they know they will have what they need wherever they go. Although they may use these items only occasionally, having them on hand spares them the frustration of having to wait a week to retrieve them from their other residence or the burden of needing to obtain them by other means.

A combination of 'shadow' and 'parked' objects

Children who prefer 'parked' objects must still carry certain things, which can eventually become 'shadow' objects over time. Tristan (aged 15) and Lewis (16) carry their computers whenever they move. They initially acquired their PCs so they could do their schoolwork and do research for their courses. Over time, however, these computers became more than simply tools, providing the two adolescents with a feeling of security and a means of escaping from the outside world. They thus became 'objects of affect' (Sacriste, 2019: 54) that Tristan and Lewis could not imagine being without for even a week.

When Tristan lived in SPC, he travelled between dwellings with a big box containing his school supplies, his laptop and sometimes his console, depending on his 'mood' and on whether he wanted to let his brother Adam (19) play with it. His brother lived full-time with their mother, who has a 'wild' island. Their mother did not spend time with Tristan when he stayed with her; moreover, Adam usually shut himself up in his room, which left Tristan alone most of the time. Since the house was isolated, it was difficult for him to go to town or to a friend's house without depending on his mother for a ride. His computer thus became a 'means of liberation' (Sacriste, 2018a: 321) for him, providing distraction from the sometimes oppressive atmosphere at his mother's house:

> The PC, every time, I'd take it because that's all I usually had to [occupy himself]. … At least at my mum's, it's all I had to do, or the TV or … so that's what I always took with me, and here [at his father's], sometimes I play with it, so I always took it with me. (Tristan, aged 15)

Lewis uses his 'computer kit', consisting of his computer, power cable and headset, as an 'object of refuge' (Sacriste, 2019: 57). Sitting at his desk in his armchair, with a blanket on his lap, helps him feel at home, although his parents' dwellings do not provide the same level of material comfort:

> In my room [at his mother's] … I have my little armchair, my computer, and I wrap up in a blanket in front of it and do my homework, or

whatever. … You see, that's really where I feel most at home. … [At his father's] I have a big desk, with lots of things on it, and my computer lost in the middle. … I feel less comfortable, in the room at my dad's … although, as I said before, it's kind of my world, so … I spend a lot, a lot of time in my room at my dad's. (Lewis, aged 16)

While the computer is associated with positive emotions, it can also have negative effects. Tristan sometimes feels bored after spending too much time on his laptop, and Lewis can feel gloomy in the morning after using the computer too late at night.

A variable pace of object transfers

The rates of circulation of 'shadow' objects and objects 'on stand-by' can vary independently of the rhythm of alternation. While children whose parents live far apart tend to take all their belongings at once when they move, as they are usually dropped off by car at the other parent's dwelling, those whose parents live close to one another have varying practices. For example, Eliot (aged 14), whose parents live on the same street, transfers objects continuously 'little by little' (de Singly and Decup-Pannier, 2016: 284), going back and forth between his parents' 'open' and 'wild' islands several times a week to pick things up or bring things back. In contrast, Remi (13) prefers to take 'everything' in one large suitcase on Sundays when he moves to his other parent's house, although the two houses (also an 'open' and a 'wild' island) are close to one another.

The ambivalence of the transition channel

In the last part of this section, we will examine how the bag or other container in which belongings are carried, which we have called a 'transition channel' in our earlier research (Merla and Nobels, 2021), has a mixed impact on the lives of mobile children. This container is the most visible object in their physical transition between dwellings. It is materially present in both dwellings as well as on the journeys between them, serving as a point of reference and an important support for the children's mobile life experience. It symbolizes continuity in movement, and acts as the link between their two residences. Moreover, it holds items that are essential for their daily lives and that help them build their identity.

The transition channel appears as the background to the children's individual lives (Sacriste, 2018a), enabling them to orient themselves socially in the space and time of each dwelling. We have mentioned Remi (aged 13), who carries his 'mobile universe' with him: that is, his clothing, shoes, Scout uniform and lessons, but also his console, rollerblades and 'things for changing wheels'. He feels secure knowing that he has all his essentials with him wherever he lives, so he never has to worry about being without something he needs.

Like Remi, Mathilde (13) travels from one dwelling to another by car with her father. She uses a large wheeled bin as a transition channel. This bin is stored in her bedroom at her mother's flat and in the dining room at her father's house. Mathilde shares the bin with her sister Clémence (15), and uses it mainly to store her school things, sports kit, toiletry bag, and some clothes she wants to have at her other parent's dwelling. When the SPC arrangement was first implemented, Mathilde's mother was reluctant to let her daughter leave the clothes she had given her at her father's house, since her standard of living was modest. To avoid conflicts or hassles due to forgotten garments, she would wash the clothes Mathilde was wearing upon arrival at her 'reef' island and keep them separate from the rest of her wardrobe. On the day Mathilde moved back to her father's house, her mother would have her wear these same clothes to ensure they would be returned to her father. Mathilde's father was not as particular about managing his daughter's belongings, seeing his dwelling as an 'open' island. Mathilde's mother therefore taught her to use the same technique at her father's house. Mathilde has since mastered this method passed down by her mother, and now uses it to her advantage by taking more clothes than she needs, surrounding herself with them wherever she goes. However: 'They always have to come back. ... They have a place, so that when you take them off, you put them there [in that place] and then you bring them back.'

The children describe these objects 'in transit' as facilitating the hardships they experience. However, they also complicate their owners' daily lives.

Manuelo (13) finds packing his belongings every week before he moves house more burdensome than the move itself. In his view, 'always taking things, moving them to one house and then moving them to the other is a real pain in the arse'. Forgetting certain things may also result in negative emotions, like lassitude and frustration. Joseph (16) feels 'kind of frustrated' when he forgets his headset and computer mouse, as these items serve as a means of relaxation and enjoyment for him. Not having necessary items for school can also be 'embarrassing' and 'stressful'.

Coping with 'parental islands'

In the first part of this chapter, we observed that the children we encountered have varying approaches to the boundaries set by their parents for their respective islands. If the parents have different types of island, for instance, a 'fortress' island and an 'open' island, the parent with the more restrictive boundary imposes certain transfer limits which are in some cases negotiable.

Although these limitations influence the children's transition practices, they do not entirely determine them.

Parents with 'fortress' islands prohibit the transfer of belongings between residences. To these parents, everything belongs to the island, and any items that they give to the child must therefore remain in their dwelling. In the rare case when items are taken to the other parent's residence (during a holiday, for example), they must be returned to their original place. Thus, children like Romane (aged ten), Marie (12), Théodore (13) and Coralie (12) prefer to 'park' their belongings, because their 'fortress' island parents (mothers for Romane and Marie and fathers for Théodore and Coralie) prefer that they not carry anything except for school-related items. These parents also ask their children to make sure they bring back anything they might carry with them to the other parent's residence. For instance, Théodore will wear clothes given him by the parent whose dwelling he is moving to, and Coralie has a school bag full of sandwich boxes that her father does not want to keep at his house, but that she keeps forgetting to leave with her mother.

Parents with 'cocoon' islands also limit the transfer of belongings between residences. However, children can negotiate some flexibility, as long as their belongings are returned to the residence where they received them. For instance, Cédric (15) may take the laptop that his mother gave him to his father's apartment for schoolwork in exceptional cases, but he must return it to his mother's house the following week. However, he normally orders his various places of residence through practices of differentiation, making use of the possessions he has in the dwelling where he finds himself. Émilie (ten) tries to have similar items in each dwelling so she can leave things in the dwelling of the parent from whom she received them. At her mother's request, she returns the clothes she is wearing when she arrives at her mother's house to her father's, carrying them in a small bag that means 'nothing' to her. However, not all children whose parent(s) have 'cocoon' islands prioritize 'parked' objects. Chloé (12) and Annelyse (ten), for instance, travel every week with objects 'in transit' that they need daily and are unable to part with. They are able to do this because their father has an 'open' island, and they receive most of their personal belongings from him. However, the few items they receive from their mother must always be returned to her apartment.

Parents with 'reef' islands allow transfer of personal belongings after some negotiation. However, they set some restrictions on what the child can take, as they want certain items to be returned to or kept in their dwelling. For instance, the father of Mélissa (ten) has specifically instructed her to return things she has received from her paternal grandparents, but has no problem with her taking other things. Mathilde (13) carries a bin every week in which she collects things she has received from her mother, who has given her permission to take them away but also insists that she bring them back.

On 'open' or 'wild' islands, parents allow children to manage their personal belongings as they see fit, without exercising any control. According to these parents, the objects belong to the child and not to the 'island'. However, children whose parents both have these types of islands may react differently to this freedom. While some, like Félicien (12) and Lewis (16), prefer to 'park' their belongings rather than taking advantage of this openness, Eliot (14) and Remi (13) carry all of their belongings with them.

We will discover later in this chapter that a broad range of structural factors can either facilitate or hinder children's material practices.

★★★

In the first part of this chapter, we learned that children tend to favour either 'parked' objects, which anchor them in each of their parents' dwellings, or objects 'in transit', which create permanence in movement and continuity between their different living spaces. As Marcoux (2001) observed of people who move house and who sort out what they want to take with them, leave behind and put into storage for a while, some children would appear to 'dwell' more in these everyday objects than in the places where they live, as it is these objects that provide them with an anchorage rather than the places themselves. The belongings that children always take with them take on a transitional character (Searles, 1986), in the sense that they are mobile points of reference that the children carry with them and return to on a daily basis. As a complement to their 'parked world', this 'mobile world' provides children with emotional security and continuity of identity in times of transition. By bringing along familiar objects, children create what de Singly and Decup-Pannier (2016: 283) refer to as a 'ritual of resistance': a symbolic representation of the continuing connection between the two spaces and two family units that facilitates a smoother transition, despite the challenges that may arise during the process.

Practices developing within a structure of opportunities and constraints

While children have some control over the objects around them, it is essential to recognize that the material practices we have described develop within a larger framework that shapes, restricts, promotes or discourages them.[8] Studies on SPC suggest that children's experience of multilocality is affected by the distance between parental residences, the age of the child and the socio-economic status of each parent (Schier, 2015). Although our study is based on a small number of children, we believe that certain other factors are also worthy of attention, including material and spatial conditions, values and educational styles, and the temporal dimension. It should be stated at the outset that these factors do not completely determine behaviour – it would be difficult to establish a direct and automatic link between a material constraint, for example, and a type of behaviour.

Material and spatial conditions include the distance between residences, the mode of transportation between them, the 'weight' of schoolwork and the socio-economic resources of each parent: these conditions influence children's decisions about whether or not to carry their belongings with them. Children whose parents live far apart may be divided into two groups: the first favours 'parked' objects, and avoids carrying things so they will not be burdened with them – or forget them at a parent's house, which would require another long journey to retrieve them. The second favours objects 'in transit', carrying their entire mobile worlds with them. In contrast, children whose parents live close to one another have no need to carry their belongings over long distances, and have more opportunity to go back and forth between their parents' residences. However, they may still prefer to move all their belongings at once, like Remi (aged 13).

The availability of a car can significantly facilitate the movement of numerous or bulky items between dwellings, regardless of distance. Nevertheless, children who have this convenience may still choose to 'park' their possessions.

The weight of school materials that children must carry, especially in secondary school, may also lead them to leave other belongings 'parked' at a parent's dwelling. For Marie (12), this choice is influenced by both her dependence on public transport (as her mother refuses to drive her) and her desire to feel less burdened, as she must already take the bus with her school bag, her sports equipment and the small bag containing the items to be returned to her other parent.

Some children respond to the constraints posed by their school materials by creating a new system that enables them to carry their belongings more easily – but only if they can travel by car. For instance, Mathilde (13) replaced her bag with a large bin that could hold all of her things and serve as a new transition channel.

The socio-economic resources of each parent also play a role in the management of children's belongings by facilitating, encouraging or discouraging certain practices. Children whose parents both have a comfortable standard of living are more likely to take 'nothing' with them between dwellings, as they may have similar items in each parent's residence. It is harder for children whose parent(s) have fewer financial resources to bring 'nothing' with them, as these parents cannot afford to replace items that are forgotten or left 'parked' at the other parent's dwelling. These children are strongly encouraged to return items like clothes to the 'right' dwelling, or to move expensive items (such as game consoles) between residences rather than duplicating them. However, a parent's modest economic situation can also have the opposite effect: limited resources can result in lack of access to a car (or reluctance to use one due to the cost of petrol), making it necessary for children to 'travel light'. Finally, children whose parents have different standards of living may cope with this imbalance by bringing certain items with them, so they can maintain the same comfort and style at both parents' residences.

The second set of factors we have identified includes the 'parental islands' and the two parents' values and educational styles, which may or may not converge. As we have described, the boundaries of the parental islands influence the children's material practices. To recapitulate, parents establish transfer limits based primarily on the degree of fusion they desire within the 'new family'. Parents with 'fortress', 'cocoon' and 'reef' islands promote the idea of the group 'we' instead of the individual 'I'. Consequently, they limit the circulation of children's personal belongings, considering that these objects belong more to the 'island' than to the children themselves. Children are therefore encouraged to 'park' the belongings they have received from this parent and to return any items they may have taken exceptionally to the other parent's residence. Conversely, parents with 'open' and 'wild' islands encourage their children's autonomy and allow them to take whatever they want from one residence to another, considering these objects to belong primarily to the children. While some children seize this opportunity to take all of their personal belongings with them, others limit transfers, confident that they can take what they need if necessary.

Some parents prioritize ecological and anti-consumerist values, either individually or in agreement with their ex-partners. These parents prefer not to consume more than necessary, and hope to instil the same values in their children: they may thus encourage children to move objects between residences rather than duplicating them. For example, Jean (13) chose to purchase a Nintendo Switch specifically because of its portability and convenience for transportation. Some parents prefer to buy second-hand items, a practice that can also lend itself to a practice of duplicating possessions and 'parking' them in each residence.

Children may find themselves in a delicate situation when one parent approves of a practice and the other does not. This may result in restrictions on certain objects being brought into the dwelling. For instance, Théodore (13) is not allowed to play Nintendo at his father's house, and must therefore leave his console 'parked' at his mother's house.

Finally, the temporal dimension is also important in children's experience of multilocality. It includes the children's age, the time since the parents separated, and the rhythm of alternation between dwellings. Of the 21 children in our study, only three were aged ten or older when their parents separated. Once the SPC arrangement was implemented, these young adolescents' parents were lenient in managing their personal belongings, allowing them to take belongings with them or leave them behind as they wished. As the other participants were younger and less autonomous at the time of separation, the management of logistics often fell on the parents at the beginning. Moreover, parents usually accompany younger children when they go out, and sometimes help them pack their things, which can limit the children's ability to choose what they want to bring with them. However, as the children grow older, the time since separation becomes longer and the alternation becomes more routine, they acquire more autonomy, becoming more responsible for their journeys and increasingly able to manage their belongings as they see fit. Chloé is 12 years old and has been moving between residences for six years. Despite her parents' initial preference that she not take anything with her between dwellings, she has been gradually taking control of her own belongings and making independent decisions about what to bring along:

> At the beginning, my parents, when I got a toy for St Nicholas' Day when I was little, they always wanted me to keep it ... in the house where I am [sic] because they always thought I was going to [forget it in the other house]. ... Before, I used to pack my things with my parents and they decided what I take [sic]. But now, on Thursday evening, well, I pack everything I need. ... And so now I'm kind of the one who chooses what I take. (Chloé, aged 12)

The temporal dimension also encompasses the rhythm of movement between residences. The shorter the period between moves is perceived to be, the less children appear to feel the need to bring their belongings with them, knowing that they will return to them soon. It should be noted that it is not so much the actual number of days spent at each residence that matters as the subjective perception of this time. For example, Lewis (16) alternates every six or eight days, but takes 'nothing' with him because, in his own words, 'a week goes by pretty quickly for me'. However, those who perceive the time between moves as 'long' tend to take their belongings with them, to not be away from them for too long.

★★★

As we have noted, the elements described here do not automatically dictate practices, and can lead to behaviour that may seem paradoxical. For instance, Mathilde takes things with her that 'belong' to one 'island', but leaves them in a specific place in the other dwelling so she will remember to take them back and avoid being reprimanded. Théodore, on the other hand, is careful to keep his two 'reserves' of clothes relatively intact, although his parents encourage him to take everything he might need with him. The meaning that children give to this way of life by means of everyday objects is constituted where the framework of opportunities and constraints formed by their family environments intersects with their own aspirations.

Travelling between islands through particular space-times

As we mentioned in the introduction to this chapter, the spaces that children traverse while moving between their two dwellings also play a vital role in their multilocal way of life.[9] In our analysis of the children's discourse, we identified three particular types of space-times: *public*, *familial* and *interstitial*.

The first two (public and familial) are transitional space-times that allow children in SPC to distance themselves from the family environment they are leaving, with its norms, values, 'parental style', activities, decor and atmosphere, and prepare themselves for the family environment of their destination.

The terminology we will adopt here allows us to consider this displacement in both its spatial and its temporal dimensions. 'Transitional space-times' constitute a kind of 'third space' (Winther, 2015: 226) which is neither the father's dwelling nor the mother's. The first type, 'public transitional space-time', refers to public, physical spaces (such as the school, the place of an extracurricular activity, a shopping street or a train or bus) that are familiar to children from the regular activities that they engage in there. 'Familial transitional space-time' refers to trips to or from a parent's dwelling accompanied by a parent and/or (full) sibling, whether by car, by public transport or on foot. For children of separated parents, these 'transitional space-times' can be understood as intermediate spaces and times, an 'in-between'. These 'in-between' space-times enable them to construct their family identity, in that they leave behind a role and status corresponding to one place of residence and prepare to play a new role on the second family 'stage', in the Goffmanian sense (Goffman, 1973). Frequenting these spaces during the move between residences can help to stabilize a life shared between two dwellings and to give meaning to the relationship between these dwellings.

Some children also travel through 'interstitial' space-times, which refer to a place of residence where they must wait before moving to the other one. Here the child is not crossing a strictly defined boundary between a 'here' and a 'there', but is temporarily situated in a space where they feel their presence is not entirely legitimate.

Children appropriate these three particular space-times and give them specific meanings according to whether they facilitate a smooth transition or upset the child's points of reference.

Public transitional space-times

On the day of a move, children may travel through 'public transitional space-times' consisting of the school, a train or bus, a shopping street or the place of an extracurricular activity. These 'transitional space-times' constitute a comforting 'non-human environment' that contributes 'to children's emotional security, to the stability and continuity of their experiences and to the development of their sense of personal identity' (Searles, 1986: 88). This environment provides a transition between two realities, internal and external, and represents 'a third aspect of life' (Searles, 1986: 79). We refer to these public space-times as 'transitional' because they enable a 'soft transfer' between dwellings.[10] Moving through a familiar place where they have regular habits and routines provides children with some degree of day-to-day stability by maintaining points of reference that give them a sense of familiarity. This makes the transfer from one parent's dwelling to the other's easier both emotionally and logistically, as the children need not make several journeys on the day of a move; they can go to school or to an activity as usual from one parent's residence, and go directly to the other parent's residence afterward. The journey between dwellings thus takes on a more 'normal' character, as each leg of the journey is a normal one, the only difference being that the point of departure is not the same as the point of return.

The school

Tristan (aged 15) considered the days of his moves to be just like any other day when he was living in SPC. On the day of transition, he would get ready 'like [he was] going to school' before leaving the house. The arrival at the other house was also routine and habitual:

> I'd go and eat something, because when you come back from school you're hungry. I'd be like … if I came back from school on any [other] day. So I'd say hello to everyone and sometimes we'd chat a bit about how things were going and what we'd done during the week, we'd do like [it was] a normal day. (Tristan, aged 15)

The conscious staging of this journey to and from school – 'like on an ordinary day' – reflects its ordinary, routine and even familiar nature, establishing the space and time of the transition as 'normal' within the child's day-to-day routine.

School plays a particularly important role in this transition phase. It is the 'transitional space-time' *par excellence*, given that the majority of the children in our study pass through their school before going to their other parent's dwelling or meeting up with this parent at the end of the day. The school is considered a centre of gravity in the family's daily life. Even after their parents' separation, none of the children we interviewed had changed schools, as their parents wanted to maintain the school as an essential anchor in their multilocal way of life. Indeed, for 12 children, both parents had either stayed in or moved to housing that was close to the schools the children attended. For the remaining nine children, one parent had moved to a town more than 20 kilometres away: quasi-egalitarian alternating rhythms were established and/or logistical arrangements were made to relieve these children as much as possible of the burdens of travel between their school and the distant parent's dwelling.

Making a smooth transition by way of the school can help children maintain their stability during major changes, such as when a parent moves to a more distant town. Coralie (12) finds that the Friday transfer via her school plays a facilitating role: 'Mum drops me off [at school] and Dad picks me up, so that changes … but I have school in between so, well … it's OK.'

However, children's perception of passing through a 'public transitional space-time' is not necessarily positive. For instance, Remi (13) does not find moving from one house to another by way of his school to be an adequate solution – on the contrary.[11] Taking personal items along while travelling can reveal sensitive information about one's family and mobile way of life, potentially leading to embarrassment:

Yes, that day [Sunday] suits me [for moving house], because I had … well, I have a friend who has to bring all his stuff to school on Mondays so his parents can come and get him. … I'd hate that, because I don't want everyone to have access to my stuff. (Remi, aged 13)

Public transport

Lewis (aged 16) finds stability and continuity in his daily life not only by means of the school he transitions through each week, but also through the journey he takes to get there. During our first meeting, Lewis placed a block on the SSNG to symbolize a 'crossing point', as he put it. This is a major roundabout where cars and several trams cross paths. He explains: 'From there, it's the same journey to school whether I'm living at my mum's or my dad's. It's just that it takes a lot longer to get there when I'm at my mum's than when I'm at my dad's' (Lewis, aged 16).

Hart (1979) points out that children do not appropriate public space in the same way as adults. The psychologist and geographer explains that the difference is reflected in the way they name locations, which refers to the way they use them. By calling this roundabout a 'crossing point', Lewis is indicating how he appropriates it and uses it to navigate his life in alternation: he connects the places where he resides by means of the multiple journeys that he undertakes between them, following different or identical routes. Lewis thus creates a 'lived space' (Di Méo, 2012), an intimate network of real and imagined places and territories. Once he has left school and has passed this 'crossing point', he becomes aware of which parental dwelling he is travelling to: this is the point where he 'leaves' the residence he is coming from and connects with the one he is going to. Part of this transitional route is the same every week, offering a certain continuity and a time for adaptation before arrival at the new dwelling.

Tristan (15) and Théodore (13) also travel independently between their residences. They each take different buses depending on whether they are going to their mother's or their father's house on Friday, the day they move house: for them, 'changing houses' means 'changing buses'. The key moment of transition is when they become conscious of which bus they need to take, as they need to think of their destination and the parent with whom they will be staying. This mental process has some disadvantages for the two teenagers, and can feel burdensome. Théodore occasionally boards the wrong bus: 'Well, the disadvantages are that you have to change weeks. I've … well, you have to change buses, and I've taken the bus to go to Mum's a few times when in fact I have to go to Dad's, or vice versa. That's one of the disadvantages.' During his bus journey, Théodore enjoys listening to music, which helps him relax before arriving at his other parent's dwelling. He explains what he likes about these autonomous trips:

> I'm less under my parents' responsibility, and so I'm more. … It's my own responsibility. … It's not the others, it's not my parents, it's me. And also, I'm more relaxed on the bus [than in the car] because I've got my headphones and so I can listen to music. … I go on my phone a bit, or I look out the window. (Théodore, aged 13)

Théodore articulates the notion that these 'public transitional space-times' are a part of his multilocal way of living and that they ensure a certain continuity in his day-to-day experience. During our interview using the SSNG, he located himself 'on the bus', because he didn't want to 'show himself once at Dad's, once at Mum's'. On the contrary, he preferred to emphasize the connections produced by his journeys on public transport.

Extracurricular activities

Coralie (aged 12) moves to her father's house on Wednesday afternoons. After school, instead of returning to her mother's dwelling, she goes to her judo class, after which she takes the train to her father's house. According to Coralie, going through this 'public transitional space-time' makes it easier for her to deal with separating from her mother:

Sometimes it's kind of upsetting to cut off the time with Mum to go to Dad's. Sometimes it's just kind of upsetting, but since I've started judo ... because before, Mum would come and pick me up at school, I'd go to her house, we'd do little things and then suddenly there was the train and I'd have to leave again and because I'd started a time with Mum, cutting it off like that wasn't very pleasant. Now that I've got judo, after that it doesn't really make a difference, because I've got judo, so I was already not with Mum. (Coralie, aged 12)

Familial transitional space-time

Some children emphasize how travelling to or from a parental dwelling accompanied by a parent and/or (full) sibling offers them opportunities for special family time in a place that is neither the father's dwelling nor the mother's, and where new practices can develop that strengthen family ties. These practices can include sharing a snack or playing games during the journey, but may also include talking about sensitive topics like tensions with members of the stepfamily. These observations reflect those of Schier (2015), who points out that the life of a 'new family' does not take place only within their dwelling, but develops through a set of new everyday practices that are also deployed outside the dwelling. According to the geographer, these include efforts to compensate for feelings of absence (making phone calls, sending cards or gifts), to facilitate mobility (planning the child's itinerary) or to help children feel at home (providing them with their own room, involving them in furnishing and decorating the dwelling, referring to the dwelling as 'their' home, inviting them to share activities). In the same vein, Christensen et al (2000) conducted a study examining how ten- to 12-year-old English children understand the concept of 'quality time' with different family members. They found that some children feel a sense of belonging to a family unit simply by being together and doing something 'as a family' in a shared space (Christensen et al, 2000: 146). The authors specify that it is 'through the dynamic and fluid movement of children in, out and around the home that their own sense of belonging to the family and the home is constituted' (Christensen et al, 2000: 153). Both Morgan (2020) and Gabb (2008) corroborate these findings. Morgan stresses that family practices are also deployed outside the dwelling, notably during car journeys. Gabb's study, by exploring experiences of intimacy and sexuality within families, reveals that the car journey to a child's school can sometimes prove to be an emotional 'hot spot' (Gabb, 2008: 138).

Inspired by this literature and based on the discourse of the children in our study, we consider these 'transitional space-times' to be 'familial' for children who make at least part of the journey[12] accompanied by a member of their 'first family'. The use of this term alludes to the 'family practices' approach proposed by Morgan (2011), which emphasizes the fluid and regular nature of family relationships. Accordingly, we can consider these spatial movements to be a novel family practice allowing parents and children to develop and reinforce their evolving relationships while travelling to or from a dwelling. Children may perceive this transition phase as quality time shared with a parent or sibling, which contributes to their feeling of belonging to the 'new family' and to their sense of home (Christensen et al, 2000). In the following pages, we will examine how the children's ages, the distance between residences and the degree of isolation of a parental dwelling influence the practice of making these journeys together.[13]

Émilie (aged ten) travels between dwellings with one or both of her parents, as she does not yet wish to travel alone. Moreover, Émilie's father lives far away, and his house is isolated and difficult to reach by public transport; consequently, he needs to take Émilie to school and to pick her up there. Despite the long distance, Émilie cherishes the quality of the time she spends with her father during their shared journeys. She describes these journeys as a 'special activity' that they experience together, like visiting a museum or their trip to a foreign city for her tenth birthday. During these trips with her father, Émilie expresses her feelings about her relationships with her stepsiblings and with her stepmother. She tells him that she sometimes feels excluded from their 'new family' because they 'don't wait for [her]' to share pleasant experiences, like choosing pet guinea pigs or meeting the neighbours' puppy. In these moments of privacy, Émilie's father reassures her about her position in the family. He suggests that she talk about her feelings with her stepsiblings Éden (ten) and Capucine (12), to let them know how much these special moments mean to her – especially since she is not always present in their house.

The situation is similar for Mathilde (13), whose father lives almost 30 kilometres from the city where she lives with her mother and where her school is located. She takes advantage of her long journeys by car with her father, or by bus with her sister Clémence (15), to discuss sensitive subjects with them. In particular, she talks about her somewhat conflictual relationship with her stepmother Alexia and stepsister Flore (15), who live permanently with her father. She considers these 'transitional space-times' to be special moments with her 'first family', where she can confide freely without fear of being overheard:

Interviewer: And so, during your journeys, you take the opportunity to …

Mathilde: To talk … to talk about the house, because there are lots of problems. … And it's a time when it's just us [Mathilde and her sister] and Dad. … We're the ones

<table>
<tr><td></td><td>[who bring up the subject], or Dad says what's going to happen with the house, and …</td></tr>
<tr><td>Interviewer:</td><td>And do you also have discussions sometimes when you're at home with him?</td></tr>
<tr><td>Mathilde:</td><td>Not a lot, because they [Alexia and Flore] are always there.</td></tr>
</table>

The parents of Joseph (16) also live almost 30 kilometres apart. The teenager considers the journeys by car with his father, who transports him and his sisters to and from his mother's town, to be 'family time'. When Joseph is not living with his father, he does not have much interaction with him, because, he explains: 'Dad, he's fine, he doesn't have too many problems, he's not too worried about keeping in touch. So we'll see each other later, and in any case, we talk a lot in the car and all. So it's fine, we still have good contact.'

Interstitial space-times

Children who pass through 'interstitial space-times' on the day of a move between residences perceive the transition more negatively than those who pass through 'transitional space-times'. They find themselves in an uncomfortable situation, being aware that they are physically present in a place where they should no longer be.

This is the case for Lewis (aged 16), who since the beginning of the school year has preferred to take the train to his mother's residence on Wednesday afternoons. This itinerary not only involves 'fewer transactions to carry out', it enables him to avoid having to deal with his 'computer kit' all morning at school: as his father lives near the station, he can easily stop at his father's apartment on the way to pick it up. He stops there only briefly, because for him the transition to his mother's house takes place when he gets out of school. He thus finds himself 'in between', being strongly present 'in thought' (Baldassar, 2008: 252) with his mother, whom he looks forward to seeing again, while being physically present in his father's dwelling, where he should no longer be:

> So, it's really … on Wednesday, so if I'm at my father's and I'm going to my mother's, I'll usually just pass through in a flash, seeing that my mother's house is far away. You know, on Wednesday, I try to have some time at her house, so in fact I try to go there pretty early. (Lewis, aged 16)

This is also the case for Joseph (16), who moves house every Friday. His sister Amandine (12) has an acrobatics class until 7:30 pm on Fridays, and he must therefore wait until that time for his father to come for him and his sisters. To pass the time, he occasionally 'squats' at his mother's house to wait for his father. His use of this term reflects the illegitimate nature of his presence in his mother's house on Friday afternoons, as his parents have decided that the transition begins in the morning when he leaves for school. Joseph is thus temporarily between two places. He is 'nowhere': no longer at his mother's, but not yet at his father's. He passes the time at his mother's house by playing online video games or watching videos; however, he never fully relaxes, knowing that this is only a transitory phase before he returns to his father's house, where he can truly settle in.

On Fridays, as Joseph is 'worn out' from his week, he is frustrated by the idea of having to change houses when he has already settled in at his mother's house:

> I used to go home to my mum's for a while [on Fridays, after school] and then I stopped doing that because it was getting on my nerves, because I don't want to move again afterwards to go somewhere else. … On Fridays, my 'objective' in quotes is just to go home, and not necessarily to move around, because I'm tired. I don't really feel like doing much of anything afterwards in the evening; it bothers me in fact. (Joseph, aged 16)

To avoid finding himself in this uncomfortable situation, he prefers to pass the time by wandering aimlessly downtown until his father comes for him:

> Since on Friday evenings I'm at my father's, I have to wait until 7:30 pm [because of his sister's activity]. I don't necessarily want to [go to his mother's house], and so I'm [not] at my mother's anymore, so, well, logically I should be somewhere else. … When I don't really want to go [to his mother's] home, I hang around with friends for a while, I'm out in the street, or I come straight home [to his father's house, by train]. (Joseph, aged 16)

The teenager chooses to wander aimlessly with his friends because he is no longer living with his mother, but has not yet moved in with his father. So Joseph would not need to either go back to his mother's house or pass the time by wandering in the streets, his father eventually proposed two alternatives that have given him some satisfaction.

One alternative is for Joseph to take the train to his father's house right after school, without going back to his mother's house, which allows him to arrive there earlier. He can thus prolong the transition he has started at school, and avoid the frustration he felt when he had to leave his mother's house shortly after arriving. Joseph is not yet very comfortable with travelling independently; he therefore sits on the train where he can read the screen showing upcoming stops. Thus reassured, he can take some time for himself by listening to music or watching a video, which he says helps him to think and clear his head. Moving from one dwelling to another through this 'public transitional space-time' helps to manage his frustrations and to facilitate the transition he initially perceived as negative.

Joseph can also meet his father and his sister Lou (six) to walk around town and have dinner together. 'That's fun sometimes too', he says. These new family routines developed in a 'familial transitional space-time' help to stabilize the life Joseph shares between his two dwellings, giving meaning to the relationship between his living spaces.

★★★

The children in our study use 'transitional space-times' and everyday objects to structure their dual living environments, thereby creating a 'lived space' (Rolshoven, 2008) that makes sense to them. As we have demonstrated elsewhere (Merla and Nobels, 2021), alternation, with its continuities and discontinuities, does not necessarily lead to instability or loss of bearings. By making use of everyday objects, children are able to structure their world, creating habits and routines – in short, creating a 'multilocal dwelling' using everyday instruments. However, this structuring is not achieved without hitches or difficulties, with objects appearing both as facilitators of transition and as constraints, burdens and sources of anxiety. Privileging personal belongings that are 'parked' in living spaces or carrying a mobile world of belongings 'in transit' contributes to creating and maintaining a particular 'aesthetic', a 'cosmology' (Miller, 2008) that we will qualify as familial. In this 'family cosmology' (Merla and Nobels, 2021), children and things are related in an orderly manner, not within a single domestic space but across a wider territory, a 'lived space', spread across several residences. Based on this cosmology, children judge the moving world around them, and themselves.

It is not so much the quantity of objects 'in transit' from one residence to another that signals children's relationships to their two residences as the weight and the practical, symbolic, identity-related and emotional functions that children attribute to these objects, and/or that the objects fulfil for them. By distinguishing between objects that are 'parked' and 'in transit' – and within the second category, between 'shadow' objects and 'stand-by' objects – and by highlighting the ambivalence of the transition channel, this chapter has revealed the specific and varied roles played by everyday objects in the logistics of transition, in maintaining continuity in movement and in anchoring children in each place of residence. 'Transitional space-times' also play important roles in the multilocal lives of children in SPC, acting as intermediaries between the social and the material to help them manage the transition between their different living spaces. They enable children to disconnect from the place they are leaving, characterized by a particular family environment, and to reconnect with the place and the family to which they are moving. In contrast, in 'interstitial space–times' (that is, the parental residence they are expected to have already left), children may feel they are temporarily losing their bearings, finding themselves in an indistinct space where they are no longer meant to be at one parent's residence but are not yet at the other's.

In the next chapter, we will invite the reader to continue our young participants' journey by addressing the question of the 'routines and rituals of return' that children develop when they have arrived at one of their 'parental islands'.

Notes

[1]   These first three sections are largely based on an article published in French in 2021 in the journal *Recherches sociologiques et anthropologiques* (Merla and Nobels, 2021). While some passages are identical, a substantial part of this chapter further develops the arguments and examples used in the original article.

[2]   Lewis (aged 16), a boy in our study, coined the term 'in transition' to describe his clarinet, which he frequently moved between his residences during the school term. We decided to change the term to 'in transit' to better capture the idea of these objects being transitory and passing through different spaces. Lewis no longer takes music lessons, and now keeps his clarinet at his father's house: we use the term 'parked' to indicate that objects are anchored in a particular living space.

[3]   We use the term 'distinguishing' here to mean recognizing the two spaces as different from one another, without necessarily emphasizing this difference or valuing one over the other. This is done primarily by means of materiality.

[4]   Romane prefers 'parked' objects. She rarely takes a piece of clothing from her mother's house, and always brings it back.

[5]   Théodore's mother has a 'reef' island.

[6]   Mélissa's father has a 'reef' island and her mother an 'open' island.

[7]   We will analyse the installation or non-installation of these objects as a 'ritual of return' in Chapter 4.

[8]   This section takes up and extends the analyses presented in Merla and Nobels (2021).

[9]   Out of the 21 children in our study, 13 travel between residences via their school. Four others change residence via an extracurricular activity. Three children return after school to the residence where they spent the last few days, and then move to the other parent's residence at the end of the day. Lastly, one child is dropped off directly at the other parent's residence on Sundays at the end of the day.

[10]   This expression was used by the father of Mathilde (aged 13) when he explained in an interview that he had chosen to make the transition from one residence to another by way of her school. It expresses the meaning that the children also give to this space–time so accurately that we have chosen to use it to summarize their discourse, even though it comes from the discourse of a parent.

[11]   Remi was the only child in our study who expressed reluctance to take his belongings with him to school, for fear that other pupils would judge him. This question could not be explored further in this study due to insufficient data, but would be worth exploring in future research.

[12]   This nuance refers to the situations where children like Lewis (16) and Félicien (12) make most of the journey on their own, before being picked up by a parent at the station. They then complete the journey together by car, arriving at the parent's dwelling shortly thereafter.

[13] The type of parental island does not affect this situation. Except for Romane's mother, who has a 'fortress' island and sees travelling as a time spent 'with the family', the other parents in charge of transitions between dwellings have 'reef', 'open' or 'wild' islands. They encourage their children to be independent and to travel as far as possible by their own means. Although they may make certain journeys with their children, their primary reason for doing so is the difficulty of accessing the place of residence in any way other than by car.

4

Routines and Rituals of Return

Specific family practices are deployed when children arrive at a dwelling where they will be residing for the next several days: we consider these practices to be 'family rituals' (Fiese et al, 2002: 382). These rituals are essential in structuring family members' everyday lives, enabling them to maintain some degree of stability during times of stress and change. In this chapter, we will examine these family rituals – which we will call '*rituals of return*' – and their role in the lives of children who alternate between residences. We hypothesize that children (re)define their places and establish a sense of belonging in their 'new families' by engaging in these stable practices upon each return 'home'.

In order to understand the difference between '*routines*' and '*rituals*', we will first examine the work of psychologists Fiese et al (2002) and the criteria they use to distinguish between the two. We will also explore other research studies, including those of Bakker et al (2015), Winther (2015) and de Singly and Decup-Pannier (2016), which focus on family rituals in the context of parental separation: these studies provide valuable insights into the central role of routines and rituals in the daily lives of separated families. We will then explore the 'routines and rituals of return' that we observed in our fieldwork, building on the insights from this previous research.

Family routines and rituals

Fiese et al (2002: 382) distinguish 'routines' from 'rituals' based on the dimensions of communication, commitment and continuity, as summarized in Table 4.1.

When people carry out a routine, they commit to actions momentarily and then forget them once they have been completed. Routines are instrumental in that they tell family members '*this is what needs to be done*'. They are repeated over time, ensuring continuity of behaviour, but without continuity of meaning. Rituals, on the other hand, symbolically communicate '*this is who we are*' as a family group. Family members are emotionally invested in

Table 4.1: Definitions of routines and rituals

Characteristic	Routines of daily living	Rituals in family life
Communication	Instrumental 'This is what needs to be done'	Symbolic 'This is who we are'
Commitment	Perfunctory and momentary Little conscious thought given after the act	Enduring and affective 'This is right' The experience may be repeated in memory
Continuity	Directly observable and detectable by outsiders Behaviour is repeated over time	Meaning extends across generations and is interpreted by insiders 'This is what we look forward to and who we will continue to be across generations'

Source: Reproduced from Fiese et al (2002: 382), with permission

these practices, which provide them with a sense of belonging both during and after the ritual activity. These practices remain in the memory, and can be relived. Rituals are repeated and transmitted from generation to generation; the meaning they are given lasts longer than the practices themselves. Their symbolic nature can be defined only by the family members themselves, making it challenging to observe rituals from the outside.

As Fiese and colleagues (2002) point out, the study of family routines and rituals can provide insights into how family life affects each member and how each individual influences the functioning of the family group. These authors emphasize that rituals consist of a practical dimension, which structures the behaviour of family members, and a symbolic dimension, which reinforces group identity by integrating the different members into the group and by giving meaning to family practices. Family routines and rituals occur within a specific cultural setting, making them potentially unique to each family.

Bakker and colleagues (2015) conducted a study in the Netherlands that examined the living arrangements and daily lives of separated families, using the concepts of 'routines' and 'rituals' developed by Fiese and her colleagues (2002) to explain how these symbolic practices contribute to 'doing family' after a separation. These authors, who consider these practices to be central to family life, explored how they function in families where separated parents live far apart. Based on interviews with 35 separated parents, the authors defined three types of separated families based on how the parents practice the rituals of the original nuclear family, like Christmas parties or children's birthdays – together, alternately or separately. The first type involves the parents 'continuing family life' (Bakker et al, 2015: 378) by continuing to practice pre-separation rituals together. In the second type, the ex-partners 'build a new life' (Bakker et al, 2015: 378) by each practising pre-separation rituals separately with their child: for example, children in these families will have two separate birthday parties. In the third type, the child participates in pre-separation rituals with 'only one parent involved' (Bakker et al, 2015: 377) – usually the mother – because the other parent is relatively uninvolved in the child's life. According to Bakker et al (2015), these types may not necessarily correspond to specific family arrangements (such as exclusive or shared physical custody), and families can shift from one type to another over time. The authors also highlight the importance of family rituals in shaping how separated families 'display' (Finch, 2007) themselves as cohesive family units.

The observation that some separated parents 'continue family life' is also made in de Singly and Decup-Pannier's discussion of 'unifying rituals' (de Singly and Decup-Pannier, 2016: 278). These rituals are described as moments that children share with both of their parents, such as having a meal together on the day of a move, that give them a sense of belonging to a family that is still united. According to these authors, these rituals help to avoid the 'splintering' of a child's identity by providing experiences shared with both parents. In parallel, they also describe 'resistance rituals' (de Singly and Decup-Pannier, 2016: 283), which refer to the transfer of objects[1] that children put in place to forge a symbolic link between their two places of residence and two families, and to make the spatial duality bearable. Finally, they observe that children may experience the transition from one residence to another as a 'ritual of passage', defined as 'a time during which a group or individual prepares or accompanies a person's passage from one condition or status to another' (de Singly and Decup-Pannier, 2016: 282). If the parents and the child emphasize continuity between the two places of residence and the two 'new families', the change of residence does not constitute a ritual, as there is no change of status; it is simply a 'new habit'. In contrast, if they emphasize discontinuity, the change of residence can be conceived of as a ritual, as the child moves from the status of 'child of their mother' to that of 'child of their father'.

Winther (2015) observes that children's journeys between their places of residence tend to become routine. The children perform the same actions and practices regularly, without paying much attention to them: (not) packing their belongings, travelling with them, saying goodbye to the 'new family' members they are leaving, saying hello to the ones they are meeting again, and (not) unpacking their belongings. According to Winther, these routines make up a 'travel grid' (Winther, 2015: 224) that provides them with a framework to follow, sparing them the need to recreate new ways of doing things at each transition. The anthropologist also notes that while some children perceive their return 'home' as an everyday practice, others see it as a '*rite de passage*' (Winther, 2015: 224) that marks a transition for both the returning children and the family members who are seeing them again.

In this chapter, we will build on the work of these authors to examine the role of family rituals in how the separated families in our study 'do family'. We will first explain how we position ourselves in relation to these studies, and how we are reappropriating the definitions proposed by Fiese and her colleagues (2002).

Following on the work of Winther (2015), we will analyse the routines and rituals that take place when children arrive on one of their 'islands'. Our focus will be on those rituals that bring members of a 'new family' together – that is, those through which parents 'build a new life' (Bakker et al, 2015) – rather than on those that 'unify' the members of the 'first family' as described by de Singly and Decup-Pannier (2016). By analysing these rituals, we will better understand how they help to (re)define the child's place within each household and reinforce their sense of belonging to each 'new family'.

Although some of the children we encountered in our study indicate that moving house has become a routine – a 'new habit' – for them, the return to each parent's dwelling holds symbolic importance for the majority. The meaning that children give to this family ritual is that of a '*rite de passage*' – which we prefer to call a '*ritual of return*'[2] – signifying a change in their status. According to Winther's (2015) conception, the term 'status' does not necessarily refer to status as the father's or the mother's child, as suggested by de Singly and Decup-Pannier (2016), but instead to the role children occupy within each 'new family' and the place they are given within the family's physical and symbolic space as 'permanent residents' or as 'guests'.

Drawing on the dimensions identified by Fiese et al (2002) (instrumental or symbolic communication, momentary or affective commitment and continuity of behaviour or of meaning; see Table 4.1), we distinguish between 'routines of return' and 'rituals of return'. In our study, we observed three different types of 'rituals of return' among the children we encountered: '*integration rituals*'; '*anchoring rituals*'; and '*(not) unpacking rituals*'. These differ according to whether children see their return to the dwelling as an ordinary or an extraordinary practice,[3] and whether the activities constituting the ritual are collective or individual.[4] They also depend on the meaning that children give to their practice of return: as something that '*needs to be done*', that defines '*who we are*' (as a 'new family') or that defines '*who I am in the "new family"*'. Table 4.2 outlines the dimensions of these 'routines and rituals of return', which will be discussed in more detail in the following pages.

While some children consider returning to a parent's dwelling after an absence of several days to be an ordinary family routine, for others, it is

Table 4.2: Definitions of routines and rituals of return

Dimension	Routines of return	Rituals of return		
		Integration ritual	**Anchoring ritual**	**(Not) unpacking ritual**
Representation of return	Ordinary	Extraordinary	Ordinary	
Practices	Individual or collective	Collective	Individual	
Communication	Instrumental	Symbolic		
	'*This is what needs to be done*'	'*This is who we are*'	'*This is what needs to be done*'	'*This is who I am in the "new family"*'
Commitment	Momentary No longer thinks about coming home	Affective, sense of belonging to the family unit Remembers coming home		
Continuity	Continuity of behaviour	Continuity of behaviour and meaning		

a symbolically charged 'ritual of return' that strengthens their feeling of belonging to the family group to which they are returning.

Routines of return: an ordinary arrival

For most participants in de Singly and Decup-Pannier's study (2016) of young people in France with separated parents, the transition from one parental residence to another represented simply a 'new habit'. We will refer to a new family 'routine' rather than a 'habit' to describe this change of residence, and more specifically, to describe children's return to the residence of the parent now responsible for them. Indeed, based on the work of Fiese and her colleagues (2002), considering a child's arrival in a parental residence as a 'routine' highlights the instrumental, momentary and continuous nature of this practice, which '*has to be done*' every week (or more frequently, depending on the rhythm of alternation). Children perceive this ordinary arrival as a regular practice that is part of the household's familial organization, and specific to each parental residence.

Eliot (aged 14) moves house every Monday after school. He collects his belongings at the residence of the parent with whom he has spent the week, then goes to the residence of the parent with whom he will now be staying. He leaves the transition channel containing his personal belongings in the entrance hall, in the same way he usually leaves his school bag, and then settles down on the sofa. Later in the evening, he unpacks his things and arranges them in his wardrobe. Returning is an ordinary, routine activity for him, and does not require extra investment in any specific task:

> I sit on the sofa or whatever, I eat, maybe I do a bit of homework if there's anything to do, and, well, otherwise nothing special. … What I do every day, you know, like when I come home from school. … I don't do anything, like, special on Mondays. When I move house, I don't do anything special. (Eliot, aged 14)

Annelyse (ten) says that whenever she returns to her father's house, whether after a day at school or a week's absence, the first thing she does is find her cat in the garden so she can pet him.[5] The girl does not attach any specific meaning to this return. She is not doing 'anything special', she says. 'I just do like … [what she] normally [does]'. Annelyse adds that she does not do 'anything special' when she returns to her mother's apartment either. She watches a film on TV with her sister Chloé (12) and their mother, or they have dinner together and chat about their past week, as they would on any other day.

Cédric (15) relates that on Friday evenings, when he returns to his mother's house, he always finds the same place set for him at the dinner table, as if this habit had not been suspended for a week. The teenager does not demonstrate any particular emotional investment in the return to either parent's residence. For Cédric, over the number of years he has been alternating, the transition has become completely routine: 'In eight years, I think I've got used to … doing this', he says. These ordinary arrivals simply blend in with the familial organization of each 'new family'.

These routine practices are purely functional and momentary. They are repeated at every change of residence, but also every day: for these children and the members of their 'new families', these practices have no particular meaning, and they are no different from those of an ordinary return from school. Marie (12) describes returning to her father's loft as if '[she] arrived [there] every day'. There is in fact no change in her daily routine: she puts her school bag in her room, greets her stepmother who is working in the office, has a snack, does some homework and then rushes downstairs to meet her neighbour in the community room, as she does every day. Lewis (16) explains that when he returns to his father's house, whether on Tuesday after school (when he moves house) or on any other day, his father is often still at work. Lewis heads straight to his room, where he drops off his school bag, sports bag and clarinet (if he has brought it from his mother's house). He then settles down at his desk to do his homework or to do research on the internet, as he does every day.

It should be noted that while arrival at a parent's dwelling is routine for some children, their return is not always perceived in the same way by members of the 'new family' with whom they are reuniting. As we will see in the section on 'integration rituals', the moment of return is invested with meaning for Lewis's and Marie's mothers and younger half-siblings, although the two adolescents see it as an ordinary, momentary stage in their daily lives.

Rituals of return

A family ritual, according to Fiese et al (2002), is a regular practice that structures the behaviour of family members, and that has a symbolic dimension in that it integrates the different members into the group and gives meaning to family practices. More than the ritual activity itself, the meaning that it takes on endures over time, reassuring the members that they belong to the family unit. As we have described previously, Bakker et al (2015) draw on the definitions proposed by Fiese and her colleagues to explore the central role of family rituals in post-separation families. These rituals enable them to 'display' (Finch, 2007) to themselves and others that they form a united family.

Based on analysis of the discourse of the children in our study, we have identified several types of family rituals that help to reinforce children's sense of belonging to each 'new family', each conveying a different symbolic meaning. 'Integration rituals' are the 'family rituals' described by Bakker et al (2015: 378). These activities bring the members of the 'new family' together, allowing them to engage in practices that show them that they still make up a family unit (*'this is what we are'*). 'Anchoring rituals' are practices that children use to anchor themselves within the parental dwelling, which they carry out on a daily basis while they are living there. The fact that they perform these rituals on the day they return thus emphasizes the habitual, mundane nature of this return, and shows that it is in no way extraordinary (*'this is what has to be done'*). Finally, '(not) unpacking rituals' are transitional practices through which children mark their place in each dwelling and each 'new family' (*'this is who I am in the "new family"'*).

Integration rituals

'Integration rituals' are moments shared by 'new family' members when children return to their dwelling. The children's return is seen as an extraordinary, festive occasion, through which the family members symbolically convey to one another who they are: a united 'new family'. The children remember these rituals, and look forward to repeating them each time they return to the dwelling.

A convivial family moment

Remi (aged 13) explains that when he arrives at his mother's house on Sunday evenings, his mother plans a meal for him and his older brothers that they particularly like, such as spaghetti Bolognese or raclette. Before supper, he sits on the sofa for a while with his mother to 'debrief' about the past week, telling her what he has learnt at school, what he has eaten at the canteen, and so on. He then takes his suitcase, which contains his objects 'in transit', upstairs to his room and leaves it there unopened. He returns to take his place at the table and to share a moment of family conviviality with his mother, brothers and stepfather, and with his three stepsisters when they are present.[6]

This moment of conviviality echoes the 'welcoming rituals' described by Hachet (2021: 166). Based on parents' experience of shared physical custody, the author shows that the transition is experienced as a moment of reunion: parents prepare for the children's arrival by stocking the refrigerator with their favourite foods, organize a small party or give the children presents. Through these rituals, parents show children that they are 'doubly present' – both physically present and available to the children now that they have returned. One parent told the researcher that it was an 'all-consuming return', because the arrival of the children – who wanted to tell him everything they had done during the past week – demanded so much energy.

The mother and stepfather of Manuelo (13) and his brother Giorgio (16) have chosen to set up a single schedule of alternation for all four of their children, meaning that everyone arrives and leaves at the same time. Thus, the two boys move house every Friday evening after school, as do their stepsiblings Sandro (15) and Elena (17). This gives the teenagers the opportunity to be physically present at the same time and to build relationships around shared activities, such as sharing takeout from a chip shop on Friday evenings:

> Here [at his mother's house], on Fridays we usually eat [takeout from a] chip shop when we get back from the week at my dad's, and then once we've done that, we have a wash and watch a film if we're not too tired, or we go upstairs and find something to do, it depends. (Manuelo, aged 13)

Like Remi, Giorgio quickly deposits the bag containing his belongings in the room he shares with Manuelo and Sandro at his mother's house. He does not empty it until the next morning, as he immediately goes back downstairs to spend the evening with the other members of his 'new family'. He explains that this time together allows them to discuss how their week has gone: 'Here [at his mother's] I also drop off my things, and I don't put them away either because often on Fridays we all get together, so we sit around the table, when we eat or whatever, we talk … we debrief about the week, you could say' (Giorgio, aged 16). These moments of sharing signify to the participants that they form a united 'new family'.

Chloé (12) explains that when she arrives at her father's house on Fridays, she immediately unpacks and installs her belongings and puts the transition channel away in her wardrobe, because she does not like her room to be messy. She then goes to the kitchen or living room and stays in these communal areas to spend time with her father and stepmother, whereas she normally spends most of her time in her bedroom:

> Well, since I don't like it when my room's a mess, I put all my stuff away in my wardrobe. And, well … and then … I don't stay in my room straight away, I go to the living room for a bit with Dad and Anaëlle [her stepmother], and I help them prepare the meal and everything, because it's been a while since we've seen each other, and we have a little apéro because it's Friday evening. And then, well … and then it's the weekend. And then, during the week, I stay in my room more. (Chloé, aged 12)

This integration ritual around the preparation of the meal and the sharing of the *apéro* echoes the '*rite de passage*' described by Winther (2015: 223) in the sense that this activity signifies to both the new arrival and the permanent residents that a transition is taking place. Chloé explains that for her, arriving at a parent's residence is a sign that she is shifting to another family environment, with different rules, routines, availabilities, atmosphere and people, and that she has to get used to this environment and find her bearings again:

> Each time, I'm in the atmosphere of my dad's place, and then I have to leave for my mum's, so it changes a bit because it's not, well, it's still kind of the same, but not really, so. … Well, you know, I still have to change, but, well … that doesn't bother me. … It's different, but I don't know why. … It's like. … Well, because there's Anaëlle [her stepmother], that changes too. … It's different people, but my dad is more, um, disorganized; he's more … you know? While my mum is all 'You have to go to bed early, you have to blah, blah, blah', and so, well … it's also different. And then my mum, as she only has the two of us [Chloé and her sister Annelyse], she asks 'Oh yeah, how was your day, blah, blah, blah?'. My dad, he asks that too. … They [her father and stepmother] also talk to each other. (Chloé, aged 12)

While an integration ritual can take place on the day the child arrives, it can also occur later. For Chloé's sister Annelyse (ten), as we have mentioned, the return in itself is more of a 'routine of return'. However, she and Chloé sometimes go to a restaurant with their father and stepmother during the week they spend at their father's house. The purpose of this outing is to spend some 'family time' together before the sisters leave again for a week. On these evenings, the girls like to sleep in their father and stepmother's bedroom, extending this 'family time' even further:

> Often, too, with Dad … well, sometimes we go to a restaurant or have a little party at home to. … You see? … It's not especially on Thursday evening, it can also be another day, when we say to ourselves 'We're all together and soon you'll be leaving' or whatever. … In Dad and Anaëlle's [her stepmother's] bedroom … sometimes when, um … we come back from the restaurant and we're all together and enjoying ourselves, well, we put a mattress in their room [for Annelyse and Chloé], and we all sleep there together. (Annelyse, aged ten)

When Annelyse mentions the 'little party at home', she is referring to the Friday night *apéro* that Chloé mentioned. While the meaning of this family moment is clear for the older girl, it is more equivocal for the younger one. The festive moment that Annelyse describes in the extract refers to both the Friday night *apéro*, which symbolizes their return, and their outing to the restaurant and the night they spend in their father and stepmother's room, which symbolize their departure. This account illustrates that it is not so much when the ritual takes place that is important, but rather the sense of belonging to a family unit that it engenders.

Félicien (12) moves to his mother's house on Wednesdays after school, and also every other Friday evening when he spends the weekend with her. While his return to her house on Wednesdays is more of a 'routine' for him, the return there on Friday evenings represents a convivial moment with his 'new family'. As we described earlier, on Wednesdays Félicien takes the train after school to his mother's house, which is more than 50 kilometres away. His mother picks him up at the station and drives him to his after-school activity. He then returns to her house, where he goes about his usual activities alone: his stepsiblings Gabin (13) and Ysaline (18) are still with their grandparents, his half-sister Jade (four) is having a nap, his stepfather is still at work and his mother goes back upstairs to work in Félicien's room, where she has set up her desk. Neither Félicien nor the members of his 'new family' have any emotional investment in this return. It is a momentary activity, and part of the family's ordinary functional organization. In contrast, Félicien says that on Friday evenings, when his stepbrother Hugo (20) and his girlfriend, who live with flatmates during the week, return to his mother's house for the weekend – as does he[7] – this return is less ordinary and more festive. He meets up 'with everyone else' in the living room, where they share a convivial moment that demonstrates their family unity.

An unsettling conviviality

While integration rituals are often experienced as pleasant and valued by both the members of the 'new family' and the children themselves, some children may perceive this enthusiasm for celebrating their return more negatively. These festive activities give an 'extraordinary' character to their arrival at their parent's residence, while they themselves may perceive this return as a routine, functional event. They may not understand the reason for so much emotional investment on the part of the 'new family' members, and may feel overwhelmed and unsettled.

As we have described, Lewis (aged 16) and Marie (12) return to their respective fathers' dwellings in the same manner as they would after an ordinary day at school: the return is momentary and of no particular significance to them. This lack of emotional investment contrasts with the attitudes of their maternal 'new family' members. Indeed, Lewis and Marie struggle to accept what they see as an excess of joy on the part of their mothers and younger half-siblings when they return after a few days' absence. Lewis says that his half-sister Clémentine (ten) 'worships' him: as soon as he steps through the front door, she throws her arms around his neck and will not let go, wanting to spend time with him and celebrate his return. Clémentine's excitement conveys her image of Lewis as a mobile, absent person who has been missed, whereas for him this return is simply part of his day-to-day life.

Marie explains that she feels like an 'intruder' every Monday when she returns to her mother's house after school. Her half-brother Oscar (six) and their mother are delighted to see her, and want to tell her all about their respective doings over the past week. In doing so, they allude to moments they have shared while Marie was away, from which she then feels excluded. She feels superfluous and out of touch, as though she does not really belong in the new nuclear family comprising the permanent residents (her mother, stepfather and half-brother). It always takes her some time to adjust to this new family environment: 'Especially at my mum's house, I have the impression – within ten minutes – that I'm an intruder, kind of like that, because … I don't know. I always get that impression when I arrive, because I was at someone else's house before' (Marie, aged 12).

Lewis and Marie are confused by this expression of 'too much' interest and enthusiasm on the part of their mothers' 'new families', while they simply want to return to the dwelling in their usual way, without any particular emphasis on this return that constitutes their 'normalcy'.[8] They would like to do what they normally do when they arrive at their mothers' houses after school: Marie likes to curl up on the sofa, and Lewis settles down at his desk. While the two adolescents see these practices as routine at their fathers' apartments, they give them a particular meaning on the day they return to their mothers' houses. As we will describe in the following section, these practices comprise an 'anchoring ritual' that helps them to take time for themselves and to integrate at their own pace with the 'new families' by whom they feel overwhelmed.

Anchoring rituals

'Anchoring rituals' are everyday practices in which children habitually engage when they return to a parent's dwelling on an 'ordinary' day, which help them to find their bearings and feel 'at home'. While children who participate in 'integration rituals' engage in 'extraordinary' activities (like a celebratory meal) that help them feel they belong to the family, those who perform 'anchoring rituals' want to demonstrate that their presence is normal and routine, as if they have never been away. They engage in their ordinary activities to convey symbolically to the 'new family' members that their return *has to be done*, and that there is nothing extraordinary about it.

Returning to one's own 'little cocoon'

As we have described, when Marie (aged 12) returns to her mother's house, she does her homework and reluctantly 'debriefs' about the past week with her mother and her half-brother Oscar (six), who are delighted to have her back. She is waiting impatiently for the chance to curl up in her spot on the living room sofa – with the remote control – to watch television. Once in place, she puts three of her favourite pillows behind her head and covers herself from head to toe with a blanket. By doing this, she leaves her personal imprint on the sofa, and gives it the symbolic meaning of a 'little cocoon' where she feels good. By following this practice of appropriation when she returns after a week's absence, as she would do after an ordinary day at school, Marie is able to regain her bearings and her sense of familiarity and comfort. This practice also communicates symbolically to the members of her 'new family' that her presence among them is completely 'ordinary'. Installing herself on the sofa in her habitual way provides Marie with comfort, warmth and reassurance, and also indicates to the other family members that she wants to be alone and not be disturbed. For example, Oscar knows that she will rarely allow him to cuddle up to her when she is settled comfortably there with her cushions and blanket. By respecting Marie's wish for peace and quiet and by allowing her to take back the 'best place' – which she considers to be hers – and the remote control, the members of the 'new family' signal that they consider her to be in her place (both physical and symbolic) within the dwelling and the 'new family', as if she had never left.

When Lewis (16) arrives at his mother's house, he heads to his room to drop off his school bag and 'computer kit', as usual. He stays there until suppertime to do homework on his computer, and to have some time for himself before he joins his 'new family'. Returning to his desk and armchair, where he can settle in comfortably and use his computer, helps him to find his bearings and ground himself in the environment of his mother's 'new family'; he does the same when he returns to his father's apartment. On the day of a move, Lewis very deliberately settles into the armchair at his desk, with his computer and a blanket on his lap, thus signalling his ordinary presence to the members of the 'new family'. This practice also gives him some relief from his half-sister Clémentine's overwhelming enthusiasm when he returns to his mother's house. He settles into his armchair when he is tired and wants to be left alone, he explains. In this cosy atmosphere, he can retreat into his own bubble, far from the world around him:

> I'm in my thing, so, well … I've sometimes realized that my mother comes to talk to me and that she gives me some information, and there's information that I've totally missed, just, well … or, a lot of times when my [half-]sister comes to ask me to do something with her, when I just want to be [in his bubble]. … Well, it's … there's a really good – a more than 70 per cent chance that I'll refuse when I'm in my armchair. … I just want to get away a little bit … be kind of in my own thing. … A lot of times, people who come to me when I'm in my armchair, however nice they might be, I just want them to go away so I can be by myself. (Lewis, aged 16)

Mathilde (13) says that one of the first things she does when she returns to her father's house is to pet her dog, whether she is returning after a day at school or a week's absence. She then greets everyone, brings in her bin and puts it in the corner of the living room, and then does 'nothing else in particular': she settles down on the living room sofa to watch TV, play on her phone or go about her usual activities with her sister Clémence (15) and their stepsister Flore (15), who lives there full-time. Flore is delighted to have the two sisters back, as she misses them very much when they stay with their mother and she finds herself an 'only child'. Although Mathilde's return may seem routine at first sight, she explains that settling down in that particular spot on the sofa means something special to her because, she says, 'It's very quiet and there's my dog, he comes to stay with me [on the sofa] and I feel really at home'. Each time she returns, Mathilde goes to the spot in the living room to which she feels attached: the part of the sofa slightly hidden by a wall, where she feels safe and comfortable, where she can mingle with others and spend time with Flore in particular, but where she can also be alone:

> [In her father's living room], it's behind a corner and it's warm [cosy] and I know how to get comfortable, and I feel good there. … It's a

corner, and there's also a blanket so I use that. There are lots of people who go by, and I like to be all by myself. (Mathilde, aged 13)

Like Marie, Mathilde returns to her ordinary routine – and resumes her place in the dwelling and in the 'new family' – by settling into her usual spot on the sofa, in her usual way.

Rediscovering one's personal world

Théodore (aged 13) moves house every Friday after school. Each week, he looks forward to returning to his bedroom at the other parent's house, as each of these rooms contains a part of his world.

> And when I'm at Dad's, for example, when I'm there for a week, I say to myself, 'Oh, I want to go back to Mum's house, to get back to my room at Mum's …' And when I'm at Mum's, well, at the end of the week, I'm like 'Oh, I'd really like to go back to Dad's house, to get back to my room …'. (Théodore, aged 13)

For Théodore, returning to each parent's residence involves an anchoring ritual. He perceives his return as something that '*has to be done*', but he invests himself emotionally through his pleasant recollection of what each of his bedrooms contains. When he arrives at his mother's house, he follows his usual routine of going to his bedroom to do his homework, play on the PlayStation and get his bearings, after which he takes a shower and changes into his pyjamas. When his mother arrives from work, he joins her in the kitchen to help her prepare dinner, which they share together as usual. His return to his father's house is also like that on any other day: he greets his father and stepmother, plays with his half-sister Delphine (seven) for a while, and then goes upstairs to his bedroom, to do his homework and to reconnect with his comics and Wii.

For Félicien (12), while returning to his mother's house can involve either a 'routine of return' or an 'integration ritual' depending on the day,[9] returning to his father's house involves more of an 'anchoring ritual'. His half-siblings, Sasha (six) and Ernest (two), are happy to have him back and would like to spend time with him. For the adolescent, however, his return is an ordinary event: he goes to his bedroom as usual, to do his homework and go about his usual activities alone. Félicien establishes clear physical boundaries to isolate himself temporarily from his father's 'new family', closing his bedroom door and ordering Sasha and Ernest to leave. In this way, he can keep them at a distance and decide when he wants to mingle with the rest of the family:

> Yes, sometimes they [his half-siblings] come in and I say, 'No, get out, get out'. … I don't let them just come into my room, like [they try

to do] all the time. ... I don't like people coming to bother me in my room, but I prefer it to be in interaction with people. They don't come into my room, but as soon as I open the door, I'm with them. (Félicien, aged 12)

Rituals of (not) unpacking

'Rituals of (not) unpacking' are the transitional practices of unpacking and installing the objects 'in transit' that some children bring along each time they move house – or of not doing so.[10] The children perceive this type of ritual as an ordinary activity. However, although it forms an integral part of familial organization, it is not a 'routine' specific to each place of residence, as it remains the same across locations. It is therefore considered to be a ritual, as the children perform it in the same way regardless of where they are. These settling-in practices communicate meaning by helping to define '*who I am in the "new family"*'. They signify to family members that the children have returned, and help the children to (re)integrate and position themselves within the dwelling and family unit. Through 'rituals of (not) unpacking', children also symbolically communicate their status within the dwelling as being either 'in transit' – present only temporarily, while waiting to leave for another place – or permanent residents, whose presence is the norm and whose absence is only temporary. They repeat these practices each time they move, and the meaning that they convey endures over time.

Not unpacking objects 'in transit'

Some children who carry objects 'in transit' with them between residences will leave the transition channel in a particular location (such as their bedroom or the living room) without unpacking or installing their belongings. The visible presence of the transition channel and the objects 'in transit' that it contains provide evidence of the child's physical presence in the dwelling.

Remi (aged 13) never empties his large suitcase when he arrives at his parent's house. He takes the things he needs from it each day, as he needs them. His mother would like him to install all of his personal belongings in his wardrobe, while his father asks him to leave the suitcase and its contents on the landing between floors rather than taking it up to the bedroom shared with his two older brothers. Remi's decision not to install his belongings in either parent's house, despite his mother's encouragement, allows him to have the same routine in both places, maintaining consistency between his two residences. He is also able to keep his clothes in the order he has established, and spares himself the effort of folding and refolding them every time he moves.

My suitcase, well … my mum asks me to empty it, but I say, 'Yeah, yeah, I've emptied it', but it's not actually emptied. It's still open, upstairs. … I leave everything in it, seeing that it's folded and that if it's unfolded, I'll have to fold it up again. (Remi, aged 13)

As we have described, Mathilde (13) finds her bearings upon return to her father's house by settling into her favourite spot on the sofa. She also puts the large bin containing her things and those of her sister Clémence (15) in a corner of the living room, where it will remain for the rest of the week. At her mother's apartment, she places the bin in the bedroom she shares with Clémence. She keeps most of her personal belongings in this transition channel, with the exception of her school materials and the few clothes she decides to wear. After wearing them, she puts her clothes 'in their place' – under the mezzanine at her mother's flat, or on her shelf in the bathroom at her father's house – to ensure she will not forget them. She explains that she and her sister are often 'too lazy' to put everything away, and that sometimes she gets lost in the mess while most of her things are 'on stand-by' in her bin:

Interviewer:	And are there things you leave in the bin?
Mathilde:	Yes, a lot … yes, but it's often when we're too lazy to put everything away. … Things like folders … empty ones, or coats, or clothes, which should actually stay here but we forget [to leave them] … or [sandwich] boxes … or chargers, but we take those pretty fast [*sic*] anyway.
Interviewer:	So, when you redo the bin, what do you do with what's left in it? Do you put it back in, or do you take it out?
Mathilde:	No, put it back in [laughs], [so] I spend my time looking for my clothes, shoes … [which are] in the bin. [Laughs.] It's me. … I like tidying up, but the bin, well, I don't really like that.

This practice echoes the tactics of 'territorializing' and 'outboxing' described by Petersen et al (2010: 268–269), which mobile people use to feel at home. The first involves marking the space of a hotel room or dwelling by placing personal effects in a visible manner, to leave a mark of one's presence. The second has two variants: the first involves preparing a bag that is adjusted and filled before each departure, but never emptied completely; the second consists of putting items to be taken along at the next departure in a bag kept in a specific place.

While Mathilde and Remi affirm their return through the visible presence of the transition channel, they also reinforce the impression that they are only passing through the parental residence, as they never empty it.

Unpacking objects 'in transit'

Other children, like Chloé (aged 12), immediately unpack and put away their personal belongings when they arrive, storing the transition channel in their wardrobe. They see this practice as an ordinary way of keeping their room tidy, while they are actually erasing all traces of their mobility, symbolically indicating to the other family members that they are taking back their place in the dwelling: they have never left, and will never leave again.

When Tristan (15) was living in alternation, one of the first things he would do on arrival, after having a snack and chatting with his mother or father, would be to go to his bedroom, put his computer on the desk and plug his game console into the television. This would allow him to go about his normal routine the next morning because, he explains, 'If I don't unpack, well, I can't do anything'. With the exception of these 'shadow' objects, the teenager preferred to leave his things 'parked', and did not take any other personal belongings with him between dwellings. To ensure that his two worlds would not mix, Tristan had adopted a 'cleanliness ritual', in the words of de Singly and Decup-Pannier (2016: 282): he would empty the transition channel, undress and have a wash, put on his pyjamas, and the next day he would put on clothes from the wardrobe in his current residence. Changing his clothes helped him to erase all traces of the previous week and to resume his place in his current dwelling and family group.

Giorgio (16) also empties his bag and puts his belongings in his wardrobe, but unlike Tristan and Chloé, he does not do this as soon as he arrives. He does not start to unpack or install his things until the following day, after he has practised the 'integration ritual' of spending the evening with his 'new family'. Annelyse (ten) also unpacks all of her belongings, but unlike Chloé, Tristan and Giorgio, who then put away the transition channel, she keeps her bag open under her desk at her father's house, or in the entrance hall at her mother's apartment. This allows her to progressively fill the bag with the items she wants to take with her the next time she moves.

The decision whether or not to keep the transition channel visible indicates to others — and to the children themselves — where they stand in the dwelling, being either 'in transit' — waiting to leave for another place — or permanent residents.

★★★

The routines and rituals of return that children establish, as well as the use of the transition channel, are ways for them to define and negotiate their place in the residence and, by extension, in the 'new family'. This topic will be examined further in the next chapter, which will consider what happens once children have settled in for a few days with one of their parents.

Notes

[1] These practices are detailed in Chapter 3.

[2] This terminology focuses on the specific moment when a ritual takes place, in this case when children travel from one place of residence to another and arrive at the residence of the parent now responsible for looking after them.

[3] 'Extraordinary' here means something that is exceptional or unusual.

[4] Even though these activities are performed individually, they are still considered rituals because they involve the other family members and affect them in some way.

[5] In their study on the sense of home among children living in shared physical custody in Australia, Campo et al (2020) found that the emotional attachment young people feel towards a place is strengthened by their affection for the pets that live there.

[6] The three stepsisters are young adults who each have their own place to live, but still occasionally spend the weekend at their father's house.

[7] On Thursday evenings Félicien stays with his mother at the residence of one of his maternal grandparents, who lives near his school, so he will not have to wake up too early to go to school on Friday.

[8] This term refers to the expression Marie's father uses when explaining how his daughter transits through school on her way to his or her mother's residence. He describes his daughter's regular transition as her 'normalcy'. Since this term refers expressly to the ordinary, habitual nature of transition practices for these children, we have chosen to use it here, even though it comes from the discourse of a parent and not a child.

[9] For Félicien, returning to his mother's house on Wednesdays is a routine of return, whereas returning there on Fridays involves an integration ritual when all the members of the 'new family' are together.

[10] While these 'rituals of (not) unpacking' concern only children who carry objects 'in transit' with them between residences, it would appear that 'anchoring rituals' are mostly (but not exclusively) carried out by those who favour 'parked' objects.

5

Making Each Island 'One's Own Island': Defining and Negotiating One's Place

A key challenge for children living in shared physical custody (SPC) is that of defining and appropriating a space of their own in each dwelling. Furthermore, they must define a symbolic place within each residence, as well as within the 'new family' unit living there. In this chapter, we will examine two aspects of this question. We will begin by highlighting the various practices that children use to make spaces their own. We will then look at how they define and negotiate their physical and symbolic place in the family – sometimes with difficulty – by managing clashes of personal 'colours'.

Appropriating a space to give it personal meaning

The children we encountered in our study appropriate space through three sets of behaviours: *marking*, *controlling* and *personalizing* (Serfaty-Garzon, 2003c). 'Marking' a space involves claiming ownership by means of inscriptions (such as a name on a bedroom door) or personal objects arranged in a unique way. 'Controlling' a space involves drawing and imposing physical or symbolic boundaries by establishing rules to grant or prohibit access to the space by certain individuals, or to determine the type of activities permitted within it. Both marking and controlling also involve the 'personalization' of a space by modifying or transforming it to reflect one's identity. Children express their personality and lifestyle through these practices of territorialization, and by doing so, they define their identity (Zaffran, 2014). These practices can be self-oriented and/or oriented towards others, and ultimately contribute to defining children's sense of place and of home in each 'new family' and dwelling.[1]

Marking one's space

The children in our study leave their imprint on their places of residence in three distinct ways: they take possession of a space by surrounding themselves with personal belongings (see also Vassart, 2006), they arrange this space in a unique way, and they spend time in the space regularly or claim an exclusive right to its use.

Surrounding oneself with personal belongings

Adolescents often consider the bedroom to be their 'home' (Ramos, 2018). Glevarec (2010b), who explored the meanings of this room among French children and their parents, observed that the bedroom has 'a central value for the younger generations, who make it a space of expression as well as of relation to the outside world' (Glevarec, 2010b: 19). According to this author, young people develop a particular 'culture' of the bedroom, which varies according to their age, through practices of privatization and individualization (Glevarec, 2010a). For the youngest (defined by Glevarec as those under eight years old), the bedroom is a place to play. Pre-adolescents (aged roughly 8–12) are particularly invested in their bedroom, which becomes a reflection of their growing autonomy while remaining under parental control. For adolescents (aged 13 and over), the bedroom becomes the place of self-expression, marking a break between the young person's personal universe and that shared with the other members of the family.

Chloé (aged 12) describes how her relationship to her bedroom at her father's house has evolved. She recounts that when she was ten years old, she expressed her wish to decorate her room according to her own tastes and to replace the furniture chosen by her father, who kept some control over her room. When she turned 12, her father allowed her to redecorate her room to better reflect her personality:

> In the corridor, well, there's a desk of my dad's, a really old-fashioned desk, and my dad likes that kind of thing, so he bought me that desk but I didn't like it. So I asked him for a long time, and two years later, well, I asked for this [more modern] desk for Christmas. ... And otherwise, I'm the one who chose everything. (Chloé, aged 12)

To feel at home, the young adolescent needs to be able to have her say about the decoration of her bedroom, and to surround herself with personal objects different from those of the family: 'Well, still, to be able to choose my own furniture and everything too, because otherwise I don't know, I don't really feel at home. And I also don't like that there are wardrobes like that with stuff from the whole family. I'd rather have my own things, you know?' (Chloé, aged 12). Children become attached to their rooms by choosing the objects and furniture around them for themselves. This material environment creates a feeling of comfort, intimacy and warmth.

Remi (13) marks the space of his bedroom at his mother's house as his own 'universe' by surrounding himself with objects that are important to him. These objects reveal his tastes and personality:

> Since I had my time when I really loved boxing, in my bedroom I had my figurines of boxers, and a boxing clock. I'm not so much into that now. There's still the clock, because I still like the clock. There are still my first figurines, on a little *étagère*. ... There's a corkboard with all little photos. ... The photo of my brothers, the photo of my little [paternal half-]sister, everything, you know? (Remi, aged 13)

The 'everything' Remi refers to when describing his personal possessions is a form of 'individual spatial expression' (Serfaty-Garzon, 2003b: 4) and a 'support for [his] singularity' (Sacriste, 2018a: 314). These 'memory objects' (the clock, figurines and photos) ensure continuity in his life by bringing together elements of the past and the present.

Some children are particularly fond of such 'memory objects' that they associate with both of their parents and with their time as a 'first family' before the separation. Cédric (15) treasures the cuddly toy that his two parents gave him as a very important keepsake. Tristan (15) keeps all of his mementos from his parents, including a mask from Venice. He is particularly fond of this mask, which he received when his parents returned from Italy, one of their last trips as a couple before they separated.

Eliot (14) has 'rebuilt' his 'little spot' in the part of the family dormitory formerly occupied by his older brother. This dormitory is a large mezzanine shared by the members of his maternal 'new family'. It is a space 'where there are still [en]closures, but it's less ... closed room', Eliot explains. Each family member has a slightly more private space, separated by curtains or partitions, which they each decorate in their own way. When his older brothers Gauthier (20) and Henri (18) left the house – or at least the dormitory, Eliot wanted to change 'rooms' to occupy Gauthier's old space, which included a double bed. He 'rebuilt [his] room there' by surrounding himself with exactly the same significant objects:

> I took the things that were in my room, photos or souvenirs or whatever, and I put them on the walls. I kind of put everything away, clothes and so on. ... There's a big map of the world that was already in my room before, and, well, some photos from basketball or souvenirs or whatever. And, um. ... There, there are my two mats that I got

when I was smaller and did gymnastics, and since then I've kept them, and there you go. And over there, there's my desk. (Eliot, aged 14)

The use of the active verb 'to rebuild' emphasizes Eliot's 'right of possession' with respect to his 'little spot'.[2] This right enables him to create a place that is 'the same' by decorating it with the same unique objects or by arranging and organizing the space (as detailed in the following section) in a way he finds meaningful. These symbolic markers, which may be moved from place to place, give meaning to the different spaces where the boy feels at home.

Arranging a space in one's own way

Children furnish and arrange spaces in ways that suit them. This assertion of a right of possession over the space is evidence of their gradual acquisition of autonomy. Indeed, Glevarec (2010b) observes that children become 'actors in a space' at the beginning of adolescence (Glevarec, 2010b: 21). They acquire a degree of control over the objects around them by acting on the space of their residences, and by making decisions about the furnishing, layout and decoration of their bedrooms and of some communal areas like the living room, the kitchen or the office. Marie explains:

> I'm the one who set everything up in my bedroom [at her father's], so I have a double loft bed and wall shelves. ... I'm the one who chose the desk. In fact, I chose everything. And the curtains, they're so beautiful! And I was able to choose from Maison Dorée [a fabric shop]. (Marie, aged 12)

Dividing the space into distinct zones

Some of the children in our study exercise a right of possession by dividing the space of their bedroom into distinct zones (Glevarec, 2010b). Romane's mother has moved into a new house where Romane (aged ten) now has her own bedroom, whereas she shared one with her brother Arthur (five) in her mother's old flat. Romane explains that she decided how to decorate her bedroom on her own:

> Now I've got a beanbag chair, I've got a little tent [the space under her loft bed, behind a curtain], I've got my own bathroom. And I've got a loft bed ... I chose everything. The whole room was in white, except for one wall which was blue. ... I picked the colours, my bed and everything. We went to pick out the bed together [with her mother], and you see ... I don't know that there's anything I didn't choose. (Romane, aged ten)

Romane has chosen to create small, distinct spaces in this personal room. Each of these spaces has its own atmosphere, depending on what she does there. In the area between her bed and the entrance, she plays with her Playmobil toys, filling this space with an imaginary world. She has placed a beanbag chair under the window at the back of her bedroom, where she sits when she wants to relax and read a book, or when she wants to cry because she feels sad or angry.

At his father's house, Giorgio (16) also distinguishes different 'spots' in his room, where he displays his various interests: 'I've got rugby photos, car photos, I've got my spot with my [audio] mixer or whatever. I've got my own "spot", or my world as I call it, with my different passions, and there you go.' The teenager personalizes this room, creating a 'world of his own' in which he makes his own choices.

Painting the walls

Some children are also invited to choose the colours of paint for their bedroom walls. At his father's house, Joseph (aged 16) has marked and personalized the space of his bedroom by choosing sober colours for the walls, in a classic style. At his mother's house, on the other hand, he had little say in the matter because the house is rented:

> At Mum's it was a rented house, so I didn't necessarily choose the decoration. But here [at his father's house], I wanted to do a white theme, really classic. And then, it actually just goes well with the colours I want to use. ... White with black. I don't really like colourful things. Or something sober like grey. ... I'm fine with anything in white, in fact. I also find that it makes the room look bigger. So I like to kind of play with the colours. (Joseph, aged 16)

Joseph wanted to 'reconstruct [his] sober bedroom, all in white, with the furniture arranged like [he] wanted', reproducing almost identically his bedroom in the house where he lived with his parents just before their separation. He was all the more upset to leave that room because he and his father had just finished renovating it, making it 'just the way he wanted it', and he had felt very much at home in the atmosphere he had created.

Mathilde (13) plans to create a 'cosy' and 'calm' atmosphere in her future bedroom at her father's house, so she can feel comfortable in her space. She plans to paint the walls white, beige and dark grey, because, she explains, 'I'm already really hyper, so if there's any exciting stuff, or colours, it's not going to work'. Children personalize spaces by transforming them and making them their own, making them reflect their past and present lives and the various facets of their personalities.

Being free to arrange the furniture

For some children, the right of possession of space is also manifested through freedom of action. They are not only invited to have their say in the decoration of their space, but they are free to change it when and how they wish. Chloé (aged 12), who chose 'everything' in her bedroom at her father's house, also appreciates being able to rearrange this room without needing to ask for permission. Amandine (12) shares her bedroom in each parental residence with her sister Lou (six): the two girls arrange these shared rooms as Amandine sees fit, as Lou has no real preferences in the matter while Amandine likes to change the layout to reflect her changing tastes:

> Before, I was on top [of the bunk bed at her father's], now it's the other way round. Sometimes we change, but, from time to time. ... At my mum's, well, we changed the position of the bed a bit because I wanted to do something different. ... Just on a whim, you feel like changing something, so you say to yourself, 'Come on, let's go, let's change things a bit because it's been a long time'. ... It's more me, because sometimes I watch videos and so I'm interested in that, and then I like to change things a bit, look at new ideas and everything for the bedroom, but my sister's not really like that. (Amandine, aged 12)

Coping with material limits on freedom

It is essential to stress that children's freedom to act remains relative, as the furnishing of their personal spaces depends on the financial means of their parent(s). Some are forced to adapt and to limit their desires more than others. Émilie (aged ten) finds that her stepsister Capucine (12) has unrealistically high expectations when it comes to decorating, given her parents' financial situation and anti-consumerist values:[3]

> At first, you know, she [Capucine] didn't complain [about having a smaller bedroom], but then for a while she got kind of fed up. So then Valentine [her stepmother] told her that ... she'd have half, or all, or a bit more than half [of the mezzanine adjoining their bedrooms, which is to be divided between the two girls], and so I think she's a bit impatient because she says to me, 'Oh, I'm going to have my place where there'll be a nice soft carpet with a beanbag chair', when, in fact, first of all, we don't really have enough money to buy her all that. We have enough money, but maybe they won't want all that for her, specifically, because they [her father and stepmother] mainly buy second-hand. And so she's not going to be very happy. (Émilie, aged ten)

Lewis (16) would like to create a 'personal spot' in his room at his father's apartment – specifically, a 'music corner', where he could settle in comfortably to play the clarinet or the djembe, store his instruments on suitable racks and thus display his passion for music. Although Lewis has control over this space, he has limited means at his disposal: his father has a modest income, and has furnished his son's bedroom with second-hand furniture. Lewis finds that he cannot create the atmosphere he wants without better-quality furniture:

> I'd like to put a little label there [symbolizing the spaces that belong to him and are important to him], but in fact it's the music corner, that's where I'd like it to be kind of my personal spot, [for his] music and all. The problem is that, like I said, the chair is often full. ... I put extra stuff on it, and that piles up. But anyway, the chair is very high. ... This one is fine [the one at the desk], it's fairly ergonomic. But this one [in the music corner] was kind of broken, we found it on the street, and it's too high, so it's not practical for playing the clarinet – or the djembe either. You don't really feel comfortable on it. I could swap [the two chairs], but I want to feel good in both cases. (Lewis, aged 16)

The importance of the physical environment's characteristics in establishing children's sense of home is clear from this account. Lewis expresses his wish to create a relaxed, calm and reassuring atmosphere by surrounding himself with objects that he would like to use more, and thus to have a certain degree of material comfort. The teenager says that one day this space will become his 'music corner', especially when he has adequate furnishings and is able to spend more time there. This statement highlights the temporal dimension that we will develop in a subsequent section, a dimension inseparable from the appropriation of a space and the attachment to a place.

Appropriative space

Children appropriate certain spaces, and are simultaneously 'appropriated by the space[s]' (Proshansky, 1976: 43). They must engage with the material environment around them, which also participates in the construction of their identity in a relation of reciprocity (Miller, 2010). The appropriative nature of space echoes the material component of the sense of space (Hashemnezhad et al, 2013) and its influence on the emotions that children may feel within it.[4]

Marie (aged 12) always curls up on the same sofa in her mother's living room. It is her favourite place to settle down because, she explains: 'That one, in fact, it's mainly ... it's in the middle [between her mother's and stepfather's usual places], and it's friendlier, I find, it's cosier too. I like to be in a little cocoon like that. And it's really comfortable.' Lewis (16) chose to move back to his old bedroom at the far end of his mother's house, where he had lived for the first few months after the family relocated there. He had subsequently moved to another bedroom, at the bottom of the stairs to the living room, so he could be closer to his mother and stepfather and thus less isolated. Two years ago, he moved back to the first bedroom, where he now feels better: this room is further from the communal areas and the other family members, which gives him more privacy; it is also brighter, and has a small alcove where he has been able to put his bed. This arrangement gives him a sense of comfort and well-being, 'where it was "cocoon" enough that way', he explains. Lewis would also like to rearrange his bedroom at his father's apartment to create a music space in the corner, because, he says, 'It's not bad, you know … it's in a corner so it's really cosy'. The decoration and the personal objects with which he would like to surround himself there (a small rug, a clarinet stand, a chair at the right height for playing his instruments) will create a special atmosphere, as will the configuration of the room.

Like Lewis, who chose a different room based on his current needs, Remi (13) '[threw] a bit of a tantrum by saying "No, I want a room with a window!" … [he] really wanted a big window because [he] like[s] it when it's cold' in his room. The adolescents identify with these material spaces even before investing in them and making them their own (Serfaty–Garzon, 2003a).

Children's physical environment can also generate more negative emotions. Lewis does not always feel comfortable in his father's apartment. He explains that there is no particular place there where he could say to himself 'I'm really here, I'm completely fine, you know?'. His bedroom there is crowded with things, dark and strangely shaped. It contrasts with his mother's house, which is always tidy, clean and bright; these characteristics make him feel at home 'just about everywhere' in her house. He says: 'When there's been a bit of sun during the day, it's nice and warm in the living room, it's pretty bright, it's really … it's pretty cool.'

Marking space through time

Children also mark places by spending time in them regularly, or by claiming an exclusive right to their use.

Regular presence

Most of the children we encountered, like Eliot (aged 14) and Lewis (16), consider that certain spaces belong to them because they spend most of their time there and because they use them regularly. The ongoing and repetitive nature of their activities in these places offers them points of reference that enable them to situate themselves and to find their place within the dwelling. While the two boys speak mainly of their bedrooms, Mélissa (ten) explains that she has appropriated the living room in her mother's apartment – and 'nowhere else' – because that is where she can read, work on crafts and spend most of her time without either being disturbed by or disturbing the other 'new family' members. She avoids spending much time in the bedroom she shares with her maternal half-siblings Ezio (14) and Olivia (17), as the room is small and does not offer her enough space to pursue her activities freely.

Being present in a place regularly gives children a sense of familiarity and security that enables them to relax and enjoy themselves there. Émilie (ten) and Tristan (15) say that they feel comfortable in a place when they have furniture that allows them to relax (like a bed or an armchair) and plenty of distractions – books and crafts materials for Émilie, or books, a PC and a game console for Tristan. This material environment enables them to pursue a hobby or to relax, alone, in their personal space.

Exclusive use

For children, being the only one who goes into a space and uses the objects there is an even more important criterion for 'ownership' than regularity of use. Anouk (aged ten) explains that her bedroom at her father's apartment is *her* space because: 'There's nobody who comes … because nobody's going to touch my stuff or anything. And because there's my guitar, and I play the guitar and no one else does.' Marie (12) and Joseph (16) also emphasize that they use 'their' spaces in a routine and habitual manner, which grants them an exclusivity of use. Marie is used to installing herself on the 'middle' sofa in her mother's living room. This is her favourite place because of its comfort and cosiness. As she always uses this sofa, '[her half-] brother has to clear out when [she] want[s] to sit there'. Joseph points out that he develops certain habits by repeating the same actions in the same space. His habitual use of these spaces provides him with reference points that enable him to find his place in the residence (for example, at the table) and to know which activities he can engage in. Joseph's routines mark his presence in the dwelling, as he always settles in the same place, and reflects the place he occupies in the communal spaces. His place is thus recognized by the other members of the family, and is no longer questioned:

[These spaces belong to him] because it's always been that way. And me, I've (quote unquote) 'self-appropriated' this space. In my bedroom, well, that's classic because that's really mine. All the things I have in it belong to me. But everything outside – the living room, the dining room, the kitchen – it's just me who's made all of that my own. It's all stuff that's become habitual. So I really don't see why I should question whether or not it belongs to me. (Joseph, aged 16)

This exclusivity of use thus leaves a symbolic imprint that keeps the other members of the family at a distance, helping to define children's place in the space and group of the 'new family'.

Controlling space and time

We will now explore the ways in which children exercise control over a space, including the time they spend and the activities in which they engage there. This control delimits their own space and time by means of physical and symbolic boundaries.

Controlling access to one's personal space

Children draw physical and symbolic boundaries, but also virtual ones, to create their own spaces of intimacy. They draw these boundaries in both their (individual or shared) bedrooms and the communal spaces of the dwelling, using objects, furniture and digital tools that enable them to create a 'bubble'.

The bedroom door: a physical and symbolic boundary

The bedroom door is an important physical boundary that children use to control space. Amandine (aged 12) explains that the door demarcates an inside and an outside, a private space and a public space – in short, a personal space and a family space:

Interviewer:	What would be the boundary between a space where you say to yourself 'This is my home, and then when I go just there, there is not my home'?
Amandine:	The bedroom door, I think it's mainly that. There's not really a boundary, but I find that when I leave my room, it's more everyone's place. While in my room it's my place, with my sister.[5] And that's how things are, you see?

The door of her private bedroom at her mother's house also plays an important role for Romane (ten), allowing her to distance herself from her family – and particularly from her little brother Arthur (five), whom she finds intrusive. The siblings have always shared a bedroom; they still share a small room in their father's flat, where Arthur 'takes up all the space'. Romane has had her own bedroom at her mother's house for only a few months, and she keeps the door to this room closed to control access – unless she forgets. Arthur is allowed in only rarely, and only when Romane gives him permission:

> He has to knock. He has to! And most of the time, I say no [he can't come in] because I want to play with my Playmobil or be alone. This is my room. And he has a room and … he's never in his room, except to sleep. Not even that, because he sleeps in Mum's bed, so. (Romane, aged ten)

Romane does not really identify with the bedroom she shares with her brother, as Arthur has many things in the wardrobe, on the toy shelf and on the floor next to their bunk bed. She therefore creates her own personal spot in her bed (the top one), where she denies access to Arthur, and marks out her own play area at the back of the room near the window. She hardly ever allows her brother to come and play with her there, considering that he already has more than enough space to play elsewhere.

Cédric (15) often goes to his bedroom when he wants to be alone, shutting the door so he will not be disturbed. The teenager wants other family members to knock before entering, but anyone who complies with this rule is welcome. This physical boundary persists symbolically when the door is open. Indeed, Cédric relates that when his father talks to him while he is in his bedroom, their interaction is rather distant. They do not talk for long, as if the father does not want to disturb his son in his personal space. In contrast, in communal areas like the living room or kitchen, the father and son talk often and at length.

Children also see entering a space without permission as a way of making it their own, as Chloé (12) describes in reference to her sister Annelyse (ten):

> Often Annelyse just walks in like that without knocking. And that makes me angry because she just takes over [*s'approprie*] my bedroom, so I get angry with her and then we argue. And my father doesn't come into my room very often, he knocks and Anaëlle [her stepmother] does too, so I don't mind as long as they ask before they come in. (Chloé, aged 12)

The sisters sometimes argue because Annelyse does not respect the boundaries that Chloé sets around her personal space. Even though Annelyse sleeps in Chloé's bedroom every night when they are at their father's house (as described in Chapter 1), Chloé does not think her sister belongs there. Chloé's feeling that she is losing control of her own space leads to arguments that allow each sister to redefine her place. In this kind of situation, Chloé and Annelyse each close the door to their respective bedrooms and prohibit the other from entering. Annelyse does not usually close her bedroom door, but does so nevertheless as a sign of retaliation and to assert her place, showing Chloé that she too has the right to control access to her space. Through materiality, the sisters reassert ownership of their respective spaces, re-establishing both the physical and the symbolic boundaries of their place in their father's house.

It is not always easy for family members to respect children's boundaries when it comes to entering their bedrooms, particularly when a room is shared with siblings. The fact that a bedroom is shared may make others feel entitled to access it freely, as if it were a communal space. However, the children see the room as their own, and would like their privacy to be respected. Amandine explains:

> I don't like it very much when people come into my room straight away, because sometimes I'm busy or something, I'm working, so I like to be focused and all. ... Before, I didn't like it much when people came in, I wanted them to knock and all before coming in, but now it doesn't bother me. ... They never did it, in fact. Never. They'd just come right in and say, 'How are you doing?' or 'Do you need any help?' or whatever, you know? (Amandine, aged 12)

Like Romane, who can decide who has access to her personal space now that she has her own room, Amandine believes that having a room to oneself legitimizes one's control over it. This 'right of possession' would give greater weight to the decision to refuse access to other family members:

> Interviewer: And what would you like about having your own space?
>
> Amandine: My sister [Lou, six] doesn't [*sic*] have to come into my room all the time to bother me, I can [*sic*] be in my room on my own, in peace, without anyone coming in to disturb me, when I'm doing my homework or whatever, you know?

Annelyse points out that this power to exclude does not apply to communal areas, where everyone is free to enter as they please:

> Everyone can choose their 'rule', in quotes, can choose what they do. It's not ... like if Anaëlle was the boss of the living room [and could make all the rules]. It's for everyone, you can come in when you want, you don't have to knock, it's really everyone's space. ... And if you want to be alone, well, you can't [in the living room]. You don't go to the living room, because everyone can go there, you go to your bedroom. (Annelyse, aged ten)

Creating privacy in a shared bedroom

Children who share a bedroom cannot use the door to establish a physical boundary. They must use other means, such as putting up a folding screen or arranging furniture, to create a space of their own. As Sacriste (2018a) observes, the arrangement of furniture in shared spaces can create personal territories by delimiting and dissociating the functions of the space.

Mélissa's mother lives in a small flat with only one large bedroom. Due to the limited space, Mélissa (aged ten) and her two older half-siblings share this room while their mother sleeps in the living room. To create a private and personal space, the mother has placed her bed in a corner of the room, with a large bookcase and a folding screen around it. This physical separation creates a distinction between the shared space and her private 'room', which Mélissa feels uncomfortable entering:

> I don't really like to go there, because … I don't really know how to explain it, but because it's kind of like her place, there [pointing to her mother's bed in the living room]. It's kind of like if it was my mother's bedroom. But her bed is her place. But here [the rest of the living room], it's not really her place. (Mélissa, aged ten)

Eliot (14) does not have any closed, completely private space. In his father's house, the wall between his bedroom and that of his brother Henri (18) is only partial, being open at the top. In his mother's loft, everyone in the 'new family' shares a single large mezzanine, which they have divided into their own 'spaces' with curtains and partitions. When his brothers Henri and Gauthier (20) moved out, Eliot decided to move into Gauthier's old 'bedroom' because it is more enclosed, which gives him more privacy. It also prevents other members of the family from disturbing him without his permission, which used to happen when he slept in his old 'bedroom':

> There [in Gauthier's bedroom], it was much more closed off. Oh yes, there's also my stepfather's dressing room here [behind the partition of his old bedroom]. So every time I woke up or whatever, I'd see him, and that didn't bother me. And he'd give me a little wave and. … There were little holes. In fact it's not a wall, it's wooden panels, so there were spaces where he could see me. It made me laugh, but after a while I wanted to change. And then I always really liked my big brother's room, so I went there. (Eliot, aged 14)

Some children arrange the furniture in their shared room to create personal spaces that they can control, and where they can find a sense of privacy. Others, like Jean (13) and Giorgio (16), symbolically divide the space by placing their beds at one end of the room and prohibiting others from entering their territory.

Virtual boundaries

Children also appropriate space by creating virtual boundaries. Thanks to information and communication technologies such as smartphones, tablets, computers or game consoles, they can escape into a virtual world where they can have time for themselves, even if other family members are present. By doing so, they create a 'virtual distance' from others (Janssen, 2021: 246), closing themselves off from their immediate environment with their music or screen, or communicating with someone more geographically distant. This is analogous to the 'bubbling' tactic identified by Petersen et al (2010: 69), in which mobile individuals use a laptop or phone to shut out and isolate themselves from external disturbances.

Remi (aged 13) shares his attic bedroom at his father's house with his two older brothers. Their beds are side by side in this large space, separated by the wardrobes that contain each boy's 'universe' and conceal them from one another's view. In the evenings, when the older boys play on their computers or game consoles and Remi lies in bed watching a video, they may forget one another's presence:

> I pick up my phone and … I watch my videos, and at the end I almost forget [my brother]'s there. … We're kind of [each] on our own side. … We're really all in our worlds. [One brother] prefers to watch history videos, I prefer really funny ones, and [the other brother]'s more into video games, and so we're kind of all in our worlds. (Remi, aged 13)

Children also use their phones, computers, tablets or game consoles to create their own 'virtual' worlds. These devices enable them to define a time to and for themselves, away from the scrutiny of others, and signal to other family members that they do not want to be disturbed. For example, Mélissa (ten) shares the one large bedroom in her mother's flat with her half-siblings Ezio (14) and Olivia (17). Each has their own bed, but no physical partitions have been installed to separate them. Being still young, Mélissa would like to play with her older half-siblings, but knows that there is no point in disturbing them when they are busy on their phone or console.

In this way, children can get away from the world around them not only by retreating to their own physical space, but also by using their connected devices. Joseph (16) explains that his smartphone enables him to 'escape into [his] freedom': to be in his own world, chatting with friends or playing games, and to forget reality for a while.

Legitimacy of access to personal spaces

In the preceding sections, we have seen that these children exercise control over the spaces they identify as their own. While some forbid anyone at all to enter their bedroom without permission, with breaches of this rule leading to disputes, others establish more nuanced rules, depending on the legitimacy they accord to the various members of the 'new family'.

Some children restrict certain family members' access to their personal space, while allowing others to enter – often members of their stepfamilies and of their biological families, respectively. Marie (aged 12) explains: 'My bedroom – it's my mum who can just come in to bring some clothes. Well, finally, only my mum can come into my room. ... My stepfather, he's never gone into my room. And my little [half-]brother – well, I don't know. ... Anyway, he doesn't come in like that.' Marie adds that she feels more or less obliged to allow access to her bedroom at her father's apartment:

> And the other bedroom [at her father's], sometimes when I'm not there they use it for the renovation project, because they still have to paint the doors and everything. So they put the doors there. ... It doesn't bother me too much, for the moment. ... They don't hesitate to go in, in any case. (Marie, aged 12)

For Glevarec (2010b), young adolescents' investment in their bedrooms is a sign of their growing autonomy, but does not mean that they are no longer subject to their parents' control. Marie allows her mother to come into her room to collect or bring back her clothes. Félicien (12) allows his father and stepmother to enter his room freely when he is not around, so they can leave his laundry and other belongings there. However, he reserves the right to refuse entry to his paternal half-siblings, aged six and two. The adults do not enter to do 'anything specific', he says, or 'anything serious' that would disturb his private space. This arrangement allows Félicien's parents to retain some control over the room by being able to enter it freely, while allowing the boy to have his own space where his parents do not act. They do not enter it when he is present, out of respect for his privacy.

Manuelo (13) sees his bedroom as his retreat, which no one else can enter. However, he does have some interactions there, particularly with his brother Giorgio (16): while he is secluded in this space of interiority, to which he tightly controls access, Manuelo remains open and outward-looking. Only his brother and his father are allowed into his room, while his stepmother must announce herself:

> My brother just comes in to talk to me, but my stepmother doesn't! She knocks, because I've always told her to. And my dad, it's rare that

he comes in, because he knows you don't come into a room like that if someone's there, or whatever. [The door is] sometimes locked, but that's rare. (Manuelo, aged 13)

Manuelo is still cautious when he allows Giorgio into his room, keeping an eye on him to ensure that his possessions are not disturbed. His suspicion stems from a desire to protect the unique and meaningful items that he keeps in this space. He explains:

I watch, I pay attention, I look to see if he's messing with anything or whatever. Even if he's my brother, I don't like it. Last time, he was sitting at my desk, but I was still watching while I played with the PlayStation. Because, well, I don't know if he's touching something [and] it's mine and he's taking it without meaning to. (Manuelo, aged 13)

Other children, like Eliot (14) and Annelyse (ten), allow all of their family members to enter their bedrooms and see no problem with their doing so. Nevertheless, Eliot says that he specifically asks his brother Henri (18) to knock before entering his room at their father's house. Annelyse makes the same request of her sister Chloé (12). For both Eliot and Annelyse, this request is made as a provocation, in response to their siblings' requirement that they knock before entering their bedrooms:

Interviewer: And do people also have to knock to get into your room?
Annelyse: No. … Sometimes I say it, but it's to say, like, well then, if I have to knock [to enter Chloé's bedroom], you have to knock too. But I always forget. [Laughs.] It doesn't bother me.

Before, as soon as my brother [Henri] … came in, we'd get angry with each other. I hated it when he came into my room. But it was the same thing. … In fact, I did that because as soon as I went into his room, he didn't like it either. So every time it was kind of a battle, and [in reality] I liked it when he came into my room, but it was just to do the same. I mainly wanted to show him that since I can't go into his room, he won't come into mine. … Gauthier [his other brother], when he came in, that didn't bother me at all, because he doesn't care if I come into his room. (Eliot, aged 14)

Annelyse and Eliot are well aware that if they do not knock before entering their sibling's room, an argument will ensue. However, they do not understand why, as their own doors are always wide open, demonstrating their readiness and willingness to welcome the other members of the family.

A variable legitimacy of access

Children can also exert control over family members' access to their belongings, independently of their degree of control over access to their bedroom. For example, some forbid other family members to use objects or furniture to which they feel strongly attached, although they welcome these people into their bedrooms. Marie (aged 12), whom we encountered in the previous section, has no problem with her father or stepmother going into her room when she is away (in the context of their ongoing renovation), because, she says, 'they don't use the armchairs, or my bed in any case … [so] it doesn't bother me'. Marie is very attached to furniture that allows her to settle down comfortably and quietly, whether in her bedrooms (like her bed and armchairs) or in communal spaces (like the sofa in her mother's living room or the tatami mat in her father's). More than the rooms themselves, Marie has made these pieces of furniture her own, defining them as her territory, 'an appropriated space' (Schmitz, 2012b: 5) that is her own and has a specific use.

Anouk (ten), Coralie (12), Émilie (ten), Lewis (16), Tristan (15) and Joseph (16) are particularly attached to their desks, because of the many hours they spend there doing things they enjoy. The first three draw or work on crafts at their desks, while the others spend time there on their computers. Joseph considers his desks at his parents' houses to be truly personal spaces, due to the many objects he keeps there and the time he spends there, particularly playing online on his laptop. He keeps other family members from approaching his desks: only his father can sit at his desk occasionally to help him with his lessons. Joseph says he prefers to keep his things to himself, out of sight of others. Émilie explains that she would feel lost without her desk, because 'everything' is on it − meaning everything that is important to her. Her games, books, sketchbooks and pencils are points of reference that enable her to feel at home in this personal space, where she feels free to pursue the activities of her choice, as and when she wishes.

The scale of the protected territory varies according to its intimate nature. Joseph wants to keep the things on his desk private, or even secret. Jean (13) does not want his sister Anouk to enter his room at their father's apartment because he does not want her going through his things. Giorgio (16) allows members of his father's 'new family' to enter his room, even allowing his brother Manuelo (13) into his bed as long as he does not go through Giorgio's things or make a mess. Giorgio does not like others to 'disturb' his space because it's '[his] own', he explains. He respects the privacy of other family members by not disturbing their things, and wants them to do the same for him.

The variability of protected territories is also apparent from the accounts of children who share their bedrooms with siblings. Remi (13) explains that his bedroom at his father's house is not entirely his, because he shares it with his two brothers. He feels entitled to control only his side of the room, where his bed and desk are, because that is where he sleeps, plays and sits. That is his place, he says. Similarly, Romane (ten) feels attached only to her bed in the room she shares with her younger brother, because she does not claim this room as her own.[6]

Establishing one's own rules and order

Children also control their space by establishing their own rules and order there. Émilie (aged ten) explains that she needs her room to be messy:

> My father tells me that I'm messy, that I should tidy my room and everything, but I can find my way around better in my mess than in … than when it's tidy, so. … There are things … it's a bit weird, but I know that, for example, there's my T-shirt that's in my bookcase, and I know it's there. That's just how things are, you know? … And when I want to put on my clothes, well, I just find them on the floor. (Émilie, aged ten)

Émilie decides to tidy her room only when she herself can no longer find her way around:

> Every month, I tidy it [her desk] and then, by the end of the month, it's messy, messy, messy! So I tidy everything up, and then it's a mess again, and it goes on like that all the time. And about once every two months, I tidy up my room. In fact, when I'm tired of it being too messed up, when there's really too much [clutter] everywhere, I tidy it up a bit. (Émilie, aged ten)

In contrast, Joseph (16) and Cédric (15) need their rooms to be tidy at all times to be comfortable there:

> In fact, I try to keep my room [at his father's] as tidy as possible. It's practically always in order. Once in a while, when I'm feeling lazy, I kind of forget to tidy it up. But generally, it's tidy. And at my mother's too. (Joseph, aged 16)

> I like it when my room is tidy. … Well, it's a bit messy, but not too messy either, otherwise I can't find my way around and that's no good. (Cédric, aged 15)

Chloé (12) also wants to maintain a certain order in her bedroom, and to have this order respected by the other members of the 'new family'. At her father's house, she allows her sister Annelyse (ten) to sleep with her in her bedroom every night, because the younger girl is afraid to sleep by herself in her own small and cluttered room. However, she insists that Annelyse put her mattress under the bed (Chloé's) as soon as she wakes up each morning, and that she take her duvet back to her own room. The younger girl never respects these conditions, and is systematically called to order: 'Annelyse, put your stuff away!'

While children must abide by the rules laid down by adults (parents, step-parents, grandparents) in communal areas, they are masters of their own rooms. Annelyse explains: '[it's where] you can keep people out, you can make your own rules and it's your place, you know – you decide'. Coralie (12) and Cédric (15) add:

We're cool [in her basement bedroom, shared with her stepsister Valérie (ten)]. But when we're upstairs [in the living room], it's a different story. You don't want to leave your things lying around too long. (Coralie, aged 12)

No, no, it's really all in my room. If there's anything of mine [in the communal rooms] my mother yells. [Laughs.] [And it's] exactly the same [at his father's flat]. Well, sometimes I leave my stuff in the living room and so does he [his father], but other than that it's usually tidy. (Cédric, aged 15)

This power of decision over one's own space is recognized as legitimate by the other members of the family. Manuelo (13), for example, feels free to do as he pleases in his room at his father's house, which he has to himself. He can put on music, watch a film or shout because he can't be heard, and no one will object to his choice of activity. Similarly, his brother Giorgio (16) says that in his room 'it's a party', because there is no outside control from other family members and because he knows the codes he has established perfectly well. He would no longer feel at home if he lost these familiar points of reference and had to adapt to new rules.

★★★

The practices we have described in this section illustrate the ways in which children appropriate a space (a bedroom, a corner of the living room, a desk, a bed) by making it their own, arranging it and restructuring it into a 'personal shell' (Félonneau, 1997: 49) that reflects their identity. These practices of appropriation demonstrate their special relationship to one or both of their dwellings, even when they are only part-time residents. Children interpret the material environments within and between which they move, and thereby transforming their dwellings into places charged with emotions and human relationships (Jorgensen and Stedman, 2001). In this way, they develop emotional ties to their dwellings and/or with specific places within them, where they feel they belong and with which they identify. The positive or negative emotions they experience there influence how they perceive and become attached to a particular space, prompting them to remain within it, to make it safer and more comfortable, or to avoid it.

Defining and negotiating one's place in the family: the importance of 'colours'

Through these practices of appropriation (marking, controlling and personalizing spaces), children are able to reactivate and renew their family relationships and their sense of legitimacy and belonging in each dwelling. What is at issue in the appropriation of space is the definition and negotiation of the child's symbolic place, not only in the dwelling but in the family unit residing there. As Marquet and Merla (2018) argue, this difficult process becomes particularly visible when space is understood as a 'central object of the sociology of the family' (2018: 141). For these authors, tensions around space reveal the inequalities, power relations and divergences that accompany the modification and re-negotiation of each ('new') family member's respective place. In this section, we will adopt this perspective to examine how children use space to influence their family relationships, and to negotiate and define their physical and symbolic place in each 'new family'. We will examine how the space of the dwelling gives meaning to family relationships, and conversely, how family relationships give meaning to the space of the dwelling.

Schiffer (1999) finds it essential to analyse artefacts (in this case, children's belongings), as the anthropologist and archaeologist notes that they play a significant role in human communication: the traces they leave can provide clues about how a place is appropriated and the activities that take place there. In the second part of this chapter, we will explore the marks and traces that children leave behind, intentionally or otherwise, the way archaeologists study artefacts. These marks and traces communicate the children's place in the 'new family' and the nature of the relationships they have with its other members.

An island of many colours

As we have described elsewhere (Merla and Nobels, 2019), Coralie (aged 12) has had her own room at both her father's and her mother's houses since the beginning of their SPC arrangement. However, she spoke very little about these two houses during our meetings. Instead, she focused on her stepfather Roland's house, where she spends most of her time when she lives with her mother and where Roland's four children – who also alternate – have come to accept her as a sister. Little by little, she has increased her symbolic space in this blended family by means of her material footprints in the house, which are considered equal to those of her stepsiblings:

> They have colours for their stuff [in the bathroom]. If they didn't, we wouldn't be able to tell what things were whose. 'That was my towel!' 'Oh, no, that was my flannel!' So it was kind of. … So Roland decided, 'You choose a colour'. Everyone has a colour, they have blue, purple and orange. And me, I chose yellow to have my colour too. (Coralie, aged 12)

Like the other children, Coralie now has her own cardboard box to store her books and little odds and ends, and she has chosen her own colour for the toilet articles belonging to her. She was eventually given her own room in her stepfather's house,[7] with her own bed, wardrobe and 'stuff'. By giving her an increasingly important physical place in the house, her stepfamily has also given her an increasingly important symbolic place in the family.

Before she had her own room, Coralie found herself constantly 'in-between' on both a physical and a relational level. Indeed, when we asked Coralie to indicate the places belonging to her on the Emotion Map of her stepfather's house, she placed a sticker on the corridor, explaining:[8]

> The corridor, because I walk around in it all the time. Yes, to go just about everywhere I have to use the corridor, so … and as there's often the washing there, I go 'chouk [imitating the sound of taking her clothes out of the laundry basket], my stuff', I go to my room with it. (Coralie, aged 12)

Coralie was constantly moving from one bedroom to another, with nowhere to settle down or to store her belongings. This constant movement was also influenced by the relationships among her four stepsiblings, aged from eight to 15, who competed to lure Coralie into their respective bedrooms to play or to sleep. At her mother's request, Coralie tried not to favour any of her stepsiblings, alternating among them as much as possible. The girl was thus constantly moving around the house, and among her relationships with her stepsiblings. The fact that she saw the corridor as her own space reflects her sense of constant movement, of cyclical mobility between and within different living spaces. During the interview with the Socio-Spatial Network Game, Coralie defined herself as the central link in the chain binding everything together: because of her regular and cyclical mobility, she connected the different residences among which she travels, and the different families who live there.

Before she had her own space in her stepfather's house, Coralie felt herself to be 'gatecrashing' there. She made efforts to fit in with this 'new family', while having the sense that she was invading the space and taking the place of other members. She kept her clothes in drawers that her stepsister Cécile had cleared out for her; she slept on a mattress on a stepsister's bedroom floor, or sometimes on a bed in the living room; she used toilet articles the same colour as those Roland's mother used when she visited. As a result, she was unable to really feel at home in her stepfather's house until she could gather all of her (yellow) things into one room: the distribution of her personal belongings among her stepsisters' rooms and the living area prevented her from establishing her own space within the house and the family unit.

Coralie has thus transitioned from being a guest – or a 'gatecrasher' who had to elbow her way into the family – to becoming a full-fledged member of the 'new family'. This integration is evident from the physical space that she has been given in the house. She now has a space of her own, which she controls and which belongs to her, because 'there aren't really any other people' who enter this previously communal room, with the exception of her stepsister Valérie (ten) who shares the room with her.

The way her stepsiblings now behave in her presence also demonstrates her integration into the family group. They are progressively and unreservedly revealing their true personalities:

> At first, the oldest one said to me, 'Yes, you know, Cécile, the one who's 13, she gets all hysterical when you're not there' and I was like [with a very surprised look] 'what the …?!' And then, like, when I start staying a bit longer, when I start gatecrashing in the family, I see her getting hysterical, and I'm like 'I understand you'. Because I said to myself, well, like that she seems perfectly normal, but when you start to … she doesn't do that with her friends. (Coralie, aged 12)

Coralie views her stepsiblings as friends with whom she can have a good time and who make her feel less lonely at weekends. While they 'kind of take [her] for a sister', she also sees herself as the third oldest sibling, who should therefore have the right to be included in decision-making before the two older ones rather than being consulted last: 'As I'm right in the middle of the pile, I'm right in between. When they go around in order from the smallest to the biggest, they often say. "Valérie, Cécile …" and I say, "Hey, I'm here, OK? I'm in between the two of them!".'

Monochrome and polychrome spaces

The colour system established by Coralie's stepfather can be used as the basis for a metaphorical distinction between shared and private spaces within a family dwelling. By assigning a specific colour to each family member, this system makes it easier to identify which items belong to whom. Coralie selected yellow as her colour, and uses bath towels and flannels in that hue, which signals that these objects are hers. This approach can be extended to all of a family member's personal belongings, which we can imagine as having a specific colour that indicates ownership. Drawing on this colour metaphor, we distinguish between 'monochrome' and 'polychrome' spaces: 'monochrome' spaces are coloured by the belongings of one specific person, while 'polychrome' spaces include multiple colours, bringing together objects belonging to different family members.

Children who gather the belongings that are important to them together in one place create a space of symbols, both significant and meaningful, that reflects their identity – in other words, they mark this place with their personal 'colour'. Identifying with these special objects, collected in one place and arranged to reflect their passions, enables them to establish and assert their position within the dwelling. In this way, these material practices create and strengthen their feeling of being a part of the 'new family'.

Exploring processes of inclusion through colour

Mathilde (aged 13) does not have to fit in with a 'new family', but must instead make room for her stepsister Flore (15) and her stepmother Alexia in her father's house. Mathilde and her sister Clémence (15) have had to share their bedroom with Flore since she and Alexia moved in with their father. To accommodate her, a third bed, desk and wardrobe have been added to their already crowded bedroom. Mathilde feels overwhelmed by the clutter in both the bedroom and the communal areas of the house, and is unsure where to find her own space. She no longer knows where to put herself, she says. While the physical space of the house was originally dominated by three colours, representing the presence of the father and sisters, two other hues have appeared on the canvas, which have started to blend with and even cover the original colours. This metaphor signifies Mathilde's struggles to find her place in the physical space of the house, and her symbolic place in her father's 'new family'. She is forced to accept the permanent presence of Flore and her stepmother at her father's house, while she herself now lives there only in alternation. However, this does not mean that she recognizes them as having 'territorial rights' (Marquet and Merla, 2018: 155): these rights belong to the first occupants of the house, and give them precedence in defining the rules of daily life. Thus, in Mathilde's view, Flore and her mother, as 'newcomers', are not entitled to have their say in the day-to-day organization of the living space – for example, in the allocation of the two new bedrooms in the attic: 'Flore [the stepsister] chose right away where she wanted to go, and I told Dad that we didn't think that was very nice because it's not her house. … Well, not completely. And he said, "No, no, you [Mathilde and her sister Clémence] can choose first".'

Flore felt entitled to choose her room first because she lives in the house full-time, while Mathilde and Clémence are away half of the time. The two sisters contest Flore's priority. In their view, their claim on the house is greater because of the childhood experiences they shared there with (both of) their parents, which are inscribed on the premises – for example, their mother's cat is buried in the garden. However, Mathilde is gradually losing this advantage, because her stepsister lives there permanently. As she is physically less present, Mathilde has the impression that her 'colour imprint' – or symbolic place – is gradually disappearing behind stronger colours (those of her stepsister and stepmother). She feels that her family territory is being invaded, but has no choice but to accept this.

The three teenagers finally reached a compromise: Clémence will keep the bedroom she currently shares with Mathilde and Flore so she can stay near her father, to whom she feels very close. The other two girls will take the new rooms in the attic, because they get on better with one another. The bedrooms were allocated based on the quality of the relationships among the three girls, and between Clémence and her father. The resulting spatial configuration thus reflects the relational closeness among members of the paternal 'new family'.

Mathilde's father and stepmother decided to renovate their house, and considered moving to a larger one, because they want to give each of their daughters a place in their dwelling – both physical and symbolic. Moving to a new house would enable the 'new family' to settle in a space free from the accumulated family memories that give the current house a particular 'colour' and add weight to decisions made by the father and two sisters.[9] The choice to renovate the house (and perhaps move to another one) shows that the adults accord each of their daughters an equal status, regardless of the time they spend in the house.

When we met Félicien (12), he was preparing to move with his father from the house where he grew up to another house. The boy expressed a great deal of regret about having to leave this house, which was filled with memories of his mother and had been renovated by his maternal grandfather.[10] The old house is also located a two-minute walk from his school, whereas the new house is in a more distant neighbourhood. Félicien explains that his father and stepmother decided to relocate so they could give each child their own room. His half-siblings Sasha (six) and Ernest (two), who live with his father full-time, have shared a room since they were born, whereas Félicien, who is there half the time, has kept the room he has always lived in.

For Coralie (12) and Mathilde, having a bed – and more importantly a bedroom (even a shared one) – is essential at an age when having a space of one's own is key to the construction of identity (Galland, 2010). Félicien, Romane (ten) and Remi (13) express the same need. Having this personal space, where they can collect their belongings and create their own 'colour imprint', enables them to feel 'at home' and 'in their place' in a residence.

Remi claimed one of the large bedrooms in his mother's house when they moved in with his stepfather. He was initially given a small bedroom, to leave the large one available for his stepfather's adult daughters who stay there occasionally. Remi contested this decision, claiming the large bedroom because he was there every other week and because he preferred its layout and large windows. In the end, his stepsisters were given the small bedroom. As Fehlberg et al (2018) found in their study of the construction of a sense of home among Australian children in SPC, the material place given to each child gives that child a feeling of belonging to the family group and of being welcome there, regardless of the duration of absence. Remi's demanding – and receiving – his own large room makes him feel recognized in his relationships with his mother's 'new family'. His mother is attempting to intensify her son's 'colour' in the house when she encourages Remi to empty his suitcase and install his belongings in his bedroom: although Remi prefers to leave his suitcase intact and thus retain his transient status, the objects with which he has decorated the bedroom he chose have established his 'colour imprint' there.

Coralie (12) gained a more important place in her maternal 'new family' when she acquired more 'socio-material weight' (Palludan and Winther, 2016: 40) – in the form of a stable (though shared) bedroom and her own colour – in her stepfather's house. Similarly, Chloé (12) describes how when her stepmother Anaëlle moved in with her father, she replaced some of his old-fashioned furniture with her own more modern pieces. Because Anaëlle replaced their familiar sofa with her own, the family members have had to redefine and re-establish their 'coloured' places on this new sofa, and these places are not yet settled.[11] Chloé does not dare to go back to her old spot, because the sofa is dominated by her stepmother's colour and her own is not yet visible. By installing pieces of furniture that reflect her tastes, Anaëlle has left her 'colour imprint' in the dwelling, gradually taking up physical and symbolic space within the 'new family'.

Giorgio (16) and his brother Manuelo (13) explain that their first days with their mother's 'new family' were difficult for everyone. Their stepsiblings Sandro (15) and Elena (17) moved into their mother's flat barely three days after Giorgio and Manuelo learned that their mother had met someone, who moreover already had two children. In one of the flat's two bedrooms, Elena had one bed to herself, while the three boys shared the other bed in the same room and the sofa bed in the living room. They took turns sleeping in these beds, in an attempt to be as fair as possible. This arrangement meant that they would sometimes sleep on sheets that someone else had used the night before, or with two boys together on the sofa bed. Manuelo had a very difficult time living with these 'strangers', and was outraged. 'I didn't get on at all with my stepfather, and all of that. I wanted him to leave.' He categorically refused to let anyone touch his belongings, and was firmly opposed to anyone he did not know sleeping in his bed. To calm the situation and to help Manuelo regain some of his territory, his mother and stepfather decided to assign him the second bed in the room where he had slept before the stepfamily arrived. The sofa was assigned to Giorgio and Sandro, who were better able to tolerate this lack of privacy. Giorgio recognizes that this spatial proximity brought him and his stepbrother closer together, and that this understanding continues:

> The parents had decided to put him [Manuelo] in a room on his own [with their stepsister] and me and Sandro together. So there was already a bond that was formed with Sandro, let's put it that way, and since then it's stayed that way, we get on very well. (Giorgio, aged 16)

The teenager also notes that the integration would have been smoother if they had had more time to adapt to this new situation:

> Everything happened very quickly, we didn't really have time to adapt. Well, now, yes, we're used to it, let's say, but … at the beginning, it's true that it was difficult because we didn't have that time to adapt, in fact – whether it was for us, Manuelo and me, or for Sandro and Elena. So we didn't have time to adapt, and there were tensions and all at the beginning, but now, as I say, we've got used to it. (Giorgio, aged 16)

Giorgio and Sandro gradually got to know one another and developed a friendship. They discovered that they shared interests including a love for football, which also brought them closer. Thus, a harmony of 'colour imprints' was created around this blending of families. The family has now moved into a new house, where each of the teenagers has their own bedroom or their own bed in a shared room. The physical space given to each demonstrates the family's inclusion of all its members.

Colour as a means of exclusion

While the presence of a 'colour imprint' can symbolize a person's inclusion, it can also keep others at a distance, as Annelyse (aged ten) explains:

> I find that the bedroom is kind of more like it's each person's little house. … It's like where all your stuff is, where it's just you who lives there, like that. I mean, who's there. Nobody else's stuff is there;

it's really your own space. While the living room, well, there, that's everyone's room, where everyone's stuff is. (Annelyse, aged ten)

Annelyse's description sums up perfectly the different ways in which children appropriate this space to create their sense of home. Annelyse takes possession of her bedroom by 'marking' the space with the 'colour imprint' of her belongings. She also takes control of the space by establishing physical and symbolic boundaries that limit access, by setting her own rules and by spending a lot of time there, alone or in the company of other members of the 'new family'.

Anouk (ten) says that her brother Jean (13) never goes into her room because 'it's a girl's room'. The boy avoids entering because he does not identify with any of the symbols there. While the 'colour imprint' of Anouk's *girly* decor allows her to be recognized as a unique individual with her own personality, it also keeps her brother at a distance. Jean feels very uncomfortable in his sister's room because, he says, 'I don't understand anything … about all these drawings, and Barbies, and girly blankets and cuddly toys'.

Chloé (12) and Eliot (14) also feel uncomfortable when they need to go into a room containing another individual person's belongings. They feel as if they are crossing a symbolic boundary and 'standing out' when they are surrounded by a colour that is not their own. In contrast, they feel at ease in polychrome communal areas, which incorporate multiple individuals' colours.

A work of multiple hands

Giving children their own colours is not enough to make them feel at home. As Walker (2020) points out, children's personal spaces need to be created materially and recognized symbolically as belonging to them by both the children and their parents. To this geographer, who sees the decoration of a bedroom as a family practice, the materiality of these rooms 'becomes active and constitutive in the re-making of the family, acting through the creation of a new affective and material domain within which [the] new blended family is formed' (2020: 218).

The ways in which children make a room, a 'little spot' or a place on the sofa their own are key to defining their place in the world. Romane (aged ten), Chloé (12), Marie (12) and Mathilde (13) are each personally invested in the decoration of their bedrooms, with the help of a parent or step-parent. This collaborative decoration contributes to constructing the girls' 'colour imprints', which in turn contribute to defining each girl's place in her dwellings and 'new families'.

As we have described, Romane has always shared a bedroom with her brother Arthur (five), but now has her own room in her mother's new house. At her father's apartment, however, she still shares the flat's only bedroom with her brother. Romane has decided to 'park' most of her belongings at her mother's house, and does not bring anything from there to her father's flat because she feels she has no real place there. She feels encroached upon by her little brother, who she says 'takes up all the space' by spreading his toys all over their shared bedroom and taking up three-quarters of their wardrobe. He also monopolizes their father (or mother) when he gets restless, makes noise and constantly demands the parent's attention. Romane is resentful of her brother, as she struggles to hold her own in her relationship with her father – but above all with her mother, who she says has eyes only for Arthur. Being invited to participate in the design, furnishing and decoration of the new house – and particularly of her own future bedroom – was a turning point in Romane's relationship with her mother. The mother and daughter were able to share many special moments together – without Arthur – while choosing the furniture and the colours for the walls. As Walker (2020) notes, the process of co-creating an individual room is a key moment, more important than the result in itself. By recognizing Romane's tastes and preferences, her mother was able to give her a place in the family in her own right, as both an individual with a unique 'colour' and a young teenager expressing the specific 'bedroom culture' of her age group (Glevarec, 2010b).

When Chloé's stepmother Anaëlle moved into her father's house, Chloé agreed to let her put certain decorative items in her own (Chloé's) bedroom, like a mirror or a photo frame. By involving Anaëlle in the creation of her personal space and accepting traces of her 'colour imprint' there, Chloé showed Anaëlle that she welcomed her and considered her to be an integral part of the family. She thus demonstrated how the negotiation of each person's place involves material and symbolic as well as relational dimensions.

Marie has her own bedroom in each of her parents' dwellings, and was invited to help decorate each room when she moved into that dwelling. At her mother's house, the adolescent was given first choice between the two bedrooms, although she did not live there full-time, and was free to decorate her room according to her own tastes. Her half-brother Oscar (six) had to accept the second bedroom, without being able to express his preference. Marie's involvement in this decision-making process enabled her to assert and establish her place within the physical and symbolic space of her mother's 'new family', where she sometimes felt like an 'intruder'.[12] At her father's apartment, Marie decorated her bedroom primarily with the help of her stepmother, who helped her to assemble furniture and to choose furnishings and decorative items that would give the room the modern look that she wanted. Marie was thus able to create different atmospheres and 'worlds' in each of her bedrooms.

While Chloé's, Romane's and Marie's accounts suggest that materiality can provide ways to integrate children and step-parents into the 'new family', Mathilde describes a situation that shows how decorating a bedroom can also exclude certain members of the 'new family'. During our car journey from her mother's apartment to her father's house (Go-Along Method), Mathilde described how she planned to decorate her newly renovated bedroom in her father's attic. Unlike the three girls who involved members of their 'new families' in decorating their personal rooms as a way of 're-making the family' (Walker, 2020: 218), Mathilde did not intend to involve her stepmother or her stepsister Flore (15) in the decoration of her room. Instead, she planned to seek advice from her mother, whose taste in interior design she appreciates. Moreover, she considered that her mother was entitled to see her room at her father's apartment and to give her opinion on its future decoration, because, she says, it is her own little spot. In this case, materiality keeps the members of her 'extra family', as Mathilde calls them, at a distance – or even excludes them – and strengthens her emotional ties with the members of her 'real family'.

The bedroom can be seen as a meeting place that allows children to establish relationships (Zaffran, 2014) and to 're-make the family' (Walker, 2020) within each household in order to be recognized as family. Collaborative decoration of this room appears to be a process in which the inclusion – or exclusion, in Mathilde's case – of different members of the ('new' and/or 'first') family can reinforce and reproduce – or weaken and destroy – feelings of family unity. Beyond the time spent together as a 'new' or 'first' family, these feelings then persist through materiality, and are therefore reinforced on a daily basis. Materiality thus plays a key role in building and maintaining these family relationships.

A clash of colours

> He [Marie's half-brother Oscar, aged six] sometimes plays with the Playmobil, but in fact he often plays here [in the living room]. He doesn't like to be all alone in the bedroom, so, well, I've put him right in the middle of the living room because he takes it over all the time. Every time, you find Playmobil, Legos, Transformers and everything in the furniture, on the floor, on the heater, so you step on it, it hurts your feet, you don't know how to get comfortable on the sofa anymore, so, you see, it's his territory, almost. (Marie, aged 12)

On the Emotion Map of her mother's house, Marie (12) placed a blue sticker representing her half-brother Oscar (six) in the middle of the living room. She explained that she likes to curl up on the 'middle' sofa (between her mother's and stepfather's habitual places) because she loves this place and considers it her own. However, she is sometimes unable to do so because the sofa is cluttered with her half-brother's toys. 'And when I ask him to take them away, he just adds more', says Marie. This rather banal situation shows that children develop strategies to maintain their presence in the dwelling and to be recognized by their siblings and their 'new families', 'by claiming material space and leaving territorial marks' (Palludan and Winther, 2016: 12). Marie also leaves 'odds and ends' (*petits brols*) on the bar, as she considers this piece of furniture to be hers. By leaving her 'colour imprint', she reaffirms her physical place when she returns to the dwelling. Her own colour reappears within the polychrome space when she reclaims her physical and symbolic place in her mother's house.

Children develop practices for negotiation of spaces that can include strategies of 'territoriality' (Félonneau, 1997: 46), based on their desire for exclusive use and symbolic control of certain spaces or objects. A territory is an 'appropriated space', in the sense that it is 'specific to a person or group of people, but also specific to a use' (Schmitz, 2012a: 5). The juxtaposition of several territories in the same space is possible, provided that 'the groups of people do not consume the same attributes of the territory and that their activities do not prevent the other group from enjoying this space as well' (Schmitz, 2012a: 5). Marie and Oscar both want to use the same attributes of a specific space (in this case the sofa in the living room), but for different functions (to rest and to play). Their intended uses are not compatible, and therefore lead to conflicts and negotiations to reinforce the boundaries of each half-sibling's territory. Marie signalled this disaccord when she drew a lightning bolt between the blue sticker representing Oscar and the white one representing herself (see Figure 1.3). The girl's desire to regain control of the 'best place' – what she considers to be 'her place' – and the remote control often leads to arguments between the half-siblings. As Marie uses this sofa all the time when she stays with her mother and feels 'at home' there, she expects the members of the 'new family' to relinquish it immediately on her return, as if she had never left.

Mathilde (13) explains how some of her returns involve conflict with her stepsister Flore (15) and her stepmother, who are full-time residents of her father's house. During the renovation of the attic, the things normally stored there were piled all over the house, waiting for new places to be found for them. Amid all this 'chaos', she describes struggling to find her place when she returned to her father's house – the house where she grew up – when she thought she would be returning to familiar reference points and habits:

She [her stepmother] got angry in fact because there was a lot of stuff on the table, but I didn't know where [she was expected to] to put things in my own house. So I really couldn't get my bearings. And she got angry. And that really got to me. … I mean, I'd start crying

because I didn't even know where I could put myself in my house.
And everything was chaotic, and I couldn't even find myself any more.
(Mathilde, aged 13)

Mathilde is forced to respect a new order imposed by her stepmother, although this order is not her own and she does not consider the house to belong 'completely' to her stepfamily. Mathilde does not concede any 'territorial rights' (Marquet and Merla, 2018: 155) to her stepmother – or, consequently, any precedence in making decisions about the dwelling's day-to-day organization. By forbidding the adolescent to put her things where she is used to putting them (on the dining room table, where she always does her homework), her stepmother is preventing her from re-establishing her 'colour imprint' in the material environment of the house. Mathilde's stepsister Flore is also denying her access to the bedroom they have shared since they moved in: Mathilde cannot put her things in their room either, because Flore does not want to be awakened in the morning when Mathilde leaves for school. Mathilde's colour is gradually fading from the polychrome spaces, being replaced by those of her stepmother and stepsister. She feels that due to her regular absences, she is losing her legitimacy to decide the rules of the house. This situation frustrates and upsets her, because, in her view, the house is first and foremost hers, not theirs. However, she is making a 'vivid' mark in the family's space by deciding to leave most of her belongings in her bin, placed in the corner of the living room. The presence of this bin signifies to the 'new family' that she and her sister have returned, and that territories must be renegotiated.

Manuelo (13) also has a conflictual relationship with his stepmother, which leads to 'clashes of colours'. According to the teenager, his stepmother 'thinks she's at home when she's not'. Manuelo's stepmother has moved into his father's house, and has been making the decisions ever since she arrived. The boy explains that she has never accepted his presence or that of his brother Giorgio (16): 'If we're not there, it's better for her.' When decisions must be made about the organization of daily life, she never asks for the boys' opinion. However, according to Manuelo, she has no right to act in this way because she is only a 'newcomer', while Manuelo and Giorgio are 'first occupants' (Marquet and Merla, 2018: 155) and should therefore have priority in making decisions.

Manuelo goes about his life pretending that his stepmother does not exist. He is enraged by her 'colour imprints' all over the house, and particularly in the office he occupied before she moved in. He feels invaded by her daily presence, not only in the house but also – and above all – in a space he considers his own. Both of them want to have exclusive use of the office, which they both consider to be their 'territory' (Schmitz, 2012a). The juxtaposition of these two territories in the same space is not possible in this case, because Manuelo and his stepmother want to use the same attributes but for different activities. The stepmother wants to use the office as her workplace, while Manuelo wants to be able to do his homework there or to use it freely for his various pursuits, like performing scientific experiments. These uses are not compatible, so each time Manuelo and his brother return, he and his stepmother engage in a process of negotiation to further mark the premises with their own colours, thus demarcating their respective 'appropriated spaces' (Schmitz, 2012a: 5). Manuelo is particularly upset by this situation because he ends up needing to move his belongings from the office to his bedroom, which he finds much less comfortable. As he can no longer divide his belongings between different rooms, he feels that he is losing control of his 'own order', that his territory has been invaded, and that his colour is gradually disappearing and being replaced with by a stronger colour that he does not like.

★★★

This chapter has highlighted the sometimes-difficult tensions and negotiations that are part of everyday life for children who must find their own place in their family groups. We have also explored how space and materiality appear as facilitators that help children (and their family members) find a place for themselves and ease tensions, but also as elements that may fuel these tensions. In the next chapter, we will see that the challenge of finding and defining one's place extends to times of absence from the dwelling, when a child is residing on the other island.

Notes

[1] It should be noted that although the processes of marking, controlling and personalizing are presented separately for analytical purposes, they are intimately linked. Some quotes used to illustrate one type of behaviour may therefore also refer to another one.

[2] The right of possession asserted by children can refer either to literal ownership of a place or thing or to behaving as if one were its owner despite this not being literally true. The right of possession is thus also moral, psychological and affective (Serfaty-Garzon, 2003c).

[3] The 'parents' here are Émilie's father and stepmother (the mother of her stepsister).

[4] This point will be explored in greater depth in Chapter 7, where we will discuss the meaning of 'home'.

[5] Amandine shares a room with her sister Lou (six) at both her mother's and father's houses.

[6] Romane feels overwhelmed by her brother Arthur (five), who takes up all the space in the bedroom they share at her father's flat.

[7] Coralie talks about 'her' bedroom, but this room is actually shared with her stepsister Valérie (ten). The room is arranged so that each girl has her own space, with her own shelves in the shared wardrobe, her own section of the desk and her own bed.

[8] Coralie is the only child who drew four houses among which she alternates: the two houses of her parents and the two houses of her step-parents. Neither of her parents lives with their new partner; Coralie therefore spends a lot of time at her stepfather's and stepmother's houses. No other children were in this situation, having parents who had

    moved in with their new partners, step-parents who had moved in with their parents, or a step-parent who did not live with the parent but spent some days in the parent's residence. None of the other children ever stayed in the home of a step-parent who did not live with one of their parents.

9   Thus, none of the family members could be considered 'newcomers' or 'first occupants' (Marquet and Merla, 2018: 155) since they would move into the dwelling together at the same time.

10   The house was renovated by Félicien's maternal grandfather while his parents were together. When they separated, his father wanted to keep it, but it has now become too cramped due to the new family composition.

11   Although we are focusing here on the objects belonging to each family member, a 'colour imprint' can also be manifested in terms of an individual's frequency of use of a given space and the control that individual can exercise over that space.

12   The girl explained that she felt this way upon returning to her mother's home after spending a week with her father.

6

Maintaining One's Place during Absence

The children we encountered in our study have adopted new family practices to maintain their connection with the 'island' they are leaving. These practices help them to feel at home not only in a single place of residence but in a wider, lived family space, an 'archipelago', where 'here' and 'there' blend and complement one another and where their presence remains symbolically strong to each 'new family' despite their absence from the dwelling.

In this chapter we will explore these varied practices, drawing on the different forms of co-presence identified by Baldassar (2008) beyond physical co-presence, namely *symbolic/'by proxy'*, *imagined/'in thought'* and *virtual*.

We will begin by analysing how children use materiality to maintain a symbolic place within the family during their days of absence. Children's presence is felt physically when they are staying in a parent's dwelling, but also symbolically when it is felt through a material trace – a 'colour imprint' – that they have left behind, which reminds the permanent residents of the children's place in the household. This is what the anthropologist calls 'co-presence by proxy' (Baldassar, 2008). The 'odds and ends' (*petits brols*) that Marie leaves on the bar in her mother's kitchen, the yellow towels that Coralie uses in her stepfather's house, the Playmobil toys scattered around Émilie's and Romane's bedrooms, Remi's boxing posters and Tristan's collections all remind the rest of their 'new families' of their symbolic presence.

We will then examine how children also remain co-present 'in thought' (Baldassar, 2008). We will see how family members' thinking about a child – or not thinking about them – when organizing family life during their absence generates feelings of inclusion in – or exclusion from – the family group.

Finally, we will discuss how children use information and communication technologies (ICTs) to maintain a sense of family unity and belonging through virtual forms of co-presence (Baldassar, 2008).[1]

Keeping one's place symbolically

In this section, we will examine how children remain present and symbolically maintain their place within the dwelling and family group through materiality, and how they remain present 'in thought' to family members during their absence from the dwelling.

Maintaining one's place 'by proxy' through materiality

The children we encountered in our study emphasize that certain spaces belong to them, and that other family members cannot access these spaces because of the material imprints – 'colour imprints' – that they leave there, which are characteristic of them. As demonstrated in the previous chapter, this marking creates a symbolic boundary whose transgression can be a source of conflict. According to our interviewees, these imprints also maintain their place in the 'new family' and in the space of the dwelling while they are away, as their boundaries are maintained even when they are physically absent.

Annelyse (aged ten) says that no one goes into her 'spot' while she is away because 'there's all [her] stuff there, so, well, the others aren't really interested in it'. Émilie (ten) corroborates this view by adding: 'when I'm not there, I don't see what they could do, other than leave my clean clothes or whatever'. As her room contains her personal belongings, the girl does not see any reason why the other residents would enter when she is away other than to leave other items belonging to her.

By recognizing and respecting these symbolic boundaries, the permanent residents show the children that they recognize their place within the dwelling and the family group. Émilie is very much aware of the role of materiality in marking personal territories. 'It's their property', she says of her stepsiblings' bedrooms, 'it's where they keep all their secrets, all their comforts and everything, so it's more personal, a bedroom'. Cédric (15) explains, 'In my room, I don't share anything, everything is mine.' Manuelo (13) points out that 'There's just my stuff [in his room] ... nobody comes in!' Gathering their personal belongings into one space and decorating that space in a unique way gives it a special 'colouring', which reflects the children's identity and gives them a right of possession and exclusive use. In this space, the children recognize themselves and are recognized by the members of the 'new family' as being 'in their place'.

As we explained in the previous chapter, the bedroom door is highly symbolic for children, for multiple reasons. It allows them to control access to their personal space, thereby demarcating a space of their own and a family space, and gives them the opportunity to distance themselves from other family members. The bedroom door also helps them to maintain their place in the family dwelling while they are away. Some children prefer to close their bedroom door when they leave for a few days, whereas they leave it open when they are present in the dwelling. Conversely, others leave the door open while they are away, but keep family members at a distance when they are present by closing the door and asking them to knock before entering. In both of these cases, they are spatially distinguishing their absence from their presence, thereby (re)establishing their place within the household.

Mélissa (ten) tidies her bedroom a little on the day she moves house, but also leaves some things lying around, like toys she has played with in the previous days or crafts she is working on and wants to finish when she gets back. At her father's house, she always makes sure to close the door to her personal room on the day she leaves, whereas she usually leaves it open when staying there. Mélissa does this to prevent her half-brother Achille (two) from entering the room while she is away, because otherwise, she explains, 'He messes up everything, he throws everything on the floor. That's not very cool.' While this practice signals to everyone that Mélissa has left the house, closing her door also allows her to maintain a symbolic presence and to control her private space by keeping her little half-brother out, even when she is away.

The order – or disorder – that children leave behind them also signals their absence to other family members, and helps to maintain their presence 'by proxy'. Émilie and Romane (ten) do not tidy their rooms at all when they leave; they simply close the door and leave the room as it is. They are reassured to find their mess – or rather, their own order – each time they return. Their belongings still resonate with their interrupted activities, as if the girls had never left, and they simply pick up where they left off. During their absence, these objects signal to others – and to the girls themselves – their position in the dwelling as 'permanent residents'. Romane adds that her mother wants her to tidy up all her 'junk' before she leaves, because the cleaning lady comes the day after her departure. However, the girl demurs, as removing these material traces from her space would be too clear an indication of her absence. She therefore chooses deliberately to leave her things as they are, forcing her mother to tidy them up.

> No, I don't tidy my room because I don't want to tidy my room. I don't like to tidy my room. It's a way of getting Mum to do it, because the cleaning lady comes, so I know she [her mother] has to tidy it. No, I don't tidy my room. (Romane, aged ten)

In contrast, Manuelo is obliged to tidy each of his bedrooms and, above all, to make his bed before he leaves. This annoys him deeply, but he nevertheless resigns himself to it. The establishment of this order, which is not his own and which is imposed on him on the day he leaves, reinforces his status as a 'regular guest' rather than a 'permanent resident'. The tidying up establishes his absence, as he is asked to return his room to the same condition in which he found it when he arrived the previous Friday evening.

Mathilde (13) and Remi (13) tidy not only their bedrooms but their whole dwellings while they pack their bags. Both adolescents go through the dwelling systematically and methodically, checking each of the common spaces. As they do this, they remove their objects and belongings from the family space, putting them in their rooms or gathering them into the transition channel to be taken to the other parent's residence. This sweep through the dwelling in search of their belongings signals to the other members of the 'new family' that they are erasing all traces of their presence. They thereby establish their absence from the dwelling, where they are only 'in transit'. This absence is made all the more obvious by the fact that the transition channel, which is never emptied and which is installed in common spaces (like the living room or stair landing), also disappears from view.

As we have mentioned, the transition channel plays an ambivalent role. Its visible presence – and that of the objects 'in transit' that it contains – attests to the child's physical presence in the residence. By (not) unpacking and (not) installing their belongings, children (re)integrate and position themselves in the dwelling. The other family members' perception of these objects reminds them that the child has returned, implying that they will need to adapt to and accustom themselves to this additional presence: each resident must redefine, or even negotiate, their place within the material environment of the dwelling, both physically and symbolically. These objects 'in transit' also indicate that the children themselves are 'in transit' and waiting to leave again for another place. When the transition channel disappears from view, this absence signals to family members that something – or rather, someone – is missing from the dwelling.

Maintaining one's place 'in thought'

In addition to co-presence 'by proxy' by means of objects that symbolically make their presence felt, children also remain co-present 'in thought' (Baldassar, 2008). This form of co-presence refers to family members' memories and projections of shared moments, which help to keep the children present in their imagination despite their physical absence. Children hope that their family members will think about them when they are absent, and will take their needs and feelings into consideration. However, while they play an active role in maintaining co-presence 'by proxy' in the practices we have just described, their co-presence 'in thought' is out of their control.

Unfortunately, we did not ask the members of the 'new families' about the thoughts they have about the children during their absence.[2] This form of co-presence is therefore illustrated here through the discourse of the children themselves, which describes certain practices implemented by members of the 'new family' that children perceive as being based on prior consideration of their needs and feelings.

An empty place on the sofa or at the dining room table can remind members of the 'new family' of an absent child's presence. Joseph (aged 16) imagines that his parents perceive and feel his presence and that of his sisters when they are absent because their 'usual places' remain empty when they are away. Family members recognize and validate these places as 'theirs' because they use them frequently:

> When we arrived [in his parents' new dwellings after the separation] … we had this idea all at the same time of each taking a place in the living room, in the kitchen, at the table. And so we've kept that. … It's more my sisters, my father and my mother who know right away: 'Joseph, he sits there. We'll put him there'. (Joseph, aged 16)

Cédric (15) always sits at the same place at the table when he returns to his mother's house. He explains that none of his three half-brothers sit there during his absence, although this leaves an empty space in front of one of the two adults. Cédric feels included because his place in the material environment and the family group is recognized and respected, even when he is absent. He continues: 'No one comes inside [his room]. Well, yes, [if] they knock before they come in. So there's no one who goes inside when I'm not there, so it's really my own space' (Cédric, aged 15). The place on the sofa or at the dining room table also represents the child's presence in the dwelling symbolically: by leaving this place empty, family members are acknowledging the fact that it represents the child 'by proxy'. These examples show that various forms of co-presence can be simultaneous and can reinforce one another: the empty chair both materially represents the child and encourages family members to think about them and respect their feelings.

Family members can also care for absent children and show them that they are still present 'in thought' during their absence by considering their alternating schedules when organizing activities or deciding on a family project.[3] For example, the parents of Marie (12) and Félicien (12) 'take an interest in their child[ren]'s well-being and preferences' (Mason, 1996: 27) by trying to schedule family activities while the children are staying with them. These children thus have the same opportunity as the other 'new family' members to participate in a brunch with an uncle and cousins, a weekend with friends or a visit with their grandparents.

In contrast, other children relate that their parents do not take their alternating schedule into account when organizing special activities. While some, like Théodore (13), cope well with this situation, others struggle with what they perceive as a lack of consideration, feeling excluded because their relatives do not appear to think of them. They have the impression that their place in the 'new family' is not recognized, and that they are seen only as 'regular guests' whose presence is a plus, but whose absence is the norm. This feeling of exclusion leads to enormous frustration and a feeling of injustice towards step- or half-siblings who are permanent residents. Émilie (ten) says that life at her father's house often goes on without her. Her paternal stepsiblings regularly participate in activities with other children from the co-operative while she is staying with her mother, such as building a communal tree house or having a Christmas party with an exchange of presents. Émilie regrets not being able to participate, but what saddens her most is that no one seems to have thought about waiting for her. She also feels left out of the life plans of her 'new family': a key example is when her stepsiblings Capucine (12) and Éden (ten) each bought a guinea pig while Émilie was with her mother, and she discovered the animals when she returned to her father's house. Because she was not included in this family project, or even informed, Émilie refuses to clean the guinea pigs' cage: they are not her animals, and she did not choose them – meaning that she did not choose them *together with her stepsiblings*. Émilie also feels excluded when members of her 'new family' do certain crafts without her, although they know these are among her favourite activities. Other examples include the 'new family' watching films that she wanted to watch with them while she is away, or going on a three-month trip abroad when she could only join them for a few weeks, as her mother did not want her to miss the start of the school year. She had 'the impression that they had done all the best things when [she] wasn't there'. Émilie feels that she is sidelined too often, and explains that she often 'goes round in circles' at her father's house, not knowing what to do or where to go. The girl struggles to establish her place in her father's household.

In a more nuanced example, the members of Lewis's maternal 'new family' decided to adopt a cat when Lewis (16) was away, even though Lewis is allergic to these animals. Nevertheless, Lewis's mother wants to ensure that he feels comfortable in her house. She therefore cleans the house from top to bottom before he returns, treating the sofas, cushions and carpets with a product that greatly reduces Lewis's allergic symptoms. In this way, she and the other members of Lewis's 'new family' maintain his presence in the house by thinking about him and by taking an interest in his health and well-being, ensuring that his bedroom door remains closed so the cat cannot slip in or helping with the deep cleaning that symbolizes Lewis's imminent return.

★★★

We have seen how children can remain co-present with their family members during their absence by means of the materiality that symbolically embodies them – 'by proxy' – or when their relatives keep them present 'in thought', taking their feelings and needs into consideration. Children also engage in virtual forms of co-presence, as we will see in the next section.

Keeping one's place virtually

While physical co-presence remains the 'gold standard' (Baldassar, 2008: 252) for maintaining and nurturing family ties, virtual co-presence can compensate at least in part for physical separation by permitting the maintenance of ties at a distance between family members dispersed among multiple places of residence.

Maintaining a close relationship with the absent parent

In their quantitative survey of how Belgian adolescents view their family configuration, Merla and Dedonder (2019) found that children in shared physical custody (SPC) communicate frequently with the parent with whom they are not living, and slightly more often with mothers than with fathers. They do so to talk about their day-to-day life, school, their emotions or the practical organization of their schedules and activities. The authors note that these children also communicate more with their parents on social networks than do those living in nuclear families.

Some of the children in our study use ICTs to maintain ties with their parents at a distance, to stay in touch or 'just to say a quick hello', as Cédric (aged 15) and Tristan (15) explain. As Licoppe (2004) points out, it is the fact of communicating with one another more than the content of the communication that reinforces feelings of closeness between relatives. These 'routinised family practices' (Morgan, 2020: 738) are deployed regularly, even daily, and nourish a sense of family togetherness.

Cédric, Giorgio (16) and Amandine (12) communicate as much with their fathers as with their mothers while residing with the other parent. None of these parents set limits on virtual contacts with their child.[4] While Cédric and Amandine text each parent (almost) daily and call them once or twice a week to chat about their day at school, Giorgio prefers to call his parents on the phone to tell them about his day or how his rugby match went.

In contrast, Joseph (16) and Mathilde (13) communicate mainly with their mothers, usually via text messages. Both mothers (who have 'reef' islands) feel the need to be in regular contact with their children, just to keep in touch. They want to be reassured that their children are doing well, but above all that their emotional ties are enduring despite physical separation:

To tell them how things are going with me, to say that things are going well with school, because I have dyscalculia and dyslexia, and

> sometimes there are things I have difficulty with, so she [her mother] wants to know how that test went and all, you know. [And with her father], a bit less, because dads ask for a bit less information, but he still does it. … And so if you forget to say something, she [her mother] gets angry. When you forget to say you're at home, she thinks you've forgotten her. (Mathilde, aged 13)

Children also contact their parent(s) when they miss them. While Émilie (ten), Annelyse (ten) and Chloé (12) communicate regularly with each parent,[5] these exchanges are usually not at their own initiative. However, they will occasionally contact a parent to compensate, at least partially, for that parent's physical absence. Some children explain that they would call or text the parent they missed most, primarily when they were younger.

> [B]ecause my parents were separated, and so at the beginning, not that it hurt me or anything, but … it took a while to adapt. So I wanted to have my father or my mother [on the phone] every day. My mother said to me, 'Check in anyway, whether with me or with Dad. I'll give you a little telephone'. (Giorgio, aged 16)

> [I call my father] for example [to] say hello. My mum often tells me 'I'll pick you up on time … well, at 3:30 pm, as usual'. And my dad, sometimes it's to ask him for something, his permission for, I don't know, something … or it's to say hello because I miss him. (Émilie, aged ten)

Émilie still asks the parent with whom she is staying for permission to use their telephone to contact her other parent. In contrast, Annelyse, Chloé and Giorgio received their own communication tools very early on (an iPod Touch for Annelyse and Chloé, and a mobile phone for Giorgio that does not allow him to go online) so that they could contact their absent parent as often as they wished.[6] Annelyse and Chloé no longer really need their iPod Touch: 'I don't really care [now]', explains Chloé. 'It happens less now. I think about her [her mother] sometimes, but not to the point where I need to call her and cry and all that. It was mostly when … I was younger', says Annelyse. Chloé no longer really takes the initiative to contact one of her parents to fill a void. She no longer feels the need to do so, because she has adapted to her way of life. She sometimes sends them WhatsApp messages to share practical information and to organize her return to their residences. However, her parents still contact her several times a week to check in and to keep abreast of her schoolwork, activities and friendships.

Although his parents – who both have 'open' islands – are open to the idea of keeping in touch during his absence, Félicien (12) contacts them only when he goes on holiday with one of them. Outside these periods, he does not feel the need to contact his other parent, as he alternates in what he perceives as a short rhythm (5/5 days) and is therefore able to have regular exchanges with each parent in physical co-presence. The longer periods of separation during holidays justify his desire to contact his absent parent to share memories and discoveries, and thus maintain a feeling of closeness. Romane (ten) also contacts her absent parent more often when she is on holiday.[7] She sends souvenir photos by email, using the tablet she has just bought with money she saved over the past year for this purpose, and calls occasionally via Skype to show her distant parent where she is staying. On a day-to-day basis, however, the girl does not contact her parents. She does not like to do so because, she says: 'When I'm feeling down or when I want my mum, or when I want my dad, I don't like [to call them]. I feel even worse when I call them.' This quote echoes the contrasting emotional consequences of regular long-distance contact as highlighted in the literature on transnational families. While new family routines involving virtual co-presence offer a form of long-distance support, they also paradoxically reinforce the feeling of absence and distance, particularly during family crises when physical co-presence seems irreplaceable (see, in particular, Baldassar et al, 2016; Nedelcu, 2017).[8] For Romane, maintaining relationships through ICTs reminds her of her mobility and of the distance separating her from her parent. Hearing or reading a message from her mother or father is not enough to make up for their absence and her feeling of lack. She prefers to think about something else, and to keep herself busy to take her mind off her feelings.

While communication tools can facilitate the maintenance of emotional closeness between parent and child, they also enable children to maintain relationships with their siblings and stepfamilies, as we will see in the next section.

Maintaining close relationships with other 'new family' members

The children in our study stay in touch with their parents and step-parents mainly through phone calls or instant messages. With their step- or half-siblings, they also keep in touch through WhatsApp messages, or through online video games that allow them to play together and share everyday events. During these games, they video call one another or chat online (using Discord, for example). As noted by Besure et al (2014), the tools that individuals use to communicate with their relatives 'differ according to the generation of the people communicating more than the content of the exchanges' (2014: 73).

Cédric (aged 15) and Mathilde (13) are the only study participants to stay in touch with their stepfathers when they are not living with them. They talk to their stepfathers when they are in contact with their mothers, both of whom have 'reef' islands. Cédric explains that having his stepfather on the phone after talking with his mother is a 'normal', 'usual' occurrence. Mathilde also shares everyday events with her stepfather, because he is part of the family WhatsApp groups with her sister Clémence (15) and both of her parents. Her stepmother does not get on at all with her mother and does not want to be part of the group, Mathilde explains, which means that she is not kept informed of the teenager's doings. In these groups, Mathilde shares information pertaining to the maths lessons that her stepfather gives her, or makes specific requests that concern both her father and her stepfather.

Tristan (15) is another exception in our study, as he is the only participant who does not have the same living arrangement as his brother. When we first met Tristan, his brother Adam (19) had been living exclusively with their mother for two years, while Tristan continued to change residences every Friday. Tristan therefore saw his brother every other week until he asked to live exclusively with his father and stepmother. He explains that since they have each been living full-time with a different parent, he and his brother have been playing more online video games in order to keep in touch:

> To stay [in touch] a minimum, so we can communicate and all, sometimes we play games together, that's how we talk. ... On our computer [*sic*], we've got a program, it's a bit like Skype, so we call each other by voice call, you know? ... That got more frequent after I decided not to go there [to his mother's house] any more. Seeing that we saw each other less, of course we needed to talk more. (Tristan, aged 15)

Tristan's account echoes the findings of Gulløv and Winther (2021) on sibling relationships in separated and blended Danish families. The anthropologists show how daily practices, routines and material dimensions form and shape these sibling relationships, and family relationships more generally. The regular movement of children living in SPC makes it difficult to maintain the kind of daily practices and routines that ensure regular meetings and shared activities. As a result, it is up to the children themselves to maintain contact and to establish close, familiar relationships despite the physical distance separating them from other family members. Tristan's testimony highlights the 'active effort' (Gulløv and Winther, 2021: 311) that he and Adam make to maintain their brotherly relationship despite the distance separating them, which, according to these authors, makes their ties fragile and vulnerable.

Other children also make an 'active effort' (Gulløv and Winther, 2021: 311) to maintain ties with their half- and stepsiblings who live permanently with their parent, or who, like them, alternate between two dwellings. Coralie (12) deeply regrets that she and her stepsiblings do not have the same alternating schedule. Social networks enable her to maintain and strengthen her relationships with her two older stepsisters, from whom she is often separated:

> Often I kind of miss them. I want to see them, and as I've got WhatsApp and the two bigger girls have got phones, I can send them WhatsApp messages. I've already had long chats with the 13-year-old, long, long, long chats. We record voice messages, well, to go faster. (Coralie, aged 12)

Coralie also plays collaborative online games with her stepsister Cécile (13). Félicien (12) does not yet have a mobile phone, and maintains his relationship with his maternal stepbrother Gabin (13) by playing online video games together when he is living with his father. While video games often appear to help form and strengthen sibling bonds, they can also weaken them when they lead to virtual arguments, as Manuelo (13) explains:

> I'm OK with my half-brother [his maternal stepbrother Sandro, 15]; I get on well with him. Sometimes we both gripe [about one another] because, when he's at his mum's, I don't know if you know the game Fortnite? Well, he plays that game there, but we log in with the PlayStation account there [at Manuelo's mother and stepfather's house], both of us. So if I log in, that disconnects him, then he logs back in, and there are two of us [with the same problem], so sometimes we grumble about that. (Manuelo, aged 13)

Children's age is a determining factor in maintaining these virtual links. ICTs are not accessible to all of the children in these blended families, particularly the youngest. Marie (12) never asks her mother to put her half-brother Oscar (six) on the phone, because 'he's too young'. Cédric explains that he could not contact his six-year-old half-brother even if he wanted to, because 'the little one isn't on social networks'. The previous excerpts also show that Félicien and Coralie maintain contact only with their half- or stepsiblings who are the same age or older, as the younger ones do not have mobile phones or are not allowed to use them because of their age. When half- or stepsiblings are less than seven years old, the question of maintaining relationships at a distance via ICTs does not arise. This is also the case for Mélissa (ten), Théodore (13), Lewis (16), Eliot (14) and Remi (13), who prefer to spend quality time with their younger half- or stepsiblings when they are physically co-present – like playing together after school. Remi also engages in co-presence 'by proxy', displaying a photo of his paternal half-sister Elsa (23 months) in his bedroom at his mother's house. This portrait reminds him that they are both part of the same 'new family', even though they live apart.

However, having older half-siblings or stepsiblings does not mean that children necessarily contact them. Maintaining ties at a distance depends first and foremost on the quality of the relationship that they establish when they are together physically.[9] When they have positive relationships (as is the case for Coralie and Félicien and their respective stepsiblings), they are more inclined to maintain them and to nurture a shared sense of belonging through virtual co-presence. Conversely, when situations are more conflictual, children avoid contact. Mathilde does not try to contact her paternal stepsister Flore (15) when she is staying with her mother. Their separation allows her some distance from Flore, because, she says, 'Staying with my half-sister [stepsister] for weeks on end is a long time, and also with her character, which is very difficult. So we're happy to come here [to her mother's flat].' Being away from one another for a few days helps to ease tensions and to preserve the bond between them, as Mélissa (ten) also attests:

> Things are better now [in terms of getting on with her half-brother Ezio (14)]. But before, we were always arguing, you know? But now it's starting to get better. … Ah yes, now I know why [I told you that] it was better on Monday and Tuesday [her new alternating rhythm]. Because with my [half-]brother, we argued too much, and so like that we saw each other less. And I think it's changed something, because now we fight less, and sometimes we share good times together. (Mélissa, aged ten)

Mélissa and her maternal half-brother Ezio (14) are constantly at loggerheads about their respective territories, and have a difficult relationship. They both struggle to find their physical and symbolic place with their mother. Ezio and Mélissa argued and provoked one another continuously during the week they lived together; this situation encouraged their mother to change the alternation schedule so that they would not be present on exactly the same days. Since then, Mélissa has lived with her mother every Monday and Tuesday, with Ezio and her half-sister Olivia (17) being present there every other week. Thus, during the week when the four of them are present at their mother's apartment, the half-siblings only spend two days together. Mélissa goes to her father's house on Wednesdays after school, and Ezio and Olivia stay the rest of the week alone with their mother. Mélissa is still young and has only recently received a mobile phone, and she has no virtual links with her half-siblings. The absence of communication at a distance contributes to dampening conflicts and facilitating family relations.

The maintenance of relationships at a distance also depends on whether or not virtual contact is seen as routine. Cédric and Giorgio (16) do not consider virtual exchanges to be a regular family practice. The two teenagers send messages only occasionally, to talk 'nonsense' or to give or receive comfort in exceptional situations – like when Giorgio's stepsiblings' maternal grandmother passed away. The boys would rather spend time with their half- or stepsiblings in physical co-presence:

> My big [half-brother], yes, we talk from time to time, but not, well. … Anyway, we see each other every other week, so that's fine. … He's got his life and I've got my life too. (Cédric, aged 15)

> [They communicate] Not so much, no. … No, we send each other little messages or whatever, but it's just bullshitting, or whatever, but otherwise. … When they're over there, well, this particular period, yes, because, like I say [*sic*] they've got problems on the other side [the death of their maternal grandmother]. So I sent them a message to say that I was there if they needed anything, things like that. But otherwise, we see one another here. I don't, we don't keep in touch when we're at the other parents' houses. (Giorgio, aged 16)

The existence and frequency of virtual contact also largely depends on how children appropriate communication tools such as the telephone, computer, iPod Touch or tablet. The mobile phone occupies a special place in this respect, as we will discuss in the next section.

Focus on the mobile phone

The mobile phone is particularly interesting for studying family practices because, as observed by Morgan (2020), its use can give rise to 'routinised family practices' that extend the sense of home beyond the walls of the dwelling and reaffirm the extent of family space. Some children have an instrumental relationship with their mobile phone, seeing it mainly as a useful tool for performing practical tasks like calling or texting a parent. Others have a more affective relationship with their phone, being strongly attached to this 'object of affect' (Sacriste, 2019: 54).

'My phone is really practical for me'

Children who have an instrumental relation with their mobile phone talk about it only as an object useful for organizing their daily lives. They use it to plan their return to a parent's residence, to organize a future event, or to communicate with their parents about things they might have forgotten when they left or that they should bring back to the 'right' island. Children like Lewis (aged 16), Félicien (12), Annelyse (ten) or Mélissa (ten) do not perceive their phone as what Sacriste (2019: 54) calls an 'object of affect': such objects provoke positive or negative sensations and emotions only for those who mobilize and appropriate them, which is not the case for these children.

Lewis rarely uses his smartphone to communicate with his absent parents, who have 'open' and 'wild' islands and therefore do not limit virtual contacts, 'except in specific cases' – if there is an event to organize and he cannot wait a week to talk to the parent concerned, or before he returns to his mother's house so he can plan his journey according to whether or not she can pick him up. During his journeys, the teenager prefers to do nothing and to look out the window of the tram or underground; he does not listen to music or play games on his smartphone. He explains: 'My phone, you see, it's really practical for me. ... No, I don't really use it excessively.'

Félicien and Mélissa each have a 'little telephone with buttons' that was given to them for safety reasons. Félicien received his phone when he started travelling alone by train between his two dwellings, and Mélissa received hers when she started taking the tram to school on her own from her mother's flat. Annelyse received her sister Chloé's old iPod Touch so that she can communicate freely with her mother or father when she feels the need.[10] However, none of these children actually use these tools. They do not even perceive the presence of these objects in their daily lives, neither using them nor appropriating them. They forget to recharge their device, or leave it at the bottom of a bag and forget its existence. As a result, the three young adolescents communicate very little – if at all – with their distant parents. They do not want to borrow the phone of the parent they are staying with, because this phone does not belong to them and it annoys them to have to ask permission to use it.

'My phone, it travels around with me'

Other children are much more attached to their phones. This attachment is more than simply emotional; they are also – and above all – 'attached' to it in the sense proposed by Sacriste (2018a): they are linked to this object by feelings of closeness and affinity, but also connected to it in the sense that it is permanently associated with them. For Sacriste, this attachment stems from the appropriation of this object, the familiar and routine use that individuals make of it and the memories and experiences that it embodies. For these children, their phones are 'shadow objects' that 'stick to them', accompanying them wherever they go, as Coralie (aged 12) and Théodore (13) made clear during the Socio-Spatial Network Game interview. When Coralie explained that she 'revolves' among the houses of her parents and step-parents, she pointed out that her phone always 'travels around' with her from one place to another (Figure 6.1). Théodore constructed a spatial and family configuration on the game board that included the two places

Figure 6.1: Socio-Spatial Network Game (Coralie, aged 12; photo taken from her vantage point)

Figure 6.2: Socio-Spatial Network Game (Théodore, aged 13; photo taken from his vantage point)

where he lives, his 20-year-old sister's student accommodation and the town where he goes to school. To symbolize his movements between all of these places, he placed a bus in front of the block representing the school, and next placed a small picture of a mobile phone topped with a black pawn symbolizing himself (Figure 6.2). He explained that 'I take the bus to my dad's and my mum's … and so [here I am], on the bus, with my phone'.

Children who prefer 'parked' objects, like Marie (12), Théodore and Coralie, and see their phone as an 'object of affect' told us that they always take it with them when they move house. In contrast, those who are strongly attached to their phones but prefer objects 'in transit' did not say explicitly that they took their phones with them, with the exception of Chloé (12). For these children, travelling with their phones seems so natural that they do not find it necessary to mention it in the interview, despite their strong attachment to the device.

'Shadow-object' phones can be considered as 'supports for anchoring' (Sacriste, 2018a: 316). These stable and familiar objects accompany children wherever they go, be it between their dwellings or between their school and extracurricular activities. While we described 'shadow objects' as 'everyday companions' in Chapter 3, mobile phones appear specifically as 'companions on the road', as Marie's mother put it. She used this term to define the role Marie's smartphone plays in her daughter's life as an independent adolescent girl. This terminology echoes the research conducted by Benjelloun (2018) on the use of the smartphone and its many roles in the lives of French people who consider themselves 'addicted' to it. The author shows that these individuals see the smartphone as a 'companion' that helps them feel less alone and in which they can confide. It gives them a sense of emotional and physical security (in case of emergency), and enables them to keep in touch with distant people and to escape from the burdens of everyday life. Most of the children we encountered also expressed a strong attachment to their mobile phones. Marie even told us, 'I love it, my phone'. Unlike those who see their phone as a practical instrument only, children who are attached to their phone see it as an 'object of affect' (Sacriste, 2019: 54) that they mobilize and appropriate to the point of transforming it, in some cases, into an intimate 'personal territory' safe from the gaze of others. For Manuelo (13), having his own smartphone means that he now has his own private virtual space, and no longer needs to delete his conversations with his friends from his father's or mother's phone.

These children's phones also represent a 'means of liberation' (Sacriste, 2018a: 321), allowing them to amuse themselves and to break free of the world around them by playing games, listening to music or watching videos and to continue the conversations that they have started with their friends at school.

When they maintain relationships at a distance with family members, some children make practical use of their 'companion on the road' to plan or organize events or activities, while others also use it as a 'means of reassurance' (Sacriste, 2019: 59) to find comfort in their distant parent, thus maintaining a close relationship at a distance. In the first category, we find Théodore and Coralie, who do not necessarily communicate with their absent parent 'unless we have to organize things', as Théodore explains.

Coralie adds that she only uses her phone to exchange information about Scout meetings with her mother by email. As Christensen (2009) notes in her study of the role of mobile phones in Danish blended families, even if these communications are only practical or functional, their regularity helps to maintain a close relationship between parent and child. When children manage organizational issues at a distance as they would have if they had been physically co-present with their parent, they are in true virtual co-presence.

Marie used to communicate rarely with her parents by phone; she would only send or receive a few messages about things she needed to bring back or wanted to have taken to the other parent's dwelling. However, since obtaining her own mobile phone when she started secondary school, the adolescent has been communicating more frequently with her mother. Whereas she did not previously have any contact with her mother (who has a 'fortress' island) while she was staying with her father (who has a 'reef' island), Marie now calls her mother or sends her WhatsApp messages when she has conflicts with friends or with her father, who she says 'has a bad temper'.[11] Although they are not physically co-present together, the girl says that she still feels supported, listened to and comforted by her mother. Marie also explains that she now systematically informs her mother of her imminent arrival on the day she moves house. When she arrives on her mother's street, Marie texts her mother to find out whether she is home. Although Marie does not use these terms, this practice can be interpreted as a way for her to anticipate her arrival and remind her maternal 'new family' that she is back – before she has even walked through the door – to avoid her feeling of being an 'intruder'.

★★★

In this chapter, we aimed to describe how family relationships and practices unfold in a multilocal context. We have seen that these relationships and practices endure and expand beyond the walls of the dwelling in an immaterial and interconnected space. The study of these practices has enabled us to document their contribution to the ways multilocal children 'do family', and to the construction of a sense of home and a feeling of family belonging that extend across several places of residence. In the next chapter, we will focus on understanding the distinct ways in which children experience this sense of home.

Notes

[1] Also known as 'connected presence' (Licoppe, 2004: 153).

[2] There are few references in the literature dealing with the thoughts that family members have – or do not have – about absent children. Hachet (2021) addresses this issue indirectly in his book on the experience of SPC from the parents' point of view and the way in

which they reconcile their times 'with child' and 'without child'. The author describes moments when parents think about their child, including the welcoming rituals that they perform when the child arrives. In one example, a father makes sure his refrigerator is stocked with his son's favourite foods before he arrives. Another example refers to a child's bedroom left empty in the child's absence: for some parents, this room lives on as if the child were present.

3   Thinking about absent children and taking their needs and feelings into consideration is a form of 'sentient activity' (Mason, 1996: 27) that 'take(s) an interest in the behaviour' of the child, 'interpret(s) his habits or needs', and 'pay(s) attention and respond(s) to his needs', even when the child is not present. This concept blurs the distinction between 'caring for' and 'caring about' by highlighting that the practices of caring for a child are often combined with thoughts and feelings about the child.

4   Cédric's father and both of Giorgio's parents have 'cocoon' islands, Amandine's father has an 'open' island, and Cédric's and Amandine's mothers have 'reef' islands.

5   These children's parents do not set limits on virtual contacts. Émilie's mother has a 'cocoon' island and her father a 'reef' island; Annelyse and Chloé's mother has a 'cocoon' island and their father an 'open' island.

6   When children do not have their own communication tools, the degree of parental conflict has an influence on virtual communication practices, as it may encourage or limit opportunities for contact. When the level of conflict is low, parents call each other regularly to discuss their child and other matters. These exchanges give the child the opportunity to talk to the parent they are not residing with once the parents have finished their conversation. However, not all children take advantage of this opportunity, and do not necessarily maintain virtual contact with their other parent. In more conflictual situations, where ex-partners communicate mainly by email or instant message, these opportunities are less frequent, but not entirely non-existent. Some parents find alternatives, such as providing a basic mobile phone or creating a WhatsApp group specifically for exchanges with the child, to allow children to maintain contact with the other parent without needing to involve them.

7   Romane's father has an 'open' island and her mother a 'fortress' island.

8   Merla and Dedonder (2019: 11) note a lack of consensus in research on the facilitating nature of online parent–child communication in post-separation families. They note that 'while some authors show that using Skype or FaceTime can lead parents and children to feel "closer" (Wolman and Pomerance, 2012), others point to the fact that virtual contact with a non-custodial parent between visits can be experienced as superficial and frustrating, particularly when the technologies are not working properly (Gollop and Taylor, 2012)'. While the advantages and disadvantages have not yet been clearly identified, existing research points in particular to 'an increase in quality time with the non-custodial parent, and a minimization of the geographical distance separating the child from his or her parent'. The disadvantages identified 'include interference from the other parent, interparental conflicts that could negatively affect the effects of communication and/or be reactivated by these continuous virtual contacts, and possible tensions between ex-partners over access to technology and the sharing of equipment and connection costs'. According to their own survey data, Merla and Dedonder note that 'interparental conflicts do not influence the level of child-parent communication'.

9   This observation is also made in the literature on transnational families (see Madianou, 2016).

10   We decided to include this device, even though it is not strictly speaking a mobile phone, because Annelyse uses it in the same way Mélissa uses her 'little phone with buttons'.

[11] Marie's mother is confused by this more regular contact. She does not want to communicate with her daughter outside the days when they live together, and she would like to re-establish these limits so that this will not happen very often. At the same time, she feels uncomfortable about not supporting her daughter when necessary. During her interview, she said that she was fine with her daughter contacting her when things were not going well, but did not want it to happen too often. These increased contacts have occurred only since Marie got her own phone.

A 'Singular-Plural' Sense of Home

We have seen in the previous chapters how children in shared physical custody (SPC) construct a sense of home at the convergence of multiple components and dimensions. Children who live multilocally occupy different positions in each of their residences, and feel a distinct sense of belonging, attachment and identification with each of them. In this chapter, we will show that children develop a 'singular-plural' sense of home at the intersection of spatial, familial and individual dimensions. This sense of home links both the geographically distinct places and the 'new families' that occupy them into an 'archipelago'. As an idea 'localizable' (Douglas, 1991: 289) in space, this sense of home ensures a certain degree of security and stability for mobile children.

The notion of a 'singular-plural' home is rooted in the relational approach to space that we are adopting in this work, which invites us to conceive of the home as being simultaneously unitary, plural, interconnected (Löw, 2015) and in relation to other spaces (Remy, 2015). Each 'island' is thus envisaged as distinct, and also as connected to the other 'island'. This interconnection generates a sense of home that is both 'singular' – unified and inclusive – and 'plural' – embracing a multiplicity of places that form a coherent whole. In this way, each 'island' is thought of as being in relation to the other in a singular 'archipelago', and also as forming a distinct whole. Within the 'archipelago', the child assigns a particular meaning to each 'island' based on its material, relational, emotional and appropriative components.[1] We are thus considering two interconnecting levels: the 'micro' level of each 'island', which can be invested with differently inflected, plural senses of home, and the 'macro' level of the 'archipelago', made up of 'islands' connected to form a singular, all-inclusive home.

To do this, we will examine how each child maintains – or does not maintain – a particular affective bond with each 'island'. Our analytical model draws on and adapts the three-dimensional concept of the sense of home and attachment to place proposed by Hashemnezhad and colleagues (2013), based on an extensive interdisciplinary literature review. The 'material dimension' of their model includes tangible aspects of the dwelling such as its size, layout and furnishings. The 'behavioural dimension' concerns the functional aspects of the living environment, such as the activities and practices that are pursued in different spaces and the relationships that develop in those spaces. Finally, the 'emotional dimension' relates to the subjective meaning, satisfaction and attachment that individuals associate with a particular place (Hashemnezhad et al, 2013: 6).

As shown in Table 7.1, our model incorporates some of these dimensions, and complements them based on our observations. We distinguish four components – *material*, *relational*, *appropriative* and *emotional*, for each of which we focus on specific dimensions. The 'material component' includes the imposed decoration of the place (wall colours, furniture and decorative elements not chosen by the child), the configuration of the spaces (the number and size of the rooms; the smell, temperature and luminosity of the premises) and the perceived level of physical comfort (quality and quantity of furnishings, whether or not the child has their own room). The 'relational component' encompasses family practices carried out in physical, virtual and symbolic co-presence as well as the quality of the child's relationships with the members of the 'new family'. The 'appropriative component' includes practices of appropriation such as marking, controlling and personalizing space, as well as the child's regular presence in the space and use of it for individually valued activities. Finally, the 'emotional component' includes the positive and negative emotions, meaning, satisfaction and attachment associated with the place of residence or with an appropriated space within it, and the resulting sense of belonging and identification with that place or space. Each component corresponds to different 'modes of experience', which we will define in the following pages.

By analysing children's discourses on these components and dimensions for each of their dwellings, we noticed that the children systematically defined[2] their tie to one residence in relation to their tie to the other. The 'islands' are thus thought of together, in an interconnected way: children give them a singular meaning, made up of plural dimensions, which forms what we have called throughout this work an 'archipelago'.

This technique also enabled us to observe that children can experience their ties to each 'island' differently. Children develop distinct ties with each 'island' because they experience its material, relational, appropriative and emotional components distinctly. As shown in Table 7.1, the ways in which the first three components (material, relational and appropriative) are perceived and experienced give rise to a sense of home that may be physical,

Table 7.1: Definition of a 'singular-plural' sense of home

Component	Dimensions	Mode of experience	Definition
Material	• Imposed decoration: wall colour, furniture and decorative objects not chosen by the child • Configuration: number and size of rooms, smell, temperature, luminosity • Perceived level of physical comfort: quantity and quality of furnishings, individual or shared bedroom	Physical sense of home	• Perception of the physical environment • Material structure's suitability for the child • Opportunity to engage in personally valued activities
Relational	• Family practices in physical co-presence • Family practices in symbolic and virtual co-presence • Quality of relationships with the members of the 'new family'	Familial sense of home	• Familiarity created while present in the dwelling • Familiarity maintained during absence • Warm atmosphere
Appropriative	• Practices of appropriation: marking, controlling and personalizing space • Regular presence in the space and use for individually valued activities	Personal sense of home	• Self-definition and self-expression
Emotional	• Positive and negative emotions associated with place of residence or appropriated space • Meaning, satisfaction, attachment associated with place of residence or appropriated space • Sense of belonging and identification with place of residence or appropriated space	The emotional component traverses the three modes of experience	

familial and/or personal. The last component (emotional) traverses these three modes of experience.

Concretely, children may feel a *'physical'* sense of home based on the material component of an 'island', depending on how comfortable they feel with the physical environment of the dwelling (imposed decoration or furnishings, configuration of spaces, perceived level of physical comfort). According to this perception, children will consider that the material structure of the place suits them – or does not, and that it offers them the opportunity to engage in activities that they personally value – or does not.

Children can also develop a *'familial'* sense of home on an 'island', seen as a whole, based on its relational component. This is the case when the dwelling is experienced as a familiar space where they share common habits, emotions and knowledge with the members of the 'new family'. They perceive it as a warm, welcoming space formed by regular family practices and satisfying relationships, both physically and at a distance.

Finally, children may feel a *'personal'* sense of home through the appropriative component. This is the case when they feel at home in a space of their own on the 'island', where they regularly spend time and engage in individual activities that they value, and which reflects aspects of their personality and where they experience peace, stability, familiarity, security, intimacy, comfort, belonging and memories. Like Sixsmith (1986),[3] we consider that the materiality of a place contributes to self-definition and enables self-expression, particularly through the practices of appropriation by which children affirm their identity.[4]

Our research focuses on how multilocal children create a 'singular-plural' sense of home in which each 'island' is viewed in relation to the other, giving a unified and inclusive meaning to the 'archipelago' they form. At the same time, the 'archipelago' consists of two distinct 'islands', each with its own material, relational, appropriative and emotional components that are experienced distinctly. Children's global sense of home (at the 'macro' level) is thus formed at the intersection of the personal, familial and physical senses of home experienced at the 'micro' level of each dwelling.

This conceptualization echoes Serfaty-Garzon's definition of home in the context of mobility, where: 'The value of dwelling itself no longer resides in the reference to a stable place or anchoring point, and its unity is lost in favour of a more complex configuration of several homes with differential and sometimes complementary qualities' (2006: 11). The children in our study have a 'singular-plural' sense of home in which each 'island' is conceived of both as being in relation to the other and as forming a distinct whole. They experience each residence distinctly, feeling at home in different ways on each of their 'islands'.

We applied the consolidated analysis grid presented in Table 7.1 to our participants to identify the kinds of relationship that each child has with their residences, in order to understand how children think of their parental dwellings when they compare and contrast the two and when they describe their emotional attachment to each of them. This way of understanding the meaning of home extends the exploratory work of Sixsmith (1986), who stressed the importance of examining the pre-eminence of one mode of experiencing 'home' over another. Our analysis shows which sense(s) of home predominate in each residence, and how different senses of home can combine in the experiences of children in SPC. We identified five distinct forms of 'archipelago' among our participants, which are detailed in the following subsections.

'Archipelagos' comprising a 'personal and physical' home and a 'familial' home

A number of children, including Giorgio (aged 16) and Félicien (12), described feeling at home in a predominantly personal and physical sense in one residence and in a primarily familial sense in the other.

Giorgio describes his particular relationship with each residence as follows:

> I feel at home in the whole house too [his mother's], but I mean, I don't have my personal privacy. … Because yes, it's, it's the house where I live, so yes, I feel at home and I have … I … I feel comfortable, or whatever, but it's not a private space for me [in contrast to his father's house], you know? (Giorgio, aged 16)

This quote reflects the 'singular-plural' nature of his sense of home. Each residence has its own distinct qualities, and is thought of in relation to the other. During our interview with the Emotion Maps, Giorgio explained that he does not necessarily feel 'better' at his father's house, where he has his own bedroom, than he does at his mother's house, where he shares his attic bedroom with his brother Manuelo (13) and stepbrother Sandro (15). He does not feel 'better' there, but 'different'.

At his father's house, Giorgio feels personally and physically at home. He finds the house comfortable and well suited to him, as he has his own bedroom that he has appropriated and that constitutes his 'private space'. His privacy is respected there because the other family members do not enter without his permission and do not touch his things. This room contains all 'those little things' that characterize him and mark the space as his own. He has surrounded himself with objects reflecting his tastes and passions to create '[his] own world', in his words. This room allows him to pursue activities that he values personally, like using his audio mixer to create his own music or arranging his collection of model cars in a display case. This feeling is reinforced by the fact that his father's house is part of his personal history: it is the house where he grew up, built by his grandfather, and is close to his activities and his network of friends.

At his mother's house, Giorgio is not attached to any particular personal space. He finds this house less comfortable because he shares a bedroom with his brother and stepbrother. He has not 'parked' any personal belongings there. However, he feels attached to the house as a whole, because it has a pleasant atmosphere and because his relationships with his stepfather and with his stepbrother and stepsister (Elena, 17) are good. While the appropriative and material components strongly influence the meaning that Giorgio gives to his father's house, the relational component is important in defining the meaning of his mother's house. Here, family practices play an 'active role' (Morgan, 2020: 735) in transforming the dwelling into a familial home. In this way, Giorgio defines a 'singular–plural' sense of home when he combines and considers his living spaces as a coherent whole, while demonstrating that each residence has its own particular and distinct meaning according to its material, relational, appropriative and emotional components.

Due to a lack of space in her house, Félicien's mother has set up her office in her son's bedroom. So as not to disturb her, Félicien spends most of his time in the communal areas of the house. His mother works in the bedroom on Wednesday afternoons, the day Félicien returns to her house, and at certain weekends: at these times, he does not allow himself to enter his own room. Félicien goes into his bedroom only to sleep. He does not appropriate this room because his mother needs to be able to enter it freely to work, but also because it is often cold there, and the room does not 'interact' enough with the rest of the house. It is on the third floor, and he must pass through three doors to get there from the ground floor: he avoids going there because he feels too isolated from the rest of the 'new family'. Félicien has not decorated this room, which contains only a few paintings he did with his mother ten years ago, just after his parents split up. He feels at home 'kind of all over the house', and above all in the living room, 'because that's where I go the most often with everyone'. He explains:

> In fact, what I need most of all is for people to be there. That everyone's there. I like it when the whole family is there. ... That they're, everyone's in the living room, I don't know ... that we're all together, you know? That we're talking together, all seeing each other, you know? (Félicien, aged 12)

This quote illustrates the importance of the relational component in the meaning Félicien gives to his mother's house. Félicien does not feel at home in this house either personally (because he does not make it his own) or physically (because he finds it uncomfortable, and its configuration does not suit him). Nevertheless, he feels at home there in a familial sense thanks to his satisfying relationships with the members of his 'new family'. These relationships play an active role in defining Félicien's sense of home, as they give him a sense of belonging to the place and of fitting into this space and this family group.

Félicien feels more at home in a personal and physical sense at his father's house. He has appropriated his private bedroom there, where he keeps his childhood mementos – like the drawings he has pasted on the walls. He exercises control over this space by refusing to let his half-siblings enter; he likes to be alone there and to be able to pursue his activities freely. This bedroom is on the second floor, on a corridor that leads to the stairs to the living room. Félicien is strongly attached to this room, which suits him better because it is closer to the communal living areas. He closes the door to his room when he wants some distance from the other 'new family' members, but he can still hear them and so does not feel completely detached from family life. He explains that he feels more at home in this bedroom than in the one at his mother's house:

> Because it's much more in interaction with everyone [at his father's house], so I just need to open my door and ... I go down the stairs and I'm already there, you know? While at Mum's, I open the door, I'm in the corridor, I open another door, I go down the stairs, and then I open another door. ... It's mainly interaction with the others. ... It's [that] when I go out [at his father's house], I'm with them right away. ... I like being [close to them]. (Félicien, aged 12)

This strong identification with his father's house was visible when Félicien talked about his travels during our interview with the Socio-Spatial Network Group (SSNG) (Figure 7.1).

During the interview, Félicien placed blocks on the game board to symbolize the houses of his mother (on the left), father (on the right) and (separated) maternal grandparents (on the right, with orange pawns) and added pieces symbolizing the members of each 'new family', the pets and the means of transport he uses to get from one house to the other. He then described returning 'to [his – that is, Félicien's] house' when referring to his father's house, and 'to the other house' or 'to Mum's' when referring to his mother's house. His use of the first-person possessive in the first case and the

Figure 7.1: Socio-Spatial Network Game (Félicien, aged 12; photo taken from his vantage point)

definite article in the second attests to his differing identification with these two places: one refers to a personal home that contributes to self-definition and self-expression, and the other to a familial home defined by the quality of relationships and by its convivial atmosphere.

Like Giorgio, Félicien is not necessarily content having little (or less) at his mother's house, and he does not consider one residence 'better' than the other, but simply different. In this way, he constructs a 'singular-plural' sense of home in which each dwelling is invested with a distinct sense of home, and is connected to the other in a singular 'archipelago'.

Émilie (ten), Anouk (ten), Mélissa (ten), Chloé (12) and Jean (13) all feel at home in a personal and physical sense in their bedrooms at their respective fathers' dwellings. At their mothers' dwellings, these children feel at home in a familial sense, as they enjoy spending time with the members of their 'new families'; however, the relatively low level of comfort they perceive there prevents them from identifying with or appropriating these places, and hence from feeling physically or personally at home.

Émilie says that she feels at home at both her mother's and her father's houses. As our analysis progressed, it became clear that she has distinct relationships to each of these dwellings. Because she lives alone with her mother, Émilie prefers to sit with her by the fire on the living room sofa rather than staying upstairs in her bedroom, where she is often cold; her Playmobil toys and craft projects have taken over the dining room table. She feels at home in a mainly familial sense at her mother's house, whereas at her father's house, she feels at home in a mainly personal and physical sense. She spends most of her time in her recently renovated bedroom at her father's house, which she finds very comfortable with its new furniture, soft carpet and beanbag chair. The space suits her and allows her to engage in the activities she enjoys. This room is also a personal home with which she identifies: she has decorated it with care according to her tastes, has organized it in her own way, and strictly controls access to it. Émilie systematically closes the door to this room, where she has put up a sign for her stepsiblings that reads 'Knock!'.

Anouk also feels at home in both her mother's and her father's apartments. In her mother's flat, she spends most of her time in the living room, where she and her mother play board games together regularly. Her mother moved into this flat after the separation, and Anouk shares a bedroom there with her brother Jean, which reduces her appreciation of her material environment. Her bed is in a corner, but she has not made this corner 'her own': it is decorated with 'nothing special' – only a few frames hanging on the walls and a lighted sign displaying her first name. She explains that she really likes to be in her bedroom at her father's house, and that she is less often in the living room with him. As her father has kept the family flat, Anouk has kept her childhood bedroom there, with all of its memories. The walls are painted in her favourite colour, and she has put drawings of flowers everywhere. Anouk is particularly attached to her bed, and also to her desk, where she does her crafts and homework. She makes sure it is 'always in order', the way she likes it. She appreciates that this room is 'her space', where 'there's no one who goes inside' except her father when he helps her with her lessons. Anouk thus feels a personal and physical sense of home in her father's flat, based on its appropriative and material components. In contrast, she feels at home in a familial sense with her mother, thanks to the quality time they spend together.

Similarly, Mélissa feels an emotional bond with both of her residences, feeling at home in both. 'There's no one place [residence] that's special', she explains. Her feeling of home is different on each 'island': at her father's house, where Mélissa has her own bedroom, this room has become her personal and physical home. She finds it comfortable, and it suits her because she can be alone and pursue the activities she enjoys without being disturbed by her half-brother Achille (two). She appropriates this room by marking it with personal objects and by exerting some control over it. In her mother's flat, Mélissa feels at home in a familial sense. She is attached to the living room, and 'nowhere else … because it's the only place where [she] spend[s] a lot of time' – with her mother, doing crafts or watching a film, or with her half-brother Ezio (14) and half-sister Olivia (17) on the rare occasions when they play a board game with her. She avoids staying in the flat's only bedroom, which she shares with her half-siblings, because its layout and clutter prevent her from engaging in her preferred activities.

The SSNG interview with Chloé showed particularly clearly how she defines a 'singular-plural' sense of home, encompassing the meanings of her individual 'islands' in a unified whole. We asked her to construct the places that are important to her on the game board, starting with where she feels at home. Chloé placed two yellow cards on the board to symbolize her residences. She then placed a pawn symbolizing herself in the centre of the board and, next to it, a picture of a telephone and a die representing the belongings 'in transit' that she carries with her (Figure 7.2).

Chloé explained that she did not put these three symbols on either of the yellow cards because she feels at home in both places: 'It's not just my dad's house or just my mum's house, it's kind of both.' This symbolic construction reflects the 'singular-plural' nature of the sense of home that she feels towards her residences. She went on to describe her relationships with each residence individually. She explained that she feels at home at her father's house – in a personal sense – because she identifies strongly with her bedroom there, which she has been able to decorate as she wishes. With her mother, she is living in the flat of her maternal grandparents (who are currently living in France) until her mother's new house is ready. Chloé, her sister Annelyse (ten) and their mother are thus surrounded by furniture and

Figure 7.2: Socio-Spatial Network Game (Chloé, aged 12; photo taken from her vantage point)

decorative objects that do not belong to them and that they did not choose. Although the wardrobes in her bedroom are filled with her clothes, Chloé cannot choose her own furniture or remove 'the whole family's stuff' that is lying around. As a result, she does not feel very much at home, because she would rather have only her own things around her. This was possible at her father's house, as he agreed to remove the 'old' furniture that she no longer wanted from her bedroom.[5] Nevertheless, the adolescent feels at home in both of her parents' dwellings, because she feels at home in her mother's flat in a familial sense. Chloé explains this feeling by describing how she spends most of her time downstairs in the communal rooms, where the sisters and their mother watch television together, chat while the mother is cooking, and spend time at the dinner table. These regular, everyday family practices nourish the emotional bond that she feels towards this dwelling.

Jean (13) also feels at home in each parental dwelling, in different ways: 'My home? There are two places, my father's and my mother's. … Here [at his father's], it's my bedroom where I really feel at home. But at my mother's, I feel … everywhere, I feel good too.' Jean identifies strongly with his father's flat, where he lived before his parents separated. Like his sister Anouk, he has kept his childhood bedroom there as it was. He has invested heavily in this space, decorating it with personal objects and creating a personal space reflecting his tastes and passions. The floor is littered with toys, and he can barely move without stepping on a toy soldier. He has painted the walls and furniture in his favourite colour, and has installed his rock collection, holiday souvenirs, Lego and Playmobil toys. In contrast, Jean does not value the material dimension of his mother's flat. He finds it less comfortable because he shares a bedroom with Anouk, and because he does not identify with the flat, he has not appropriated specific places there. The shared bedroom is soberly decorated: the walls are white, and there are few personal objects in the corner around Jean's bed – only a book or a few Legos on the windowsill. Although his parents allow him to carry personal items between dwellings, Jean prefers to 'park' his belongings at his father's apartment, which is filled with memories of the ten years he spent there with his parents: he makes do with a few things at his mother's flat so that he can keep his room at his father's as it has always been. This personal home is cluttered with 'memory objects' (toys, souvenirs) (Sacriste, 2019: 58), in contrast to his room at his mother's flat. When his sister is away, Jean spends time on his phone in their shared bedroom. He often sits in the living room playing PlayStation or board games with his 'new family', fostering a familial sense of home.

'Archipelagos' comprising a 'personal' home and a 'familial and physical' home

Other children feel at home in a predominantly personal sense on one 'island' and in a primarily familial and physical sense on the other.

Lewis (aged 16) experiences the material environment of his residences in terms of their decoration, the size of the rooms and his perceived degree of comfort, which strongly influence how he feels about each dwelling and the physical sense of home he feels there – or does not feel:

> At my father's, my bedroom is actually a lot bigger, especially [the ceiling is] a lot higher. At my mother's, my room is more or less the same size [as the room where the interview took place] and at my father's, it's really much bigger, so it gets cold very quickly, there's kind of a lot of space, so it's not 'We're good in our little room', you know? I've got a big desk with lots of things on it and my computer lost in the middle. … I feel less comfortable in my room at my father's. (Lewis, aged 16)

Lewis does not feel physically at home in his father's triplex, which he finds uncomfortable and unwelcoming with its large rooms. His experience of the material environment has a negative impact on the relational component, as he feels less inclined to leave his room to spend time with his father and half-brother because of the 'total chaos' that reigns in the apartment. Nevertheless, he identifies with his bedroom and manages to feel at home there in a personal sense: 'though, as I said before, it's kind of my world, so I spend a lot, a lot of time in my room at my father's'. Lewis also feels attached to this apartment because it is in the city, as he defines himself above all as a 'city person'. The apartment gives him a great deal of independence and freedom of movement:

> It's more a place that suits me. ... There [at his mother's], it's really the countryside. ... I'm much more a city person than a country person. ... When I'm in B., I've got easier access to certain activities and everything. ... I feel more independent. I can go out and come home whenever I want. I know the neighbourhood and everything. There [at his mother's], there's not really a neighbourhood, but I know it a bit. But I don't know, it's kind of like a little world, kind of detached from everything, where I'm peaceful, but where I go to get away from things. But basically, I feel more [at home] there [at his father's]. (Lewis, aged 16)

Lewis is also attached to his mother's house, although he finds it suits him less because of its isolation and distance from his school, friends, cultural activities and the city where he grew up. Despite these disadvantages, he experiences positive emotions there, and feels attached to the 'little world detached from everything', as he calls it, where he can 'get away from things'. Lewis identifies with his bedroom at his mother's house as well, and particularly with his armchair and his bed where he has the feeling of being in a 'little cocoon'.

According to Lewis, 'there are no common denominators' in the decoration of his two bedrooms. However, although the two rooms are very different in terms of size, light and temperature and offer him different levels of comfort, he has put the same type of furniture in both rooms. Each contains a large desk at which he spends a lot of time drawing and working on his computer, an armchair and a synthesizer for composing music. While in his father's apartment he spends most of his time in his bedroom – his 'personal' home, in his mother's house he also likes the communal rooms, where he feels at home in a familial sense. He says that 'in general ... in my mother's house, it's pretty much everywhere that I feel at home'. He enjoys being in his mother's living room: its layout and the quality of his relationships with his mother, to whom he is very close, and with his stepfather and half-sister (Clémentine, ten) create a warm, relaxed atmosphere. The material component of the dwelling evokes positive emotions for Lewis, and enables the residents to spend time together in shared spaces. In this way, Lewis's two dwellings are ordered into a 'singular-plural' home, forming a unified whole while remaining unique and distinct from one another.

Marie (12) feels comfortable in her mother's house thanks to the orange colour of the walls, which creates a warm atmosphere, and the modest size of the house, which she feels has a positive influence on her relationships there: 'It's small, and it's not that I prefer "small", but I prefer it [the house] to be a bit too small rather than too big. That way *we're more together*, and I like that.' Marie feels at home in this house both physically, based on the level of comfort she feels, and in a familial sense, because being together is what matters most to her. She spends most of her time in the shared spaces, and has made the 'middle' sofa in the living room – her 'little cocoon' – her own. Curled up on 'her' sofa, she can stay close to the 'new family' members who sit with her, or who are in the adjacent dining room/kitchen. Marie goes to her bedroom only to sleep or to read, or when a friend comes over. She has decorated this room summarily, with bookshelves on the wall and mementos from her maternal grandmother, like cuddly toys and raffle prizes they won together. The girl is attached to her mother's house mainly due to the family practices that take place there and the resulting warm, friendly atmosphere:

> Maybe I feel more comfortable at my mum's than at my dad's. ... I don't know, it's an atmosphere that I prefer at my mum's. I mean, it's mostly, my dad's often, well, not in a bad mood, but I don't know, he's got kind of a bad temper. And my stepmother is often in the office, so it's not very lively. And since here [at her mother's] there's my [half-] brother [Oscar, six], and he's smaller, he plays and stuff, and that livens up the atmosphere. (Marie, aged 12)

Marie finds the atmosphere to be less comfortable in her father's loft, because of her father's difficult temper and her stepmother's working all day. As a result, she is often alone, or with the other children in the co-operative. Apart from these times with friends, Marie stays in her room, which she has transformed into her personal home. She has chosen the colour scheme and the 'modern' furniture, and has created a comfortable space with a sofa and cushions under her loft bed. She has also built her own cardboard furniture. She perceives her places of residence as distinct from one another, and nurtures this difference because she likes the fact that 'it's different', she says.

When we asked Manuelo (13) where he felt at home, he replied 'at Dad's', but immediately added that he feels better at his mother's:

> At Dad's house, but I feel better here [at his mother's]. ... At Dad's house, because Dad's house is on my grandfather's land – my

grandfather who passed away – and he's the one who built it, and all, so I don't want to leave it – the house – because it was his land, he had his garage downstairs. He built it, so he put his hands on the house. And so for me, it's my house. (Manuelo, aged 13)

Manuelo feels personally at home in his father's house because of the family history it embodies: he has lived there all his life, his grandfather built it and it is filled with shared memories from before his parents separated. He is very attached to this house steeped in memories, and reinforces this sense of home by appropriating his bedroom there, decorating it with objects that reflect his passions. The walls are painted in the colours of his favourite football team, and he keeps his PlayStation and gaming accessories there. Manuelo is also attached to his mother's house, where he feels at home in a familial sense thanks to the satisfying relationships he maintains there. He finds the atmosphere warm and caring, and he feels listened to, understood and respected: 'And I feel better here [at his mother's] because here, if I have a problem, I can talk about it, while at my dad's, he'd shout, he'd get angry straight away. There's more talking here than at my dad's.' Manuelo also feels at home physically in his mother's house, where he feels more material comfort and can pursue his activities freely:

And homework and all that, that's better here, because at my dad's, I don't have a desk, I only have the PlayStation. Here [at his mother's], I've got everything on it [his desk], and I can put lots of stuff inside it. And at my dad's, my bedroom's always kind of a mess because everything's on top of everything else. (Manuelo, aged 13)

His bedroom at his father's house contains most of his mementos and other cherished objects. However, it is very cluttered, and he finds it less comfortable than the room he shares at his mother's new house with his brother Giorgio (16) and stepbrother Sandro (15). He has a desk in this room where he likes to pursue his various activities, and where he can arrange his personal belongings as he wishes – like his tablet, favourite pens, video games and charger. The only thing Manuelo takes with him to his mother's house is the tracksuit in his favourite football team's colours. He surrounds himself with objects similar to those he has at his father's, but which he must share with the other boys. Manuelo spends his pocket money on high-quality joysticks, a headset and other PlayStation accessories which he keeps at his father's house, making do with lower-quality equipment at his mother's house where he must share it. In this way, the adolescent thinks of each of his places of residence in relation to the other, including them as parts of a coherent whole while seeing them as distinct from one another.

Eliot (14) clearly demonstrated a 'singular-plural' sense of home during the SSNG interview.[6] After receiving the initial instructions, he placed a medium-sized green card on the board, on which he then placed two small pink cards symbolizing the two places where he lives:

> So this [the first pink card] is like for my home, where I feel really … [it's] my mum's apartment. I even put two places [putting down the second pink card], my dad's and my mum's, with obviously my brothers and my little [half-]sister at my dad's and, at my mum's, just with my two brothers and me. (Eliot, aged 14)

He went on to explain: 'The green card is where I feel at home and, where I feel at home, there's my dad's and my mum's.' This construction shows that he sees each dwelling as connected to the other and that they form a whole together (symbolized by the green card). In the interview, Eliot also explained how he experiences each place of residence separately. He needs to be surrounded by family members, especially his brothers Henri (18) and Gauthier (20), to feel at home. The teenager attests to a familial sense of home in his mother's loft when he emphasizes the activities he shares with his mother and brothers there, which transform the dwelling into a convivial home:

> [At the dinner table at his mother's apartment] often the whole family's there, talking, laughing and so on. It can last until 10 pm, while we eat at 7 pm. And I like being here [in the TV room] because we often watch a film with Sandrine [his brother Gauthier's girlfriend] and also with the whole family. (Eliot, aged 14)

Eliot feels at home in his mother's loft in a familial sense, thanks to its warm and cheerful atmosphere. He also feels at home in a physical sense, as his stepfather has entirely renovated this dwelling using fine materials; moreover, he greatly appreciates the material comfort he feels in his part of the dormitory, where he has a double bed and a desk. However, he sometimes feels less at home there in a personal sense, because he has only been living in this apartment for five years. Conversely, he feels at home in a personal sense in his father's house, where he was born and where he spent his entire childhood, even if the atmosphere there is sometimes strained: his father is under a lot of pressure at work, which makes him nervous and irritable.

Eliot differs from the other children described in that his personal sense of home is linked not to specific rooms or places, but to his entire dwellings. He does not attach much importance to his bedrooms, where he goes only to sleep or do his homework; he prefers to stay downstairs in the communal living areas of both dwellings. At his father's house, where he feels at home in a personal sense, he uses the living room sofa to get his bearings and to take some time for himself. At his mother's apartment, where he feels at home in a familial sense, he prefers a chair in front of the wood-stove where he can chat and spend time with other members of the 'new family':

> At my mum's, it's mostly by the fire, and at my dad's, it's on the sofa. That's always my place, in front of the fire; I pull up a chair and I sit there. And at my dad's, it's on the sofa. I lie down on it. … Sometimes I sleep, sometimes I do nothing, sometimes I'm on my phone, sometimes I watch a series, sometimes I just stay there doing nothing and close my eyes. Nothing … [whereas in his bedrooms] I'm hardly ever there, except to sleep, sometimes to do my homework when it's late. But otherwise, no, it's very rare in any case. (Eliot, aged 14)

Eliot thinks of his places of residence in an interrelated way, and describes his particular relationship with each: in one dwelling, he has a familial and physical sense of home based on the quality of his relationships, the warm, friendly atmosphere and the physical comfort he finds there. In the other, he feels at home personally because of the personal and family history binding him to this childhood home, where he finds all his familiar references.

'Archipelagos' comprising a 'personal, familial and physical' home and a 'familial' home

Within their 'archipelago', some children feel at home in a personal, familial and physical sense in one dwelling, with no predominance of any one mode of experience, and in only a familial sense in the other: in this dwelling, they value their family relationships, but their negative relationships to the material and appropriative components of the dwelling prevent them from feeling physically or personally at home there.

Romane (aged ten) feels at home in both parents' dwellings because in each one, she has a bedroom and one of her parents is present:

> [She feels at home] well, here [at her father's] and at my mum's, and at my [old] flat, but now I don't go there anymore seeing that it's been sold. … [To feel at home,] I need a room, either with my brother or on my own. When I know that I'm at home, well, often my parents are there. (Romane, aged ten)

After the separation, Romane's mother kept the flat where Romane and her brother Arthur (six) grew up. A few months ago, the three of them moved into a house her mother had bought and refurbished, which is two streets away from her father's rented flat. While Romane feels at home in each parent's dwelling, she does not have the same relationship with her two 'islands'. During the SSNG interview, she built her residences with blocks, indicating the importance of her old flat and her mother's house with small disks. She explained: 'That, that's my flat. Well, my old flat, because now I've moved out. But it's still an important place. … This is my new house with my mum. Here [at her father's], it's a place you rent, so it's not so important.'

The interview with the Emotion Maps provided a deeper insight into each residence, showing that Romane feels particularly at home – in a personal, physical and familial sense – in her mother's house. She feels at home physically because she is very comfortable in this newly renovated, light-filled and tidy house. She feels at home in a familial sense thanks to the satisfying relationships she maintains – particularly in the living room and kitchen because, she explains, 'here, we spend time together with my brother and my mother, reading stories and everything'. Finally, she feels at home in a personal sense in her single bedroom, which she has decorated according to her tastes and divided into areas dedicated to her favourite activities, like playing with Playmobil toys and drawing. She also controls access to this room, keeping her little brother at a distance.

In contrast, Romane finds her father's flat uncomfortable because the bedroom she shares with her brother is too small, and she does not like how it is decorated. Her father, who has a modest standard of living, has decorated the room with furniture and objects given to him by friends, most of whom have sons. As a result, the room contains mainly 'boy' things, which Romane considers to belong more to her little brother. Romane is rather feminine, and does not identify with this space, where she feels overwhelmed. She therefore makes do with very little in this shared room, where she feels no positive emotional connection and which she finds less comfortable than her room at her mother's, which she 'loves'. She feels at home only in a familial sense because her father is there, and because she likes to be in the living room where she 'shares things with [her] brother and [her] father while playing video games' and they 'fight with [her stepmother]' on her father's sofa bed.

'Archipelagos' comprising a 'personal and familial' home and a 'personal' home

The children in this last category feel at home in a predominantly personal sense on both 'islands', and also in a familial sense on one of them.

Théodore (aged 13) does not identify with either of his parents' houses as a whole, but primarily with his two bedrooms. He talks about his residences in a detached tone, using the definite article and naming them according to their locations: 'the house in L.' where his father lives and 'the house in C.' where his mother lives. The adolescent prefers to define himself as not belonging to either residence in particular. During the SSNG interview, he placed a pawn symbolizing himself and a picture of a telephone together on the game board, next to a miniature bus near the block representing his school, and explained:

> Well, because that's how I go to Dad's and Mum's [by bus]. That's how I can travel to both of their houses. And I wouldn't like to show myself once at Dad's and once at Mum's, no. So I'd rather put myself on the bus. Like that, you know I'm taking public transport to go to my parents' houses. (Théodore, aged 13)

While Théodore does not see his parents' houses as points of anchorage where he feels he belongs, he is strongly attached to his two bedrooms, with which he identifies and where he feels personally at home. Each room contains a part of his private universe, to which he looks forward to returning each time he moves: 'One of the advantages is that I change all the time. In other words, I'm not always used to a particular room, a particular house. I change. Sometimes I go here, sometimes I go there. So I have my two rooms.' Théodore's bedrooms contain objects that enable him to pursue activities that are different but that he enjoys equally, like a PlayStation at his mother's house and comic books at his father's. He has painted the walls of both bedrooms in his favourite colour, which makes them look relatively similar.

The relational component is also important in defining the sense of home for Théodore, who feels at home in a familial sense as well at his mother's house: 'It's 'cooler', I feel better here [at his mother's]. I'm more relaxed. I'm less stressed. Whereas at Dad's house, I'm always like "You've got to do this, you've got to do that". I'm under more pressure.'

Mathilde (13) shares her two bedrooms with her (step)sisters. She feels at home in a personal sense not in a bedroom, but in a specific area of each dwelling:

> Where I feel really, really at home is in my bed at Mum's. And there [at her father's], that spot [her place in the corner of the living room sofa, which is hidden by a wall]. … Because there [in her bed on the mezzanine at her mother's], it's higher up and there's almost no one there, not everyone can see where I am and you don't hear much [noise]. … And there [on the sofa at her father's], it's behind a corner and it's warm [cosy] and I know how to get comfortable, and I feel good there. (Mathilde, aged 13)

At her mother's apartment, Mathilde feels personally at home in her bed on the mezzanine of the bedroom she shares with her sister Clémence (15).

She has created a 'little spot' there, decorated with objects that reflect her tastes and her passions for photography and drawing. Being up high, she feels hidden from view and removed from family life. She also feels at home in a familial sense at her mother's residence, as she has good relations with her mother, sister and stepfather.

Mathilde does not feel at home in the room she shares with Clémence and their stepsister Flore (15) at her father's house, because 'there's not much room for me'. At present, she does not feel at home in this house in a familial sense, because relations are strained with her stepmother and her stepsister who live there permanently. Nevertheless, she has created a more personal spot on the sofa in the living room, where she can settle down with a blanket and her dog. She feels at home there – in a personal sense – thanks to the calm atmosphere and the fact that her dog comes to stay with her there.

When we met Mathilde, this house was being renovated: her father was converting the attic into two new bedrooms so the three teenagers would each have their own room. Mathilde is wagering heavily on the future layout of the house, which should feel less crowded and more comfortable. She believes this will make living together easier:

> I have the impression that it's going to get better. ... Because there we were always together, we didn't have any place where we could be alone. And now things are going to be much better. I think we're going to have fewer problems because it was really ... well, it was full, you know, my house. And it's because we had to take everything from upstairs [in the attic] downstairs [in the living room]. But we took out a lot of things. And so now we're going to buy some cabinets to put lots of things in, and it will get better. (Mathilde, aged 13)

The new layout will give her a place of her own in the near future:

> I've really got something for myself. I'm kind of far away from things, and I'm upstairs. Because now we sleep next door to Dad and [her stepmother] Alexia's room, and I want to have something where not everyone has to come. ... And when I go upstairs, it's going to be a lot quieter. It's going to be great. (Mathilde, aged 13)

Mathilde is already planning her future bedroom, which she cannot wait to paint in light colours and to decorate with cushions to create a cosy space and a soothing atmosphere. She looks forward to being able to get away from family life by going to her bedroom, where she can do what she pleases, recharge her batteries, find the calm she needs to unwind and take time for herself by listening to music.

Amandine (12) sees each of her bedrooms as a 'little house'. She has made each of them her own by decorating them with personal objects, and feels free to pursue her activities there undisturbed:

I don't really have a preference for my bedroom at my mum's or my dad's, but I feel comfortable. … It's kind of like my own little house, like that. I like to do my own things, you know, I feel good there. … Even if I'm in the same room as my sister [Lou, six], she's often downstairs, so I stay in the bedroom and then I do kind of what I want. (Amandine, aged 12)

Her brother Joseph now enjoys changing houses and returning to each of his rooms – his personal homes – at regular intervals:

Well, I mean, that doesn't bother me. I even like to change houses like that. Changing environments, in fact. … On one hand, it's a bit of a paradox, because I like to be kind of a homebody, to stay inside, at home, and not move. On the other hand, I need to change environments a bit. It's good for me, actually. I don't like to stay in the same room all the time. I like to stay in the same room that belongs to me – so my bedroom – as much when I'm here [at his father's] as at Mum's. But I do like to 'change', in quotes, even though I'm always in my room. It's kind of like that, in fact. That's why I like to stay in my own place. (Joseph, aged 16)

This feeling of being at home is slightly more pronounced at their mother's house. She lives in the city where Joseph and Amandine grew up, whereas their father has moved nearly 35 kilometres away. Both teenagers go to school in their hometown. Their network of friends is concentrated there, and they are 'more used' to being and moving around in this town. Joseph says, for example:

I feel better at my mum's because it's closer to the school, you know? It's closer to my environment, my neighbourhood, my friends. I have lots of friends around my mum's house, and maybe, I think it's psychological, but I feel better there. So, then, here – I'm fine at Dad's, but I think I'm closer to an environment … closer to everyday life [at his mother's], you know? (Joseph, aged 16)

The brother and sister spend more time in their bedrooms at their father's house, while at their mother's house they gather more often around the large dining room table to study or to play a board game with other family members. These practices help to transform the space of their mother's house into a familial home. In this way, they both define a 'singular-plural' sense of home, seeing their living spaces as interrelated while distinctly evaluating the relational component of each one.

An 'archipelago' comprising a 'personal, familial and physical' home and a 'non-home'

Tristan (15) is an exception in our study, showing that children may not feel at home in any sense on one of their 'islands'. During the SSNG interview, Tristan refused to place his mother's house on the game board. When asked why, he explained: 'In fact, I don't really feel at home there, so that's kind of why. [Although] yes, she herself [his mother] still means a lot to me.'

To feel at home in a familial sense, Tristan needs to be among people he likes, and needs there not to be a 'bad atmosphere'. We first met him a month after he began residing exclusively with his father, as he could no longer stand the conflict with his stepfather Augustin, who was present at his mother's house at weekends. These tensions made him feel uncomfortable in his own house, where he could not do what he wanted when his stepfather was there – like play on the PlayStation in the living room, watch TV, or shower when he wanted to. Furthermore, Tristan shared only rare moments with his mother, who had a 'wild' island and spent most of her time on her computer. The scarcity of quality time spent together prevented Tristan from feeling at home in a familial sense. Tristan also experienced a low level of material comfort at his mother's house. When Augustin's father came to stay with them, Tristan had to give up his bedroom and bed to him and sleep on a mattress in the living room. The adolescent was not personally invested in his bedroom, as he did not have exclusive use of it and finally did not use it much. He explained: 'It's hardly decorated at all. ... I've got two posters on the wall, that's it. ... I don't care, I'm hardly ever there. Just to sleep, so I don't really care, you know?' Moreover, his mother did not have the money to spend on decorating his room. He therefore preferred to play online video games in the living room or to chat with his mother in the kitchen when his stepfather was not around.

In contrast, Tristan feels at home in a personal, physical and familial sense at his father's house. His father and stepmother recently moved into a new house that he finds comfortable. Tristan has chosen beautiful wallpaper for his bedroom there. He has decorated this room with mementos of his 'first family' and other personal objects, like his penknife collection, and he has divided it into different activity zones. He also likes to spend time watching TV or chatting with his father and stepmother in the communal living areas.

Tristan's requesting and being granted full-time residence with his father undoubtedly reflect his difficulties in feeling at home in his mother's house and the imbalance between his two 'islands'.

A 'singular-plural' home as a vector of opportunities rather than fragmentation

Some children, such as Mélissa (aged ten) and Mathilde (13), are ambivalent about their multilocal way of life. These two girls appreciate their alternation between 'islands', but would prefer that their parents were still together. Mélissa, who enjoys her weeks away from her half-siblings, does not find it 'super cool' that her parents are apart. Mathilde, who also appreciates the time away from her stepfamily, is still having difficulty with the parental separation, even though it dates back ten years. She has trouble talking about it:

> It's been since I was 3, so I'm used to it, but still, it's kind of ... Well, I'm very happy like this, but it's also kind of difficult [to talk about it] because I've also had a lot of difficulties. When I was with my mum, I missed my dad, and vice versa. You see? (Mathilde, aged 13)

Romane (ten) does not really see any advantages in her parents being separated. She would prefer to have a single residence where she could gather all her belongings and be with both her parents at the same time, although she knows this is no longer possible.

However, many of the children in our study like to alternate between two places that offer them different material (and personal) environments and different family relationships. For these children, their two residences provide the opportunity to withdraw for a few days and distance themselves from each 'island' and its inhabitants, which enables them to rejoin the members of their 'new family' more easily afterwards and to maintain better relationships in physical co-presence. This observation echoes the findings of studies on relationships between adults and ageing parents (Merla, 2012; Leider and Janssen, 2014), which show that distance and separation are sometimes beneficial to the creation and maintenance of emotional ties. In our study, we observed that the 'imposed' distance from each 'island' and its inhabitants also helps to create a bond between children and the members of their 'new families'.

Coralie (12) moves house every Wednesday, and spends every other weekend with each parent.[7] She often lives in the house of her mother's partner Roland, whose four children move house every week. Because of their unsynchronized alternating rhythms, Coralie is sometimes sad and frustrated at having to leave for her father's house when her stepsiblings arrive at her stepfather's the same day. However, these few days away are beneficial to her, giving her a chance to relax and unwind, away from the constant noise and bustle of her large 'new family':

> Sometimes at the weekend, when I don't go to their house, it feels kind of empty because sometimes there's lots of noise [there], lots

and lots of noise. And sometimes [it's] really quiet. So, you're there at Dad's, it's kind of like a break. I rest a bit at Dad's, and [then] at Mum's, 'Woohoo!' (Coralie, aged 12)

Mathilde (13) appreciates being away from her father's house every other week. Her stepmother and stepsister Flore (15) live there permanently, and Mathilde does not want to spend too much time under the same roof as Flore, who has a 'very difficult' personality. SPC allows her to distance herself from her stepsister, which makes their life together easier and helps them to have a better relationship. Similarly, Émilie (ten) has a good relationship with her paternal stepsiblings Éden (ten) and Capucine (12), precisely because they are separated for a few days a week. She sometimes quarrels with one or the other of them, but these disputes are less frequent than those between the brother and sister because, Émilie says, 'they're together more'.

Cédric (15) likes to get away from each 'island' for a week. The physical distance allows him to take a step back from the habits, ways of functioning and character of each parent, with which he sometimes finds it difficult to cope. He likes to 'change the scenery a bit' and to rediscover the positive aspects of each residence on a regular basis:

> Well, being around your mother's character all the time, it's, er … you know. [Laughs.] And being around your father's character all the time, that's also, well, you know. Like that, you change. And it's with the house too: you're getting stuck in your routine somewhere, and then you go to the other house, and yes, that changes. (Cédric, aged 15)

For his part, Giorgio (16) stresses that he would not want to return to his life before his parents separated:

> In fact, I'd find it hard to go back to the life I had before, with my parents [together], with a nuclear family, you know? … It feels weird being … I don't know … I wouldn't know how to go back to a normal family any more … now that I'm moving from one place to another. (Giorgio, aged 16)

The teenager appreciates the varied character of this way of life:

> And even at Mum's and at Dad's, it's not that there are two different mentalities, but we live differently, it's like. … My stepmother doesn't have kids, so I live with just my father and my stepmother. There are kids here [at his mother's], so it's a different way of life, let's just say. We do things at Dad's that we don't do with Mum, and vice versa. So that's what's good, it's a bit more varied than when there were the four

of us with Dad, Mum and my brother. It was monotonous, let's say, always the same. So this is what I actually prefer. (Giorgio, aged 16)

Similarly, Théodore (13) and Mélissa (ten) prefer to change residences every week (or twice a week for Mélissa) to distance themselves from their younger half-siblings, with whom they spend a great deal of time at their fathers' houses. Going to stay with their mothers offers them a breath of fresh air that helps them to continue this investment in their sibling relationships:

Théodore:	She [his paternal half-sister Delphine, seven] is always very happy to see me again because she has fun with me and she doesn't like to be alone, an only child. She likes to keep busy, so she prefers it when I'm around.
Interviewer:	OK. And so you're all alone here [at his mother's] during the week?
Théodore:	Yes, that's right. So I'm kind of quiet. … I'm kind of freed I can do more what I want, what I feel like doing, and less looking after Nine [Delphine].

That doesn't bother me either. What I like when I leave my little brother [Achille, two] is that I don't hear him for two days and that he stops crying, and that, that's cool. Because he's great and he's cute, but sometimes it's really a pain. (Mélissa, aged 10)

Thus, although it is difficult for some children to be separated from one of their parents for several days, alternating between two places of residence can also be seen as an opportunity for children. Their regular absences allow them to maintain positive and friendly relationships with the members of each 'new family', and to bring a breath of fresh air to their daily lives each time they return home.

Notes

[1] When they talk about their attachment to each of their residences, the children in our study rarely say that they prefer one or the other, or feel more attached to one or the other. While they see each residence as distinct, it is not defined as being 'better' than the other.

[2] This may be due, at least in part, to a methodological effect. During the interviews, our methodological tools encouraged children to talk about their life experiences with each parent, between and within households.

[3] The model we present here echoes in part that proposed by Sixsmith (1986), based on a study of the sense of home among 22 graduate students. The social psychologist considers that home can be experienced in personal, social and physical ways. The 'personal home' is seen as an extension of the self, appearing as 'a central emotional and sometimes physical reference point in a person's life which is encapsulated in feelings of security, happiness and belonging' (Sixsmith, 1986: 290). The physical aspects of the place (the layout,

the presence of objects, and so on) are seen as essential to self-definition because they allow self-expression. The author stresses that knowledge of the place and memories of important events experienced there strengthen the emotional ties that people feel towards it. This space is an integral part of their personal history and identity. The 'social home' is defined by the presence of others and by the relationships established with friends and family members in a place. It is a place of 'entertainment and enjoyment of other people's company' (Sixsmith, 1986: 291). Finally, people define a 'physical home' when the material structure of the place suits them, in the sense that it offers them a certain degree of physical comfort and the opportunity to carry out activities that they value personally (Sixsmith, 1986: 292). While these modes of experience are described separately, the author points out that in reality 'each home features a unique and dynamic combination of personal, social and physical properties and meanings' (Sixsmith, 1986: 294).

4   In Chapter 5, we presented various practices of appropriation (marking, controlling and personalizing a place) that children may (or may not) use within their dwellings, thereby illustrating how they create (or do not create) a 'personal home' (Sixsmith, 1986), a world of their own (Serfaty-Garzon, 2002) where they can express themselves as they are.

5   This testimony echoes how practices of appropriation change according to the age of the children, as described in Chapter 5. While Chloé was initially happy having her bedroom decorated with her father's furniture, at around the age of 12 she asked for more modern furniture that better reflected her tastes.

6   The photo of Eliot's SSNG appears in Chapter 1 (see Figure 1.2).

7   Coralie alternates every 2/5/5 days. Every week, she lives with her mother on Mondays and Tuesdays, with her father on Wednesdays and Thursdays, and with each parent every other weekend (Friday to Sunday).

Concluding Reflections

In this book, we examined the construction and maintenance of a sense of 'home' among 21 Belgian children living in shared physical custody (SPC). Our aim was to gain a better understanding of how these children construct and define their place within each of their dwellings, how they come to terms with and appropriate this multilocal way of life, and ultimately, how they articulate these places of residence and families into a 'global home' that synthesizes their multiple senses of belonging. Along the way, we noted the obstacles and difficulties they encountered and the practices they implemented on a daily basis in – and between – two living environments marked by distinct material characteristics, family configurations, cultures and 'parental styles'.

A 'singular-plural' sense of home

Our central question was that of how children in SPC make themselves 'at home'. The answers we have found confirm the multiplicity of dimensions that come into play in the creation and maintenance of a sense of home. Our work has brought to light a variety of ways in which places are occupied, appropriated and given meaning. It has also shown the extent to which this work of (re)constructing a sense of home is intimately linked to the relationships that children have with those around them, and to the position they occupy – or would like to occupy – in their families. We confirm Campo et al's observation that for children, home is a 'fundamentally relational idea and experience, referenced to the presence of significant others and the feelings and activities associated with them' (Campo et al, 2020: 316). By making use of everyday objects, marking the space with their 'colour imprint' and exercising some control over their appropriated territories, children structure their material and family universes, defining and negotiating a place in – and belonging to – their two living spaces and family groups while asserting their own developing identity.

In the first chapter of this book, we wrote that we considered the 'sense of home' to be a unique sense of identity, stability, security, peace and belonging to one or more places – and by extension, to the people, objects and ideas that inhabit that (or those) place(s) (Winther, 2009). For the children we encountered, this sense of identity, security and belonging can be constructed in different ways, and derives – cumulatively or exclusively – from their sense of the suitability of the physical configuration of a place, the quality of relationships and the atmosphere prevailing there, or the possibility of appropriating a territory 'of their own' that reflects their tastes and personality. Our findings also confirm that 'home' does not stop at the limits of a single residence, but can extend to encompass multiple distant, contrasting locations in a sense of home that is both singular and plural, like an 'archipelago' made up of multiple 'islands'. Moving back and forth within this space can be experienced as a burdensome constraint – but also as a resource, when this alternation allows children to take some often-needed distance from members of their 'new family', to change atmosphere in order to come back refreshed, or to engage in different relationships and activities that allow them to test and commit to different ways of being themselves.

Multilocality, socialization and habitus formation

By studying children's sense of home in SPC, we have identified skills, strategies and ways of being, doing and feeling that are specific to this particular life context, demonstrating that SPC constitutes a specific context of socialization. To transpose Wacquant (2005: 316) to the context of our study, SPC involves children's development of 'enduring dispositions or trained abilities and structural inclinations to think, feel and act in determined ways' that enable them to 'respond creatively to the constraints and demands of their environment' of multilocal living. We contend that this socialization equips children with a '*multilocal habitus*' (Merla et al, 2021b), which we have defined elsewhere as 'a set of potentially contradictory habits, patterns and dispositions' (2021b: 40) that enable children to navigate multiple frames of reference. These habits and dispositions also 'help to define the contours of family and family inclusion at local and global levels – "here", "there", and "in-between" – through various forms of co-presence, and multisensorial, symbolic, virtual and material practices, which produce common knowledge and experiences' (Merla et al, 2021b: 40).

The children in our study showed us how a 'multilocal habitus' can involve multiple ways of being, doing and feeling. These include ordering a world in movement and creating continuity in alternation through the management of personal belongings that are 'parked' or 'in transit'; investing in transitional spaces that make it easier to move between dwellings; engaging in 'routines and rituals of return' – which are sometimes poorly understood by permanent residents; marking, controlling and personalizing spaces to meet one's needs; and ensuring a continued presence during periods of absence through objects, symbols and virtual contacts. Through these various practices, the family is itself 'in movement': the children's mobility and intermittent presence trigger a constant (re)negotiation of roles, places and territories. Thus, the family is constantly 'done', 'undone' and 'redone'. This dynamic character is a constant in the lives of these children. How SPC is experienced and organized changes over time, depending in particular on the children's age, residential relocations, or the arrival or departure of members of the 'new families'. Children and family members must learn to adapt to these changes; they must also learn to cope with the network of temporal, material, familial and spatial opportunities and constraints that influence how they 'do family' and construct a sense of home in the context of SPC. These opportunities and constraints offer children certain resources they can mobilize to manage this way of life on a daily basis, but may also confront them with obstacles and limitations that make things more difficult or complicated. Our work explored the agency of children who, within the limits of their possibilities, deploy strategies and practices to manage these constraints, accommodate them, and shape a world that suits them better. It remains to be seen whether socialization to a multilocal way of life (and thus, the formation of a 'multilocal habitus') equips children with specific forms of capital that they will be able to mobilize as adults to manage the mobility and multilocality that may characterize their professional, intimate or residential trajectories. Kaufmann and colleagues (2004: 750) claim that the experience of mobility can equip social actors with mobility capital (or 'motility'), which they define as 'the way in which entities access and appropriate the capacity for socio-spatial mobility according to their circumstances'. This capital comprises three dimensions: access, competence and appropriation. 'Access' refers to the economic and socio-spatial conditions under which available means of transportation and communication can be used. 'Competence' refers to skills acquired through socialization, most importantly acquired skills for mobility and organizational skills like the capacity to plan and coordinate activities through space and time. 'Appropriation' refers to the meanings that agents give to available mobilities. It is shaped by strategies, values, motives and habits, and constructed through the internalization of norms and values (Kaufmann and Widmer, 2005: 201). In our view, socialization to a multilocal way of life can equip children not only with mobility capital, but also with another form of capital more directly linked to learning how to anchor themselves in multiple places and to maintain meaningful social relationships in a multilocal context.

It is important to bear in mind that not all children face the same opportunities and constraints, and that they also differ in their capacity to respond to them. This qualitative and largely exploratory study has brought to light a multitude of factors that will need to be studied in greater depth in the future, using a broader population and quantitative methodologies. It has also raised a number of questions: what links can be detected between 'parental islands' and the socio-economic profiles of the parents concerned, or the length of time that has elapsed since separation? Are the practices of carrying a 'mobile world' – or taking 'nothing' between dwellings – more prevalent in certain social groups? Does the children's gender affect the practices adopted? How does the degree of conflict between parents influence children's possibility of experiencing a 'personal' or 'familial' home? How does the distance between residences – and between residences and places of sociability – affect the quality of children's relations with each parent? How does the decision to welcome a step-parent into an existing dwelling – or, on the contrary, to move into the step-parent's dwelling, or move together to a new location – influence how children define and negotiate their physical and symbolic place in the 'new family'?

Beyond the Belgian case

Our research has the potential to shed light on many situations, in Belgium and elsewhere, but also has its limitations. For the children we encountered, who had spent a large part of their childhood alternating between two residences, life in SPC had become routine – a way of structuring their personal and family lives that they experienced on a daily basis. Our study was also conducted in a social and legal context in which divorce, parental separation and SPC have become commonplace. It will therefore be necessary to compare our findings with those from contexts less favourable to SPC to see how children's sense of 'home' may be affected by a lack of institutional and social recognition, and by more traditional visions of gender roles in post-separation parenting. Comparisons with other contexts must also consider how domestic and public spaces are culturally defined and inhabited: the interior of the dwelling is less invested in some countries than in Belgium, mainly due to the characteristics of their housing stock and cultures that favour outdoor living. In their study of SPC in the Piedmont region of northern Italy, where much of the housing stock consists of relatively small flats where children usually share a bedroom, Merla and Murru (2023; see also Merla and Murru, 2021) show that the neighbourhood is a key place in which children invest and where they construct their identity. Nevertheless, for many children, their mother's dwelling remains their key reference point. According to the authors, this is largely the result of gender inequalities in Italian family law and in the labour market, as well as the organization of the school system (Merla and Murru, 2021). The courts usually award the family residence to the mother after separation, and mothers are more likely to adapt their working hours to family life than fathers because of gender inequalities in the labour market. One consequence is that mothers are more available to prepare meals for children – who finish school at 1 pm – and to supervise their homework afterwards. As a result, children tend to return to their mother's dwelling every day after school, regardless of the rhythm of alternation, with her residence acting as a 'homework house' (Merla and Murru, 2023: 21). These children therefore 'tend ... to consider their mother's dwelling as their "primary residence", and their father's dwelling a "secondary residence"' (Merla and Murru, 2021:11).

Key lessons for practitioners

Legal and youth welfare practitioners have observed that our results are likely to be representative of the situation of children living in SPC in Belgium and other European countries that have integrated SPC into their legal system. It is not possible to verify this hypothesis due to lack of data; however, in a recent study, 86 per cent of Belgian adolescents in SPC said they were 'satisfied' with their custody arrangement. They also had the lowest levels of conflicts between parents reported among children with separated parents, as well as high levels of feeling 'at home' in both of their parents' residences (Merla and Dedonder, 2019; Merla, Dedonder and Baar, 2022): these findings tend to confirm the perception that SPC is experienced as relatively non-problematic in many cases. Practitioners are aware that they have little contact with separated families in which life is going relatively well, seeing, as it were, only the tip of the iceberg. By showing them how young people deal with SPC on a daily basis, our study can provide them with tools to inform their practice. These include the typology of 'parental islands', which can be used with parents – and children – to identify how they actually function and how they would like to function; the lens of everyday objects, which offers a very concrete way to examine the issues involved in the logistics of alternation, drawing attention to the meanings children attach to the objects around them and to their material practices; the variety of ways in which space and places are appropriated, and the underlying issues of belonging and inclusion. More generally, this work shows how children create points of reference in order to adapt to change and movement, to generate stability and to appropriate a way of life that diverges from the normative sedentary model of residence: this is all the more important as stability is a major criterion in the assessment of SPC applications by the courts (Merla, Dedonder and Baar, 2022). It also shows that 'home' does not depend solely on the degree of material and architectural comfort that can be offered to a child, and challenges the idea that children cannot feel at home if they do not have 'their own' bedroom.

As we noted in Chapter 1, a key issue in public debates on SPC is its relevance and applicability in cases of family violence. The families we encountered were not involved in legal disputes around child custody at the time of the interviews. The ex-partners got on relatively well, despite some tensions, and to the best of our knowledge these families had no history of domestic violence. Consequently, our analyses do not allow us to address the issue of living in SPC in a context of extreme conflict and/or violence – or of maintaining a sense of home in such a context. There has been virtually no research on this latter issue, apart from an exploratory study by Fehlberg et al (2023) of how Australian children who have experienced domestic violence (specifically, directed towards their mother by their father) feel 'at home' in their abusive father's home following parental separation. Their four case studies show – as does our research – that children's sense of 'home' is constructed in relation to the places themselves, the activities that children can pursue there that contribute to the appropriation of these places, and the relationships that develop there. For these children, however, the question of 'home' is particularly complex. As for many children with separated parents, this question involves a desire to maintain a relationship with each parent and to love and treat them fairly, but in the context of domestic violence, this involves tremendous emotional work to make sense of the abusive father's behaviour and to continue the relationship with him. This specific context and this emotional work inevitably weigh on children's possibility of feeling 'at home' in their parents' residences. We can also assume that situations of extreme conflict that do not include domestic violence significantly affect how children can cope with moving between places, maintain a sense of belonging to each residence/family and ultimately develop a global sense of home.

Broadening the scope of analysis to include more family configurations, spaces and significant others

The practices, processes and dynamics that we have presented in this book extend beyond the context of SPC. We can hypothesize that some of the practices and issues that emerged in our work in relation to the appropriation of space, the relationship with objects, the negotiation of territories – and more generally, the place of each person in the family – may concern all children, whether they live in nuclear, blended or monoparental families. We are thinking in particular of territorial conflicts between siblings over the 'best' bedroom or spot on the sofa; the refusal (or granting) of access to an individual bedroom (or appropriated 'corner' of a shared room) to a family member; the difficulty of feeling at home in a space arranged and decorated in a way a child does not find suitable; the tactics used to create bubbles of privacy in shared spaces. Our findings call for the development of a sociology of childhood and youth that considers space a key entry point for the study of family relationships, particularly among siblings. Our findings could also inspire future work on other forms of multilocality that children experience: we are thinking in particular of children who live for part of the year in boarding schools, or with grandparents, or abroad in extended visits to members of a transnational family. For these children, the questions of attachment to places, their appropriation and, more broadly, feelings of belonging are also important.

Finally, we could not conclude this work without noting that children do not develop a sense of 'home' only in their parental residence(s). Indeed, in their analysis of the meaning that French and Portuguese teenagers attribute to their mobility in cities, Ramos and de Singly (2016) show that, at an age when young people are gradually detaching themselves from their family identity to construct their own identity, movements among friends – without adults – represent an important stage in their process of individualization. This spatial independence allows them to take refuge in the interstices of the city to amuse themselves and do as they please in 'their own little world' – their 'home' – far from adult supervision, where they can define an autonomous self without being reduced to the identity of 'child of'. Moreover, Authier and Bidou (2005) emphasize that the study of blended families is not limited to analysing the relationships between parents and children. It is also important to examine the role of children's relationships with grandparents, uncles, aunts, cousins and other relatives in 'doing family'. The authors note that while the parental dwelling is one of the spaces in which family identities and ties are constructed and strengthened, other residential family spaces (a second home, a holiday village, a relative's house) and non-residential spaces (such as urban public spaces) should also be considered when investigating the relationship between family and space.

References

Ahmed, S. (1999). Home and away: Narratives of migration and estrangement. *International Journal of Cultural Studies*, 2(3), 329–347.

Ahrons, C.R. (1979). The binuclear family: Two households, one family. *Alternative Lifestyles*, 2(4), 499–515.

Amphoux, P. and Mondada, L. (1989). Le chez-soi dans tous les sens. *Architecture et comportement*, 5(2), 135–150.

Austin, W.G. (2018). Parental gatekeeping and child custody evaluation: Part III: Protective gatekeeping and the overnights 'conundrum'. *Journal of Divorce & Remarriage*, 59(5), 429–451.

Authier, J.-Y. and Bidou, C. (2005). Éditorial. La famille dans tous ses espaces … ou presque! *Espaces et sociétés*, 1(120–121), 7–14.

Bacon, K. (2018). Children's use and control of bedroom space. In S. Punch, R. Vanderberck and T. Skelton (eds), *Families, Intergenerationality, and Peer Group Relations* (pp 85–105). Singapore: Springer.

Bakker, W., Karsten, L. and Mulder, C. (2015). Family routines and rituals following separation: Continuity and change. *Families, Relationships and Societies*, 4(3), 365–382.

Baldassar, L. (2008). Missing kin and longing to be together: Emotions and the construction of co-presence in transnational relationships. *Journal of Intercultural Studies*, 29(3), 247–266.

Baldassar, L., Nedelcu, M., Merla, L. and Wilding, R. (2016). ICT-based co-presence in transnational families and communities: Challenging the premise of face-to-face proximity in sustaining relationships. *Global Networks*, 16(2), 133–144.

Benjelloun, A. (2018). Je Smartphone! In V. Sacriste (ed), *Nos vies, nos objets. Enquêtes sur la vie quotidienne* (pp 109–116). Villeneuve d'Ascq: Presses universitaires du Septentrion.

Berman, R. and Daneback, K. (2020). Children in dual-residence arrangements: A literature review. *Journal of Family Studies*, 25(1), 2–17.

Bernardi, L. and Mortelmans, D. (2021). Introduction: Advances in research on shared physical custody by interdisciplinary approaches. In L. Bernardi and D. Mortelmans (eds), *Shared Physical Custody* (pp 5–21). Cham: Springer.

Berthier, N. (2010). *Les techniques d'enquête en sciences sociales. Méthodes et exercices corrigés* (4th edn). Paris: Armand Colin.

Bessière, C., Biland, E. and Fillod-Chabaud, A. (2013). Résidence alternée: la justice face aux rapports sociaux de sexe et de classe. *Lien social et Politiques*, 69, 125–143.

Besure, C., de Stexhe, Y., Druant, C., Rinschbergh, F., Merla, L. and De Mol, J. (2014). Coprésence physique, coprésence virtuelle et liens familiaux en situation migratoire. In L. Merla and A. François (eds), *Distances et liens* (pp 63–82). Louvain-la-Neuve: Academia.

Biland, É. (2023). *Family Law in Action: Divorce and Inequality in Quebec and France*. Vancouver: University of British Columbia Press.

Blunt, A. and Dowling, R. (2006). *Home*. London: Routledge.

Bonnin, P. (1999). La domus éclatée. In P. Bonnin and R. De Villanova (eds), *D'une maison à l'autre* (pp 19–44). Paris: Creaphis.

Bourdieu, P. (1979). *La distinction, critique sociale du jugement*. Paris: Minuit.

Bourdieu, P. (1997). *Méditations pascaliennes*. Paris: Seuil.

Bovill, M. and Livingstone, S. (2001). Bedroom culture and the privatization of media use. In S. Livingstone and M. Bovill (eds), *Children and Their Changing Media Environment: A European Comparative Study* (pp 179–200). New York: Routledge.

Braver, S.L., Ellman, I.M., Votruba, A.M. and Fabricius, W.V. (2011). Lay judgments about child custody after divorce. *Psychology, Public Policy, and Law*, 17(2), 212–240.

Brunet, F., Kertudo, P. and Malsan, S. (2008). *Étude sociologique sur la résidence en alternance des enfants de parents séparés*. Paris: CNAF, Dossier d'étude n° 109.

Bruno, L. (2018). National self-image as an obstacle to ensuring children's rights in the context of domestic violence and family law: The case of Sweden. *Journal of Social Welfare and Family Law*, 40(4), 426–440.

Campo, M., Fehlberg, B., Natalier, K. and Smyth, B. (2020). The meaning of home for children and young people after separation. *Journal of Social Welfare and Family Law*, 42(3), 299–318.

Casman, M.T., César, A., Waxweiler, C. and Mezabi, D.C. (2010). *Évaluation de l'instauration de l'hébergement égalitaire dans le cadre d'un divorce ou d'une séparation*. Recherche commanditée par le Secrétariat de l'État à la Politique des Familles: Université de Liège.

Christensen, P., James, A. and Jenks, C. (2000). Home and movement: Children constructing 'family time'. In S.L. Holloway and G. Valentine (eds), *Children's Geographies: Playing, Living, Learning* (pp 139–155). London: Routledge.

Christensen, T.H. (2009). 'Connected presence' in distributed family life. *New Media & Society*, 11(3), 433–451.

Clerc, M. (2014). Le positionnement sur l'échelle des niveaux de vie. *Insee Première*, 1515, 1–4.

Côté, D. and Gaborean, F. (2015). Nouvelles normativités de la famille: la garde partagée au Québec, en France et en Belgique. *Canadian Journal of Women and the Law*, 27(1), 22–46.

Cretin, L. (2015). Dossier: Résidence et pension alimentaire des enfants de parents séparés: décisions initiales et évolutions. In J.-L. Tavernier (ed), *Famille et couple* (pp 41–49). Paris: Insee.

Csikszentmihalyi, M. and Rochberg-Halton, E. (1981). *The Meaning of Things: Domestic Symbols and the Self.* Cambridge: Cambridge University Press.

Danic, I., Delalande, J. and Rayou, P. (2006). *Enquêter auprès d'enfants et de jeunes. Objets, méthodes et terrains de recherche en sciences sociales.* Rennes: PUR.

de Singly, F. (2006). *Les Adonaissants.* Paris: Armand Colin.

de Singly, F. and Ramos, E. (2010). Moments communs en famille. *Ethnologie française*, 40(1), 11–18.

de Singly, F. and Decup-Pannier, B. (2016). Avoir une chambre chez chacun de ses parents séparés. In F. de Singly (ed), *Libres ensemble. L'individualisme dans la vie commune* (2nd edn) (pp 275–296). Paris: Armand Colin.

Di Méo, G. (2012). Éléments de réflexion pour une géographie sociale du genre: le cas des femmes dans la ville. *L'information géographique*, 76(2012/2), 72–94.

Douglas, M. (1991). The idea of a home: A kind of space. *Social Research*, 58(1), 287–307.

Duchêne-Lacroix, C. (2013). Éléments pour une typologie des pratiques plurirésidentielles et d'un habiter multilocal. *e-Migrinter*, 11, 151–167.

Duchêne-Lacroix, C. (2014). Habiter plusieurs logements habituels: éléments conceptuels d'une pratique plurielle. In P. Hamman, M. Blanc, C. Duchêne-Lacroix, T. Freytag and C. Kramer (eds), *Questionner les mobilités résidentielles à l'aune de la multilocalité* (pp 33–60). Strasbourg: Neothèque.

Eurostat (2023). *Divorceindicators*, October. Retrieved from https://ec.europa.eu/ eurostat/databrowser/view/DEMO_NDIVINDcustom_685155/bookmark/ table?lang=en&bookmarkId=cc90d043-4364-4937-99df-d356174f973b

Fehlberg, B., Natalier, K. and Smyth, B. (2018). Children's experiences of 'home' after parental separation. *Child and Family Law Quarterly*, 30(1), 1–21.

Fehlberg, B., Natalier, K., Smyth, B.M. and Campo, M. (2023). Exploring the 'best interests' principle: 'Home' after parental separation for children and young people who have experienced domestic abuse. *Australian Journal of Family Law*, 36, 23–37.

Félonneau, M.-L. (1997). *L'étudiant dans la ville. Territorialités étudiantes et symbolique urbaine.* Paris: L'Harmattan.

Fierens, J. (2008). Photo de famille. L'image de la famille à travers les mutations récentes du droit civil belge. *Journal du droit des jeunes*, 278, 23–31.

Fiese, B., Tomcho, T., Douglas, T., Josephs, K., Poltrock, S. and Baker, T. (2002). A review of 50 years of research on naturally occurring family routines and rituals: Cause for celebration? *Journal of Family Psychology*, 16(4), 381–390.

Finch, J. (2007). Displaying families. *Sociology*, 41(1), 65–81.

Flaquer, L. (2021). Shared parenting after separation and divorce in Europe in the context of the second demographic transition. In A.-M. Castrén, V. Česnuitytė, I. Crespi, J.-A. Gauthier, R. Gouveia, C. Martin, et al (eds), *The Palgrave Handbook of Family Sociology in Europe* (pp 377–398). Cham: Springer.

Fransson, E., Hjern, A. and Bergström, M. (2018). What can we say regarding shared parenting arrangements for Swedish children? *Journal of Divorce & Remarriage*, 59(5), 349–358.

Gabb, J. (2008). *Researching Intimacy in Families*. Basingstoke: Palgrave Macmillan.

Gabb, J. and Singh, R. (2015). The uses of Emotion Maps in research and clinical practice with families and couples: Methodological innovation and critical inquiry. *Family Process*, 54(1), 185–197.

Galland, O. (2010). Introduction. Une nouvelle classe d'âge? *Ethnologie française*, 40(1), 5–10.

Glevarec, H. (2010a). *La culture de la chambre. Préadolescence et culture contemporaine dans l'espace familial*. La Documentation française, coll. 'questions de culture'. Paris: Ministère de la culture – DEPS, EAN: 9782110975409.

Glevarec, H. (2010b). Les trois âges de la 'culture de la chambre'. *Ethnologie française*, 40(1), 19–30.

Godbout, É., Parent, C. and Saint-Jacques, M.-C. (2015). Positions taken by judges and custody experts on issues relating to the best interests of children in custody disputes in Quebec. *International Journal of Law Policy and the Family*, 29(3), 272–300.

Godbout, É., Saint-Jacques, M.-C. and Ivers, H. (2018). Après la séparation, avec qui les enfants devraient-ils vivre? Une analyse de l'opinion québécoise. *L'Année sociologique*, 68(2), 393–422.

Goffman, E. (1973). *La présentation de soi. La mise en scène de la vie quotidienne I*. Paris: Minuit, 'Le sens commun'.

Gulløv, E. and Winther, I.W. (2021). Sibling relationships: Being connected and related. In A.-M. Castrén, V. Česnuitytė, I. Crespi, J.-A. Gauthier, R. Gouveia, C. Martin, et al (eds), *The Palgrave Handbook of Family Sociology in Europe* (pp 301–319). Cham: Springer Nature.

Gyger Gaspoz, D. (2014). Donner voix à l'espace physique: lorsque la chambre perpétue et écrit l'histoire de l'adolescent au travers d'objets significatifs. Le cas des jeunes en itinérance géographique. *Strenæ*, 7, 1–13.

Hachet, B. (2014). Les calendriers et les agendas de la résidence alternée. Structure et plasticité des territoires temporels des parents. *Politiques sociales et familiales*, 117(1), 29–44.

Hachet, B. (2021). *Une semaine sur deux. Comment les parents séparés se réinventent*. Paris: Les Arènes.

Hakovirta, M. and Rantalaiho, M. (2011). Family policy and shared parenting in Nordic countries. *European Journal of Social Security*, 13(2), 247–266.

Hakovirta, M., Meyer, D.R., Salin, M., Lindroos, E. and Haapanen, M. (2023). Joint physical custody of children in Europe: A growing phenomenon. *Demographic Research*, 49, 479–492.

Hart, R. (1979). *Children's Experience of Place*. New York: Irvington.

Hashemnezhad, H., Heidari, A.A. and Hoseini, P.M. (2013). 'Sense of place' and 'place attachment'. *International Journal of Architecture and Urban Development*, 3(1), 5–12.

Janssen, C. (2021). Transition numérique: la solitude du lien. *Cahiers de psychologie clinique*, 2(57), 239–263.

Jorgensen, B. and Stedman, R. (2001). Sense of place as an attitude: Lakeshore owners' attitudes towards their properties. *Journal of Environmental Psychology*, 21, 233–248.

Kaufmann, V. and Widmer, E. (2005). L'acquisition de la motilité au sein des familles: État de la question et hypothèses de recherche. *Espaces et sociétés*, 2(120–121), 199–217.

Kaufmann, V., Bergman, M.M. and Joye, D. (2004). Motility: Mobility as capital. *International Journal of Urban and Regional Research*, 28(4), 745–756.

Kellerhals, J. and Montandon, C. (1991). *Les stratégies éducatives des familles*. Paris: Delachaux et Niestlé.

Kellerhals, J., Perrin, J.-F., Steinauer-Cresson, G., Vonèche, L. and Wirth, G. (1982). *Mariages au quotidien: inégalités sociales, tensions culturelles et organisation familiale*. Lausanne: P.-M. Favre.

Kusenbach, M. (2003). Street phenomenology: The go-along as ethnographic research tool. *Ethnography*, 4(3), 455–485.

Leider, B. and Janssen, C. (2014). La distance au cœur du lien. De la différenciation des générations au sein de la famille. In L. Merla and A. François (eds), *Distances et liens* (pp 17–37). Louvain-la-Neuve: Academia.

Lenel, E. (2018). Introduction. In E. Lenel (ed), *L'espace des sociologues. Recherches contemporaines en compagnie de Jean Remy* (pp 7–16). Toulouse: Érès.

Licoppe, C. (2004). 'Connected' presence: The emergence of a new repertoire for managing social relationships in a changing communication technoscape. *Environment and Planning D: Society and Space*, 22(1), 135–156.

Ligue des Familles (2020). *Le baromètre des parents de la Ligue des familles*. Bruxelles: Ligue des Familles.

Lincoln, S. (2014). 'I've stamped my personality all over it': The meaning of objects in teenage bedroom space. *Space and Culture*, 17(3), 266–279.

Löw, M. (2015). *Sociologie de l'espace*. Paris: Maison des sciences de l'homme.

MacDonald, K. and Greggans, A. (2008). Dealing with chaos and complexity: The reality of interviewing children and families in their own homes. *Journal of Clinical Nursing*, 17(23), 3123–3130.

Madianou, M. (2016). Polymedia communication among transnational families: What are the long-term consequences for migration? In E. Palenga and M. Kilkey (eds), *Family Life in an Age of Migration and Mobility: Global Perspectives through the Life Course* (pp 71–93). London: Palgrave.

Mallett, S. (2004). Understanding home: A critical review of the literature. *The Sociological Review*, 52(1), 62–89.

Marcoux, J.-S. (2001). The refurbishment of memory. In D. Miller (ed), *Home Possessions: Material Culture Behind Closed Doors* (pp 69–86). Oxford: Berg.

Marquet, J. (1991). *Nomisation et réalité dynamiques: contribution à la sociologie compréhensive* (PhD). Louvain-la-Neuve: Academia.

Marquet, J. (2008). *La famille à l'épreuve de la rupture conjugale.* Bruxelles: Les Cahiers du CEPESS.

Marquet, J. (2010). Couple parental – couple conjugal, multiparenté – multiparentalité. Réflexions sur la nomination des transformations de la famille contemporaine. *Recherches sociologiques et anthropologiques*, 41(2), 51–74.

Marquet, J. and Merla, L. (2015). *L'intérêt supérieur de l'enfant dans la mosaïque familiale: ce que cela signifie pour les enfants. Rapport final.* Bruxelles: OEJAJ.

Marquet, J. and Merla, L. (2018). L'espace, un objet central de la sociologie de la famille. In E. Lenel (ed), *L'espace des sociologues. Recherches contemporaines en compagnie de Jean Remy* (pp 141–166). Toulouse: Érès.

Mason, J. (1996). Gender, care and sensibility in family and kin relationships. In J. Holland and L. Adkins (eds), *Sex, Sensibility and the Gendered Body* (pp 15–36). London: Macmillan.

Massey, D. (1994). A place called home? In D.B. Massey (ed), *Space, Place and Gender* (pp 157–173). London: Polity Press.

Merla, L. (2012). Salvadoran transnational families, distance and eldercare: Understanding transnational care practices in Australia and Belgium. In T. Geisen, T. Studer and E. Yildiz (eds), *Migration, Familie und Soziale Lage. Beiträge zu Bildung, Gender und Care* (pp 295–312). Wiesbaden: Springer VS.

Merla, L. (2018). Rethinking the interconnections between family socialization and gender through the lens of multi-local, post-separation families. *Sociologica*, 12(3), 47–57.

Merla, L. and Dedonder, J. (2019). *Configurations familiales post-divorce/séparation en Fédération Wallonie-Bruxelles: le point de vue des adolescent·e·s.* Rapport de recherche MobileKids, Louvain-la-Neuve: UCLouvain.

Merla, L. and Nobels, B. (2019). Children negotiating their place through space in multi-local, joint physical custody arrangements. In L. Murray, L. McDonnell, T. Hinton-Smith, N. Ferreira and K. Walsh (eds), *Families in Motion: Ebbing and Flowing through Space and Time* (pp 79–95). Bingley: Emerald Publishing.

Merla, L. and Murru, S. (2021). Families facing the Italian lockdown: Temporal adjustments and new caring practices in shared physical custody arrangements. *Journal of Family Research*, 34(1), 429–457.

Merla, L. and Nobels, B. (2021). Gérer l'alternance, ordonner un monde en mouvement: les pratiques matérielles des enfants en hébergement égalitaire. *Recherches sociologiques et anthropologiques*, 1, 171–197.

Merla, L. and Murru, S. (2023). *Les enfants en garde alternée: rapport final du volet italien du projet MobileKids*. Rapport MobileKids, Louvain-la-Neuve: Cirfase, UCLouvain.

Merla, L., Baar, M. and Dedonder, J. (2020). *Séparations parentales et hébergement alterné égalitaire en Belgique: Cadre juridique et regard de praticien·ne·s du droit*. Rapport de recherche, Louvain-la-Neuve: UCLouvain.

Merla, L., Dedonder, J., Nobels, B. and Murru, S. (2021a). The SOHI: Operationalizing a new model for studying teenagers' sense of home in post-divorce families. In L. Bernardi and D. Mortelmans (eds), *Shared Physical Custody: Interdisciplinary Insights in Child Custody Arrangements* (pp 155–180). Cham: Springer.

Merla, L., Nobels, B., Murru, S. and Theys, C. (2021b). Presentation. 'Doing family' in and through space: Towards a multilocal habitus? *Recherches sociologiques et anthropologiques*, 1, 25–45.

Merla, L., Dedonder, J. and Baar, M. (2022). Traitement judiciaire des demandes d'hébergement égalitaire en Belgique: critères d'évaluation et normativités familiales. *Revue trimestrielle de droit familial*, 2, 227–253.

Meyer, D.R., Carlson, M. and Alam, M.M.U. (2022). Increases in shared custody after divorce in the United States. *Demographic Research*, 46(38), 1137–1162.

Michaud Delahaye, P. (2009). La résidence alternée ouvre des perspectives de métissage singulier. *Spirale*, 1(49), 153–161.

Miller, D. (2008). *The Comfort of Things*. Cambridge: Polity Press.

Miller, D. (2010). *Stuff*. Cambridge: Polity Press.

Mincke, C. and Montulet, B. (2019). *La société sans répit. La mobilité comme injonction*. Paris: Éditions de la Sorbonne.

Morgan, D. (2011). *Rethinking Family Practices*. Basingstoke: Palgrave Macmillan.

Morgan, D. (2020). Family practices in time and space. *Gender, Place & Culture*, 27(5), 733–743.

Nedelcu, M. (2017). Transnational grandparenting in the digital age: Mediated co-presence and childcare in the case of Romanian migrants in Switzerland and Canada. *European Journal of Ageing*, 14, 375–383.

Paillé, P. and Mucchielli, A. (2021). *L'analyse qualitative en sciences humaines et sociales* (5th edn). Paris: Armand Colin.

Palludan, C. and Winther, I.W. (2016). 'Having my own room would be really cool': Children's rooms as the social and material organizing of siblings. *Journal of Material Culture*, 22(1), 34–50.

Petersen, M.G., Lynggaard, A.B., Krogh, P.G. and Winther, I.W. (2010). Tactics for homing in mobile life: A fieldwalk study of extremely mobile people. *MobileHCI*, 7(10), 265–274.

Poittevin, A. (2005). Une lecture des espaces pour lire les liens fraternels. *Espaces et sociétés*, 1–2(120–121), 61–77.

Price, J. (2002). The apotheosis of home and the maintenance of spaces of violence. *Hypatia*, 17(4), 39–70.

Proshansky, H.M. (1976). Appropriation et non-appropriation. In P. Korosec-Serfaty (ed), *Appropriation de l'espace. IAPS* (pp 34–49). Strasbourg: Université Louis Pasteur.

Ramos, E. (2018). *La chambre à l'adolescence à l'ère des écrans connectés. Ancrage spatial et mobilité numérique.* Paris: Les chantiers Leroy Merlin Source.

Ramos, E. and de Singly, F. (2016). La construction d'un espace 'à nous': la mobilité spatiale à l'adolescence. *Les Annales de la recherche urbaine*, 111, 58–67.

Recksiedler, C. and Bernardi, L. (2021). Are 'part-time parents' healthier parents? Correlates of shared physical custody in Switzerland. In L. Bernardi and D. Mortelmans (eds), *Shared Physical Custody* (pp 76–102). Cham: Springer.

Remy, J. (2015). *L'espace, un objet central de la sociologie.* Toulouse: Érès.

Rolshoven, J. (2008). The temptations of the provisional: Multilocality as a way of life. *Ethnologia Europaea Journal of European Ethnology*, 37(1–2), 17–25.

Sacriste, V. (2018a). Conclusion: Les objets comme supports d'existence. In V. Sacriste (ed), *Nos vies, nos objets. Enquêtes sur la vie quotidienne* (pp 313–322). Villeneuve d'Ascq: Presses universitaires du Septentrion.

Sacriste, V. (2018b). Introduction. In V. Sacriste (ed), *Nos vies, nos objets. Enquêtes sur la vie quotidienne* (pp 13–38). Villeneuve d'Ascq: Presses universitaires du Septentrion.

Sacriste, V. (2019). Les objets face aux épreuves de l'existence moderne. *Sociographe*, 5(Hors série 12), 42–65.

Schier, M. (2015). Post-separation families: Spatial mobilities and the need to manage a multi-local everyday life. In C. Aybek, J. Huinink and R. Muttarak (eds), *Spatial Mobility, Migration and Living Arrangements* (pp 205–224). Cham: Springer.

Schier, M. (2017). A multi-methodological approach to multi-locally living children in post-separation families. Paper presented at the Researching Multi-local Children: Methodological and Ethical Issues conference, 3–5 April, Louvain-la-Neuve.

Schier, M., Hilti, N., Schad, H., Tippel, C., Dittrich-Wesbuer, A. and Monz, A. (2015). Residential multi-locality studies: The added value for research on families and second homes. *Tijdschrift voor economische en sociale geografie*, 106(4), 439–452.

Schiffer, M.B. (1999). *The Material Life of Human Beings: Artifacts, Behavior and Communication*. London: Routledge.

Schmitz, S. (2012a). Le 'mode d'habiter': analyse de l'usage d'une notion émergente en géographie. In B. Frelat-Kahn and O. Lazzarotti (eds), *Habiter. Vers un nouveau concept?* (pp 35–45). Paris: Armand Colin.

Schmitz, S. (2012b). Un besoin de territoire à soi: quelques clés pour un aménagement des espaces communs. *Belgeo*, 1–2.

Searles, H. (1986). *L'environnement non humain*. Paris: Gallimard.

Serfaty-Garzon, P. (ed) (2002). *Dictionnaire critique du logement et de l'habitat, sous le regard des sciences sociales*. Paris: Armand Colin.

Serfaty-Garzon, P. (2003a). *Chez-soi. Les territoires de l'intimité*. Paris: Armand Colin.

Serfaty-Garzon, P. (2003b). Le chez-soi: habitat et intimité. In M. Segaud, J. Brun and J.-C. Driant (eds), *Dictionnaire critique de l'habitat et du logement* (pp 65–69). Paris: Armand Colin.

Serfaty-Garzon, P. (2003c). L'appropriation. In M. Segaud, J. Brun and J.-C. Driant (eds), *Dictionnaire critique de l'habitat et du logement* (pp 27–30). Paris: Armand Colin.

Serfaty-Garzon, P. (2006). En mouvement. Le chez-soi à l'épreuve des mobilités. In P. Serfaty-Garzon (ed), *Un chez-soi chez les autres* (pp 7–40). Montréal and Paris: Bayard.

Sixsmith, J. (1986). The meaning of home: An exploratory study of environmental experience. *Journal of Environmental Psychology*, 6, 281–298.

Sodermans, A.K., Matthijs, K. and Swicegood, G. (2013). Characteristics of joint physical custody families in Flanders. *Demographic Research*, 28(29), 821–848.

Solsona, M. and Ajenjo, M. (2017). Joint custody: One more step towards gender equality? *Perspectives Demografiques*, 8, 1–4.

Steinbach, A. (2019). Children's and parents' well-being in joint physical custody: A literature review. *Family Process*, 58(2), 353–369.

Thomson, E. and Turunen, J. (2021). Alternating homes: A new family form: The family sociology perspective. In L. Bernardi and D. Mortelmans (eds), *Shared Physical Custody* (pp 23–26). Cham: Springer.

Turunen, J. (2017). Shared physical custody and children's experience of stress. *Journal of Divorce & Remarriage*, 58(5), 371–392.

Van Houcke, F. (2017). *Législation sur l'hébergement égalitaire: 10 ans après … Analyse – mars 2017*. Bruxelles: Coordination des ONG pour les droits de l'enfant.

Vassart, S. (2006). Habiter. *Pensée plurielle*, 2(12), 9–19.

Wacquant, L. (2005). Habitus. In J. Becket and M. Zafiovski (eds), *International Encyclopedia of Economic Sociology* (pp 317–321). London: Routledge.

Wagener, M., François, A. and Merla, L. (2021). Mères seules, la fin de la stigmatisation? *Sociétés en changement*, 12, 1–8.

Walker, A. (2020). 'I don't know where all the cutlery is': Exploring materiality and homemaking in post-separation families. *Social & Cultural Geography*, 23(2), 210–226.

Weller, S. (2012). Evolving creativity in qualitative longitudinal research with children and teenagers. *International Journal of Social Research Methodology*, 15(2), 119–133.

Wellman, B. (2018). Foreword: The family has become a network. In B. Barbosa Neves and C. Casimiro (eds), *Connecting Families? Information and Communication Technologies, Generations, and the Life Course* (pp xv–xx). Bristol: Polity Press.

Widmer, E. and Favez, N. (2012). *Capital social et coparentage dans les familles recomposées et de première union.* Genève: Université de Genève.

Widmer, E., Kellerhals, J., Lévy, R., Ernst, M. and Hammer, R. (2002). *Cohésion, régulation et conflits dans les familles contemporaines.* Rapport final n°5004-047772-1. Zürich: Seismo.

Widmer, E., Kellerhals, J. and Lévy, R. (2006). Types of conjugal interactions and conjugal conflict: A longitudinal assessment. *European Sociological Review*, 22(1), 79–89.

Winther, I.W. (2009). 'Homing oneself': Home as a practice. *Home and Space*, 4(2), 49–83.

Winther, I.W. (2015). To practice mobility – on a small scale. *Culture Unbound*, 7, 215–231.

Zaffran, J. (2014). La chambre des adolescent(e)s: espace intermédiaire et temps transitionnel. *Strenæ*, 7, 1–9. Retrieved from http://journals.open edition.org

Zartler, U. (2011). Reassembling families after divorce. In R. Jallinoja and E. Widmer (eds), *Families and Kinship in Contemporary Europe: Rules and Practices of Relatedness* (pp 178–191). Basingstoke: Palgrave Macmillan.

Zartler, U. (2021). Children and parents after separation. In N. Schneider and M. Kreyenfeld (eds), *Research Handbook on the Sociology of the Family* (pp 300–313). Cheltenham: Edward Elgar.

Index

A

absence *see* co-presence: in thought
access 188
Amphoux, P. and Mondada, L. 9
anchoring 21, 61, 62–63, 67
  objects on stand-by as support for 71–72
  shadow objects as supports for 69–70
anchoring rituals 97, 102–105
anomic parallel parents **28**, 29, 32, 48
appropriating a space 109
  controlling space 118–127
  and family relationship 128–131
    exclusion through colour 134–140
    inclusion through colour 131–134
  marking one's space 110–118
  see also co-presence
appropriation 188
appropriative space 115–116
archipelago metaphor 20–22, 142, 164
  'personal and familial' home v. 'personal' home 177–181
  'personal and physical' home v. 'familial' home 165–171
  'personal, familial and physical' home v. 'familial' home 176–177
  'personal, familial and physical' home v. 'non-home' 181
  'personal' home v. 'familial and physical' home 171–176
  see also parental islands
association couples 26–27
association parents **28**, 29, 32, 44
Authier, J.-Y. and Bidou, C. 192
autonomy/fusion family functioning 26, 30

B

Bakker, W. 93, 97
Baldassar, L. 142
bastion couples 26
bastion parents 27, **28**, 30–32, 32–33

bedroom doors 118–120
bedrooms 9–10, 129
  co-presence by proxy 143–144
  controlling space 121–122, 123–127
  exclusion through colour 134–137
  inclusion through colour 131–134
  marking one's space 110–115, 116, 117–118
  and singular-plural sense of home 165, 166–167, 168–169, 171–172, 174, 178–180
Belgium 12–14
belonging 60, 84
Berman, R. and Daneback, K. 6, 7
Besure, C. 150
Biland, É. 5
Bonnin, P. 8
bubbling tactic 122

C

Campo, M. 186
case studies 1–4
  see also Belgium; study participants
Christensen, P. 84, 158
cleanliness rituals 107
closure *see* openness/closure family functioning
co-presence 142
  by proxy 142, 143–145
  in thought 142, 145–147
  virtual 148–158
cocoon couples 26
cocoon parental islands **31**, 35–39, 52, 75, 78
cocoon parents 27–29, **28**, 32, 55
colour 129
  exclusion through 134–140
  inclusion through 131–134
communication *see* virtual co-presence; virtual contact limits
companionship couples 27

companionship parents **28**, 29, 32, 39, 40
competence 188
conflict
  between parents 5, 7, 14, 23–24n12,
    53, 159n6
  with new family 138–140, 153, 181
continuity 60, 93
controlling space 118–127
couples, interaction within 26–27

D

De Singly, F. 9, 11
  and Decup-Pannier, B. 10, 60, 68, 76,
    93, 95
differentiation practices 63–64
digital media 21
  see also information and communication
    technologies (ICT)
doing family 8–9, 12, 92–93
domestic violence 6, 190–191
doubling 67
Duchêne-Lacroix, C. 20, 58

E

egalitarian shared physical custody (SPC) 13
Emotion Maps 16, 18, *19*, 129, 137–138,
    165, 177
European Union (EU) 5
exclusion 146–147
  through colour 134–140
expressiveness/instrumentality family
    functioning 26
extracurricular activities 83–84

F

fairness 64–66
familial dimensions, parental islands 53–54
familial transitional space-time 80,
    84–86, 88
family
  doing family 8–9, 12, 92–93
  institutional model 8
family functioning 25–26
family practices 84, 85–86
  see also co-presence; family rituals;
    family routines
family relationships 21, 128–131
  exclusion through colour 134–140
  inclusion through colour 131–134
  through virtual co-presence 148–158
  see also conflict; interaction within couples
family rituals 91–93
  rituals of return 94–95, 97–107
    anchoring rituals 102–105
    integration rituals 97–102
    rituals of (not) unpacking 105–107
family routines 91, 92, 93–94
  routines of return 95–97

family space 44, 49
family violence 190–191
  see also domestic violence
Fehlberg B. 7, 133, 191
Fiese, B. 91–92, 97
fortress parental islands **31**, 32–35, 52, 55,
    74–75, 78
fusion *see* autonomy/fusion
    family functioning
future research 189–190

G

Gabb, J. 84
gender roles 6, 26–27
Glevarec, H. 110, 112, 123
global sense of home 11, 164
Gulløv, E. and Winther, I.W. 151

H

Hachet, B. 29–30, 53, 55, 98
Hart, R. 82
Hashemnezhad, H. 162
home, sense of 7–12, 60, 192
  'personal and familial' home v. 'personal'
    home 177–181
  'personal and physical' home v. 'familial'
    home 165–171
  'personal, familial and physical' home v.
    'familial' home 176–177
  'personal, familial and physical' home v.
    'non-home' 181
  'personal' home v. 'familial and physical'
    home 171–176
  singular-plural 161–165, 186–187
  as vector of opportunities 182–184
house-domus 8
humility of things 68

I

identity, shadow objects as supports for 70
in-between space 21
in-between space-times 80
inclusion through colour 131–134
information and communication technologies
    (ICT) 30–32, 34, 37, 42, 46–47,
    50–51, 122
  see also digital media; virtual co-presence;
    virtual contact limits
instrumentality *see* expressiveness/
    instrumentality family functioning
integration rituals 97–102
interaction within couples 26–27
interstitial space-times 80, 86–88
Italy 189–190

J

joint physical custody *see* shared physical
    custody (SPC)

K

Kaufmann, V. 188

L

legal practitioners, key lessons for 190–191
liberation, shadow objects as a means of 71, 72
Licoppe, C. 148
limits on movement 32
  cocoon parental islands 37
  fortress parental islands 33–34
  open parental islands 44–46
  reef parental islands 41–42
  wild parental islands 49–50
lived space 20, 61, 83
living standard 52

M

Marcoux, J.-S. 76
marking one's space 110–118
Marquet, J. and Merla, L. 128
material conditions 77
material dimension, parental islands 52
material limits 114–115
material practices
  creating similarity between dwellings 66–67
  differentiation practices 63–64
  distinguishing in a spirit of fairness 64–66
  impact of opportunities and constraints
    on 76–80
  marking one's space 110–112
  object transfers 73
  objects in transit 69
  objects on stand-by 71–72
  and parental islands 74–76
  parked objects 62–63, 72–73
  resistance rituals 93
  rituals of (not) unpacking 105–107
  shadow objects 69–71, 72–73
  taking nothing along 67–69
  transition channels 73–74
Material Studies 59
materiality 59–62, 164
  co-presence by proxy through 143–145
  see also material practices
memory objects 111
Merla, L and Dedonder, J. 148
Miller, D. 68
Mincke, C. and Montulet, B. 45
mobile phones 154–158
mobility capital 188
monochrome spaces 130–131
Morgan, D. 84, 154
movement, limits on 32
  cocoon parental islands 37
  fortress parental islands 33–34
  open parental islands 44–46
  reef parental islands 41–42
  wild parental islands 49–50

multilocal dwelling 20–22, 58
multilocal habitus 187–188

O

object transfers 73
  see also objects: transfer limits
objects 58–59, 59–62
  of affect 72, 154–155, 157
  controlling access to 125
  of escape 71
  marking one's space with 110–112
  memory objects 111
  parked objects 61, 62–63, 65, 66, 67, 69,
    72–73, 77
  shadow objects 69–71, 72–73, 155, 157
  on stand-by 71–72
  transfer limits 32, 78
    cocoon parental islands 39
    fortress parental islands 34–35, 64
    open parental islands 48
    reef parental islands 43
    wild parental islands 51
  in transit 61, 65, 69, 74, 77, 105–107, 157
  see also material practices; materiality
open parental islands **31**, 44–48, 52, 53,
  54, 76
openness/closure family functioning 26, 30
ordering
  by creating similarity between
    dwellings 66–67
  objects in transit 68
  objects on stand-by 71–72
  parked objects 62–63, 72–73
  shadow objects 69–71, 72–73
  in a spirit of fairness 64–66
  taking nothing along 67–69
  through differentiation 63–64
outboxing 106

P

Palludan, C. and Winther, I.W. 10, 60
parallel couples 26
  see also anomic parallel parents
parental islands 20, 21–22, 25, **31**, 190
  cocoon islands 35–39, 52, 75, 78
  fortress islands 32–35, 52, 55, 74–75, 78
  impact on material practices 74–76, 78
    (see also transfer limits)
  influencing factors 51–56
  open islands 44–48, 52, 53, 54, 76
  reef islands 39–43, 52, 54, 75–76, 78
  wild islands 48–51, 52, 76
parental styles 27–29
parked objects 61, 62–63, 65, 66, 67, 69,
  72–73, 77
participatory methods 16–20
personal belongings see objects
Petersen, M.G. 67, 106, 122

Piedmont region, Italy 189–190
Poittevin, A. 9
polychrome spaces 130–131
practitioners, key lessons for 190–191
presence *see* co-presence
public transitional space-times 80, 81–84
public transport 36–37, 49, 68, 77, 82–83

Q

quality time 84, 85–86
quasi-egalitarian shared physical
    custody (SPC) 13

R

Ramos, E. and de Singly, F. 192
reassurance, shadow objects as a means of 70–71
Recksiedler, C. and Bernadi, L. 5
reef parental islands **31**, 39–43, 52, 54,
    75–76, 78
regulation, family functioning 26, 30
Remy, J. 59
research
    future research 189–190, 191–192
    key lessons from 190–191
research methods *see* participatory methods
research participants *see* study participants
resistance rituals 76, 93
rite de passage see rituals of return
rituals 91–93
rituals of passage 93
rituals of resistance 76, 93
rituals of return 94–95, 97–107
    anchoring rituals 102–105
    integration rituals 97–102
    rituals of (not) unpacking 105–107
routine objects 67
routines 91, 92, 93–94
routines of return 95–97
rules 126–127

S

Sacriste, V. 59–60, 121, 154, 155
Schier, M. 84
Schiffer, M.B. 128
school 81–82
school materials 77
sense of home 7–12, 60, 192
    'personal and familial' home v. 'personal'
        home 177–181
    'personal and physical' v. 'familial' 165–171
    'personal, familial and physical'
        home v. 'familial' home 176–177
    'personal, familial and physical'
        home v. 'non-home' 181
    'personal' home v. 'familial and physical'
        home 171–176
    singular-plural 161–165, 186–187
        as vector of opportunities 182–184

Serfaty-Garzon, P. 11, 164
shadow objects 69–71, 72–73, 155, 157
shared physical custody (SPC) 4–7
    Belgium 12–14
    and sense of home 7–12
sibling relationships 151–154
single parents 53
singular-plural home 161–165, 186–187
    'personal and familial' home v. 'personal'
        home 177–181
    'personal and physical' home v. 'familial'
        home 165–171
    'personal, familial and physical'
        home v. 'familial' home 176–177
    'personal, familial and physical'
        home v. 'non-home' 181
    'personal' home v. 'familial and physical'
        home 171–176
    as vector of opportunities 182–184
Sixsmith, J. 164
smartphones *see* mobile phones
social class 5
socio-economic resources 77–78
Socio-Spatial Network Game (SSNG) 16,
    17–18
    public transitional space-times 82, 83
    shadow objects 69, 155–156
    singular-plural home 167, 169–170, 175,
        177, 178
space
    family space 44, 49
    in-between space 21
    lived space 20, 61, 83
    and materiality 59
    monochrome and polychrome
        spaces 130–131
    transitional space 21
space appropriation 109
    controlling space 118–127
    and family relationship 128–131
        exclusion through colour 134–140
        inclusion through colour 131–134
    marking one's space 110–118
    see also co-presence
space-times 80–88
spatial conditions 77
spatial dimension, parental islands 52–53
spatio-temporal limits 32
standard of living 52
study participants 14–16
symbolic boundaries 109, 118–120, 135, 143

T

temporal dimension, parental islands 54–55
temporal territoriality 29–30, 53–54, 78–79
territorial rights 131–132, 139
territoriality 138
territorializing 106

time
  marking space through 116–118
  see also space-times
transfer limits 32, 78
  cocoon parental islands 39
  fortress parental islands 34–35, 64
  open parental islands 48
  reef parental islands 43
  wild parental islands 51
  see also personal belongings
transition channels 73–74, 105, 144
transitional space 21
transitional space-times 80–88

U

unifying rituals 93

V

Van Houcke, F. 13
virtual boundaries 122
virtual co-presence 148–158
  mobile phones 154–158
  relationship with absent parent 148–150
  relationship with 'new family' members
    150–154
virtual contact limits 32
  cocoon parental islands 37–39
  fortress parental islands 34
  open parental islands 47–48
  reef parental islands 42–43
  wild parental islands 51

W

Walker, A. 135, 136
welcoming rituals 98
Wellman, B. 21
Widmer, E. 25–26, 27
wild parental islands **31**, 48–51,
    52, 76
Winther, I.W. 93–94

Y

youth welfare practitioners, key lessons
    for 190–191